The Canoe Camper's
Handbook

Other Books by Ray Bearse

Vermont: A Guide to the Green Mountain State (1968)
Maine: A Guide to the Vacation State (1969)
Massachusetts: A Guide to the Pilgrim State (1971)
Centerfire American Rifle Cartridges 1892–1963 (1966)
Vermont Is Covered Bridge Country (1974)
Vermont Mountain Trails and Summits (1974)
Let It Begin Here: 1775–76 (in preparation)
Pistol and Revolver Cartridges (1967)
    (with H.P. White and B.D. Munhall)
Walther Rifles and Pistols (1962)
    (with W.H.B. Smith)

The Canoe Camper's Handbook

RAY BEARSE

Winchester Press

Copyright © 1974 by Ray Bearse
All rights reserved

Library of Congress Catalog Card Number: 73-78836
ISBN: 0-87691-094-0

Published by Winchester Press
460 Park Avenue, New York 10022

PRINTED IN THE UNITED STATES OF AMERICA

*This book is for
Janet
with much love
and for
Jack and Betty Bradish
with affection*

Contents

Preface

Canoe camping and voyaging—one of the most exciting, peaceful and rewarding of the silent sports—is the subject of this book. Kayak racing, competitive whitewater canoeing and canoe sailing are not within its scope.

This book is written with the assumption that the reader is a man or woman who knows nothing about canoe camping and voyaging. Some readers may have canoeing experience but may not have extended this experience into the areas of camping and voyaging. I hope that the experienced canoe camper and voyageur will also find something new and useful within these pages that will increase his enjoyment of this silent sport.

The fact that I have assumed the reader to be totally ignorant, not just of canoeing but of basic camping techniques, outdoor cooking, map reading, and all other aspects of the sport, does not mean, of course, that you can learn everything you need to know from this book—or from any book, or a whole library of books. Canoeing is something you *do;* you read about it and talk about it only to fill gaps in your knowledge and to avoid mistakes, not as a substitute for the activity. So I offer this book modestly, as an aid and not as an end in itself. I have done my best to be clear and straightforward, and at the same time to communicate some of the pleasure the canoe has given me—and can give you.

The book is organized as follows:

Part I—The Canoe: These chapters briefly cover the canoe's history and development. Contemporary canoe materials are discussed as are the various lengths and hull designs. A chapter is devoted to canoe nomenclature. You will learn how to outfit your canoe.

Part II—The Camp: Packs, sleeping bags, tents, clothing, footgear, general outfit, kitchen gear, and food. To make your choice easier we list brands, prices, and weights.

Part III—Canoe Techniques: You'll never become a master voyageur by studying canoe and voyaging techniques in this or in any other book. Practice makes you expert but we included basic canoe techniques which you can practice on your neighborhood pond or stream.

Part IV—Voyaging Techniques: Camping techniques, how to read a map and compass, planning your voyage, how to load and trim you canoe, pitfalls to avoid. A final chapter—a catchall—has data on various subjects, from how to keep bears from consuming your food supply to how to dry out your camera after it falls overboard.

Part V—Where to Go Voyaging: Highlights of some Canadian canoe trips, province by province. Similar data is included for U.S. canoe country plus a few states with some interesting water. The final chapter describes Quetico-Superior country with details on regulations, weather, outfitters, and other data needed before making a voyage through this fabulous region.

Appendices include a list of canoe manufacturers, a list of camping and trail food manufacturers, an equipment

checklist, lists of map and guidebook sources, and a basic bibliography of books on canoeing and canoe routes.

This volume discusses some of the less pleasant aspects of voyaging: bears, bugs, bad weather, burns, blisters, bone breaking, capsizing, and getting lost. Reading
this handbook is not a cure-all for these afflictions but
will help reduce these hazards to a minimum.

You can beat the bugs by going in a bug-free
time—usually August throughout most of canoe country—and you can avoid capsizing by properly loading
the canoe and by using a modicum of common sense.
Portage backaches can be reduced by selecting proper
lightweight equipment and foods and then by stowing
them in the right packs in the right manner.

If your holiday schedule doesn't allow you to go
voyaging in a bug-free month then you will discover
how to reduce their damnable discomfort to a minimum.

You can keep reasonably dry in foul weather—both
ashore and afloat—if you follow some simple precautions in matters of equipment, clothing and techniques.

In the matters of equipment—as in other things—
one man's experience, even if it covers nigh a half century, is not as good as the collective experience of many
others. Therefore the equipment and techniques I de-
scribe are not only those I have used myself but reflect
the combined experience of my many canoeing friends,
acquaintances and correspondents.

We included weights of various equipment—you'll
appreciate this information on portages—and current
prices of most equipment. The prices are from late 1973
or early 1974 and they are not apt to decrease by the
time this volume appears. Not all items are priced the
same in all catalogs or in all shops, but the difference is
usually slight.

One of the satisfactions of voyaging is the over-coming of minor discomforts and inconveniences like bad weather. You won't appreciate the virtues of a roomy dry tent, a comfortable down sleeping bag, a trail stove, and easy-to-fix meals until you encounter a spell of bone-aching portages and/or bad weather.

May you always have fair weather, no bug bites, short portages, downstream currents—and following winds.

—Ray Bearse
Williston-on-the-Winooski
Vermont
March 1974

Acknowledgments

Special credit goes to Janet for her always cheerful attitude no matter how long the portage, how bad the bugs or weather, or how rough the rapids or high the waves.

To the following, I am also indebted:

Colonel John Bradish and his wife, Betty, for many kindnesses, comradeship and conversation. When my regular typist fell ill and no secretarial standbys were immediately available, he took time from an already overloaded schedule to type the manuscript.

My old friend Angus Cameron for encouragement, professional criticism and personal advice based on his many years of North Country voyaging.

Frederick Pruyn, Manchester, Vermont, and Vero Beach, Florida, for assistance in many ways.

John Smith, director, Photographic Services, University of Vermont, for professional advice and encouragement.

My photographs were developed and printed by Mike Hill of the University of Vermont's Photographic Services.

Howard C. Lance, for providing the drawings and sketches.

Judge Wynn Underwood, Middlebury, Vermont, a fellow voyageur for nearly forty years.

Deane Gray, president of Old Town Canoe Company, Old Town, Maine, for supplying me with various types of canoes for testing and voyaging purposes.

John Randolph, editor-publisher of *Vermont Sportsman*, who helped finance some voyages through the purchases of articles.

Jon Marshall Waters, president of Canadian Waters and Waters, Inc., for many kindnesses and assistance which helped to make voyaging in the Quetico-Superior country such a pleasure.

Robert Elliot, master voyageur and Maine waters authority, recently retired director of the Vacation Travel Bureau, Maine Department of Economic Development.

Neil Kvasnick, proprietor of Skihaus of Vermont, Middlebury, and Sam Cutting, proprietor of Dakin's Vermont Mountain Shop, Ferrisburg, Vermont, for various assistance and for procuring equipment on many occasions on all too brief notice.

Wayne "Ricky" Larrow, Jr., Williston, Vermont, for his services as a model in the photographs showing how to get back into a swamped canoe.

Deane Peterson, Bolton, Vermont, a future master voyageur.

Space does not allow the listing of all the ministers, deputy ministers, and technical assistants of various provincial departments such as Tourism and Natural Resources in Alberta, British Columbia, Manitoba, New Brunswick, Newfoundland-Labrador, Nova Scotia, Ontario, Quebec, and Saskatchewan. Yukon and Northwest Territories officials were most helpful.

Many thanks are due to numerous post managers and officials of Hudson's Bay Company, including the Northern Stores Department.

I owe a debt to various state officials in Maine, New Hampshire, Vermont, Massachusetts, New York, New Jersey, Tennessee, Arkansas, Florida, Michigan, Wisconsin, Iowa, Illinois, Ohio, and Minnesota.

Thanks to Frank Forrester, Information Officer, U.S. Geological Survey, Reston, Virginia, for giving his agency's permission to reproduce the official USGS National Topographical Map Series' Symbols.

I thank Alfred A. Knopf, Inc., for permission to use several quotations from Sigurd F. Olson's *The Lonely Land,* the University of Minnesota Press for permission to use a quotation from Florence Page Jacques' *Canoe Country,* and to the Packsack Press for a quotation from Mark Fisher's *The Quetico-Superior Canoeist's Handbook.*

—R. B.

The Canoe Camper's
Handbook

Part I
The Canoe

1
Escape to Freedom

The movement of a canoe is like a reed in the wind. Silence is a part of it, and the sounds of lapping water, bird songs, and the wind in the trees. It is part of the medium through which it floats, the sky, the waters, and the shores. A man is part of his canoe and therefore part of all it knows. The instant he dips his paddle, he flows as it flows, the canoe yielding to his slightest touch and responsive to his slightest whim and thought . . . There is magic in the feel of a paddle and the movement of a canoe, a magic compounded of distance, adventure, solitude, and peace. The way of a canoe is the way of the wilderness and of freedom almost forgotten, the open door to waterways of ages past and a way of life of profound and abiding satisfaction.

—Sigurd F. Olson, *The Lonely Land*

A loon calling across a spruce-encircled lake . . . the aroma of sizzling bacon, flapjacks and boiling coffee . . . a deer drinking at the water's edge . . . your canoe knifing through a whitewater channel . . . the warming comfort of hot rum at the end of a long day's run against the wind . . . the pleasant hiss of the pressure lantern as it warms and lights the tent . . . the hypnotic rhythm of paddle strokes . . . the driving rain strumming its tattoo against the nylon tent fly . . . campfire smoke against the dark green pines . . . a swimming moose eyeing your craft from a distance . . . the ecstatic shock of diving into a cold spring-fed lake . . .

These are the warp and woof of our winter's golden dreams.

ESCAPE TO FREEDOM

Today's man is circumscribed top, sides, and bottom by people and problems. The two pressures are usually synonymous.

Man, be he (or she) a factory worker, a Madison Avenue advertising executive, a Washington bureau-

Regina Historic Canoe Trails Club members
prepare to portage on Lake Brabant—Reindeer Lake voyage.

crat, a doctor, merchant, student, or parent, is hemmed in by the unending demand for survival in the socio-economic jungle.

Everywhere we are surrounded by people with whom we waste time—and "Time," wrote Ernest Hemingway, "is what we have the least of."

Man is judged by his ability to survive economically in a world over which he has constantly decreasing control. Talents are wasted in accumulating useless clutter.

Somewhere, even in the heart of a timid accountant or bank clerk, beats another drummer. The drums say, "I am a man. I should not be judged solely on my value in the marketplace—but on my worth as a man.

"A few generations ago my ancestors had different values. My worth, as was theirs, should be judged, had I the courage and know-how, on my ability to live and travel through the wilderness with rifle, rod, axe, cook kit, bedroll, and canoe."

Very few of us are fortunate enough—we might not all like it—to return to the ways of the primitive past. We can, however, escape to freedom, as did Daniel Boone from the Indians, in a canoe along the watery freeways of the wilderness.

During the past few years tens of thousands of Americans have become backpackers. Now the mountain trails are crowded. Many backpackers are switching to that most romantic of all craft—the canoe. This continent has waterways to suit the desires of all who would voyage to freedom.

Americans buy nearly 100,000 canoes a year, and the number is increasing annually. Too many purchasers fail to realize that their slender craft could be a vehicle to the Freedom Trail, if they'd only liberate it from their local pond.

RURAL AREAS

Many Sunday canoe trippers longing for the chance or fortitude to make a wilderness voyage neglect the pleasures to be found on streams that may be but a few miles away from their backyard barbeque pit.

Vermont's Big Otter comes to mind. This ninety-odd-mile-long river—no great shakes as a stream—meanders through pleasant countryside with occasional views of Vermont's Green Mountains and the Taconics and the Adirondacks of Upper New York State.

The river, though never more than a few miles from a village (it passes through about a half-dozen), nevertheless has many miles of isolated canoeing. There are long stretches with no habitations. The building of dwellings close to much of the stream has been impossible because of the annual spring flooding. One might have to walk five miles to find the nearest farmhouse. You can camp most anywhere along its banks.

Probably there are similar streams in every state.

For the hesitant tyro many streams, like the Big Otter, have almost no rapids. There are a few easy portages around dams. Here also the tyro canoe camper can test his equipment, knowing that he is never far from civilization if assistance is ever needed.

There are streams like the 400-mile-long Connecticut River, which commence in the wilderness and then flow by tiny settlements, mostly based on logging and affiliated industries. Farther downstream, towns such as Hanover and Brattleboro are resupply points. Still farther downstream are cities like Holyoke, Springfield, and Hartford, and finally Long Island Sound.

Many streams provide the history-minded voyageur with sites to visit. Many rivers are an integral part of history.

Streams like the Otter and Connecticut are fine places to commence canoe voyaging. After several days of rain or bugs one may stay in a motel for a change of atmosphere, a thick steak, a whiskey sour, a bottle of wine, and a hot shower. Your wife and children, if you take them along, will enjoy the interlude.

Indoctrinate your family into voyaging the comfortable way. It may be easier, then, to get them to like more remote country.

SEMI-WILDERNESS AREAS

There is little true wilderness left for voyageurs south of the Canadian frontier. Much of it is semi-wilderness. There is disagreement among voyageurs and backpackers as to what differentiates wilderness and semi-wilderness areas as the terms often overlap.

Our version of the semi-wilderness are the great canoe areas of Maine, the Adirondacks, the great parks of Quebec Province (one has more than 5,000 square miles), Quetico-Superior area, and Southern Canada.

These areas are characterized by mapped canoe routes. You don't have to take them but it might be a good idea to test your canoe legs before voyaging into true wilderness areas. In Maine, along rivers like the famed Allagash, camping is allowed only at specified primitive campsites. This is to reduce fire hazard in the Maine woods which are the state's greatest asset.

WILDERNESS AREAS

Every ardent canoe camper hankers for a trip to

Canoeing family style: break 'em in easy-like.

"The Silent Places" or "The Great Lonesome" of the Canadian bush, be it the subarctic streams of rocky Labrador, the vastness of Northern Quebec and Ontario, or the wild, lonely rivers and lakes that slice across the northern section of Canada's prairie provinces and into the hinterlands of the vast Northwest and Yukon Territories.

It is possible to voyage through a small segment of these areas during a fortnight's holiday if you reach your shoving-off point by plane and return home the same way. The Hudson's Bay Company has a canoe charter service and will supply the gear and grub you didn't or couldn't bring along.

RENT OR BORROW?

Before investing in a canoe and camping outfit—you might be unfortunate enough not to enjoy voyaging—rent or borrow a canoe and camp outfit. Most canoe liveries have only aluminum canoes for rental. They withstand many hard knocks and require almost no maintenance.

You might borrow a canoe and gear from a friend. For ourselves, we would prefer to rent rather than be obligated to a friend or acquaintance. If anything is damaged or lost, money will satisfy the outfitter, but money cannot compensate a friend for the loss of gear that may be much treasured because of its usefulness and sentimental associations.

It is not necessary to own canoe camping equipment. The art and science of outfitting has reached maximum development in the Quetico-Superior canoe country. Here at Ely, Minnesota, and other jumping-off places you can, for a daily fee of from $10 to $14, secure an outfit including aluminum canoe, all camp gear, plus lightweight food.

Hudson's Bay Company (six months notice required) rents aluminum canoes and will place them at any Hudson's Bay Post you desire. HBCo. trading posts can supply foods (not lightweight) and gasoline for your stove and lantern.

Chapter 25 contains additional details on Quetico-Superior outfitting.

We know voyageurs who've spent more than twenty summers in the Quetico-Superior country and have always rented their outfit. Other voyageurs, like this writer, enjoy buying, testing, using, and owning their voyaging outfit.

WHAT PRICE FREEDOM?

A canoe suitable for recreational voyaging on lakes and rivers can be purchased for $300. Price depends on type, length, material, and workmanship. A well-de-

signed, finely crafted canoe for $350 is cheaper than a
$175 canoe because it will last longer and perform bet-
ter. Our basic canoe and camping outfit cost more than
$1,000, but you can do it almost as comfortably and as
efficiently for about one-half that price. Our basic approximate costs:

Canoe	$ 350.00
Paddles (3) & pole	50.00
Tent	195.00
Sleeping bags (2), pads, shells	250.00
Stove	26.50
Packs (6 Duluths, 1 basket)	215.00
Tarp	27.50
Miscellaneous: axe, cook kit, compass, etc.	100.00
Life jackets	70.00
	$1284.00

You could do it this way:

Secondhand canoe	$ 150.00
Paddles (3) & pole	50.00
Gerry Quetico sleeping bags (2) & full-length pads	97.50
Tent	75.00
Stove	12.75
Packs & bags	75.00
Miscellaneous; axe, cook kit, etc.	50.00
Life jackets	70.00
	$ 580.25

Secondhand Equipment

Some outfitters, like Canadian Waters, Ely, Minnesota, offer used equipment for sale. This gear which
sees much annual use still has a long life ahead when
used occasionally by recreational canoeists. Prices aver-

age about one-third of original cost. Examples: 28 x 30-inch Duluth packs, $12.50; Gerry Quetico sleeping bags, $12.50; 7x7-foot A-tents, $40.00. Here's a chance to outfit inexpensively. You can replace these items over the years.

The investment in any recreational pursuit depends on one's financial means. A family can readily spend a thousand dollars on a short vacation of the motel-and-restaurant sort. This is much fun but when we return from a voyage our investment, we hope, is still intact and will be for many future cruises. We're strong believers that in terms of fun and physical conditioning, and spiritually, nothing is superior to canoe travel.

Vermont (the Winooski): Writer's Camp.

IS CANOEING EASY TO LEARN?

Yes. Study basic paddle and canoe handling techniques in Chapter 14. Practice in a quiet cove or on a pond. Then venture onto a slow moving stream. Only practice and experience can make an expert, but there are thousands of canoeists who fare forth on canoe camping holidays who are not experts.

A major safety factor is the recognition of your limitations and determination not to run unnecessary risks. You must first know how to recognize what these risks are. See Chapter 17.

Every summer hundreds of canoe campers arrive at one of the outfitters in Ely, Minnesota, without ever having dipped a paddle. Two or three hours of practice with an instructor, and they depart for their holiday in the semi-wilderness.

IS CANOEING DANGEROUS?

The canoe is one of the most stable watercraft the world has ever known. People who know how to handle it have crossed continents and oceans. As with the automobile and bicycle, certain commonsense rules must be observed. The American Red Cross, because of its overemphasis of general safety rules, has created a false image of the canoe as being unstable and dangerous.

The canoe has figured in history and adventure on the North American continent from the earliest days to the present.

2
Romance of the Canoe

*"Something lost behind the Ranges
Lost and waiting for you. Go!"*
    —Rudyard Kipling, *The Explorer*

Two canoe voyages—one that took place and another that didn't—affected the political map of North
America.

The one that did was made by Admiral Samuel de
Champlain (1567?–1635), "the Father of New France,"
and one of this continent's greatest explorers. He
reluctantly accompanied his Algonquin allies into battle
against their hereditary enemies, the Iroquois. It was
early in July, 1609, when Champlain and canoeloads of
Algonquins attacked the Iroquois. The Algonquins,
aided by Champlain's firearms, defeated the Iroquois,
thus laying the foundation for a successful colony. The
irate Iroquois became allies of the English and 150
years later this alliance drove France from the New
World.

Champlain on that fateful canoe voyage discovered the great lake to which he gave his name, and dis-

Hudson's Bay Company trading posts still serve northern voyageurs after a 300-year romantic history.

covered the present state of Vermont, the Green Mountains, and the Adirondacks as well.

Champlain, blissfully unaware that he had sown the seeds for the downfall of the colony he had founded, became this continent's first major explorer to utilize the canoe in his travels.

Marquette and Joliet are probably America's best known canoeists. The Canadian-born explorer and hydrographer, Louis Joliet (1645–1700), and Jesuit missionary and explorer, Père (Father) Jacques Marquette (1637–1675), were the first to follow the Mississippi River from near its source to its confluence with the Arkansas River. They also discovered the Missouri River. Their canoes travelled on most of our major midwestern rivers.

Pierre Gaultier De Varennes, Sieur de La Verendrye (1685–1749), was the second great native Canadian explorer. After soldiering in Europe he returned to Canada where between 1730–34 he organized a chain of forts (trading posts) at his own expense to the northwest of Lake Superior.

Between 1738–44 Verendrye discovered the Dakotas, western Minnesota, Montana, Manitoba, and the Northwest Territories. Much of this exploration was done with canoes. He may have been the first native white North American to have sighted the Land of the Shining Mountains as the Big Stonies or Rocky Mountains were then called.

This man, so little known today, should be far better remembered than he is. The Province of Quebec now has a Verendrye Park—a place for semi-wilderness minded canoeists—a fitting memorial to this great explorer. His explorations led the way to a land and water route to the Pacific.

THE VOYAGEURS

The big 35-foot-long birchbark canoes were swung alongside the stone quays of Montreal near the huge stone and log warehouses that bulged with trade goods: red wool blankets, smoothbore muskets, powder, ball, lead bars, flints, steel knives, axes, tomahawks, needles, beans, mirrors, iron kettles, and copper tea pails. Goods were stowed in 90-pound bundles called "pieces."

Not forgotten were the 90-pound rawhide parfleches (pillowlike sacks) stuffed with pemmican, that staple ration of the fur brigades. A small cask of rum was stowed aboard each canoe. Every night the bourgeois—the head of the canoe brigade—would ration out drams to his pooped paddlers.

Goods were all stowed. Voyageurs had said their au revoirs to their wives, squaws or mistresses. Canoes swung into the current. Paddles dug in. Thirty strokes to the minute was standard but when necessity demanded the strokes could be increased to forty or fifty.

Sun glinted off swinging paddles. It was a long way to the annual rendezvous at Grand Portage at the head of Lake Superior.

These short, swarthy, good-natured, hard-working, hard-drinking sons of New France sang their chansons as they paddled their long way up the St. Lawrence, Ottawa, and Mattawa rivers, Lake Nipissing, Georgian Bay at the head of Lake Huron, and along the North Shore of Lake Superior to Grand Portage. Grand means big and it was big: nine weary miles over the Height of Land to the long chain of lakes and rivers that led northward.

Here at Grand Portage, the "pork-eaters" from Montreal met the usually good-natured contempt of the "winterers" from the North. Winterers were the self-endowed aristocrats of the fur trade. These hardy men were led by Scotsmen with names like MacFarlane, MacDougal or McGillivray.

Here, winterers turned in their furs and picked up their own supplies and trade goods. Drinking, wenching, singing, eating, and yarn spinning lasted a few days. Then the winterers were off to their beloved North Country and the pork-eaters laden with the winter's catch returned to the safe precincts of Montreal. Then the cycle would commence again.

A MODERN VOYAGEUR

Few of the millions watching political commentator Eric Sevareid are aware that his writing career commenced with one of this century's most remarkable canoe voyages.

Seventeen-year-old Sevareid and his high school classmate, Walter C. Port, decided to make a 2,250 mile voyage from Minneapolis to Hudson Bay via the Red River of the North, Lake Winnipeg and Nelson River. The *Minneapolis Star* agreed to pay $50 toward the voyage in exchange for a series of articles. The paper advanced money for supplies and equipment.

Four months after the *Sans Souci*—a second-hand 18-foot wood and canvas Old Town canoe—left Minneapolis, the voyageurs returned. It had been an exciting, educational, and sometimes harrowing voyage. The comrades were still friends though once, suffering from "bush fever," they had come to blows.

They left with a little knowledge about canoe handling and some elementary boy-scout-type knowledge of woodmanship; but they had survived fear, danger, hunger, cold—it was winter when they left the North—and they had come close to death and lesser disasters such as soggy flapjacks, but they had survived.

Florida's modern Seminoles demonstrate dugout canoe making.

The first leg of the voyage, along the Minnesota River and north along the Red River, was mostly through farm areas. Once they hit Lake Winnipeg, one of the world's largest lakes—actually an inland sea—they encountered high winds, rough water, and exposure beyond the protection their thin summer clothing provided.

There were compensations. Sevareid, a native of the prairies, was excited over his first views of vast evergreen forests and meetings with the Cree—his first Indians.

Finally, they arrived at York Factory—the end of their journey. They made their way 90 miles to the nearest railhead and thence back to Minneapolis where Sevareid ultimately became a newspaperman and then during World War II, a radio newsman in the China–Burma–India Theater for CBS.

Sevareid's book *Canoeing with the Cree* has become a classic. He was one of the few travelers through that area at the time who recorded their observations.

It was not an easy journey as Sevareid recalled nearly forty years later. "I knew instinctively that if I gave up . . . no matter what the justification, it would become easier forever afterwards to justify compromise with any achievement."

NEW YORK TO NOME

Two New Yorkers, Geoffrey Pope, 23, and Sheldon Taylor, 25, failed to interest Manhattan acquaintances in backing a 7,000-mile canoe voyage from New York City to Nome, Alaska. In the spring of 1939 they loaded meager supplies and ancient camp gear into a battered wood-and-canvas canoe and headed north. With this fragile logistical support they commenced their cruise up the Hudson, through the Champlain Barge Canal, down Lake Champlain (it flows north) into the Richelieu River and finally to Montreal.

Publicity sparked attention. The New Yorkers, who previously had viewed the venture with a financially jaundiced eye, anted up $400. That bought a new canoe and supplies, but there remained a problem, an elusive one that kept reappearing. It was like a dog that won't stay home and keeps popping up in the rear-view mirror.

The problem was bush fever. No two persons can withstand confinement within close quarters—and a canoe and small tent are close quarters—without unreasonable argument and sometimes blows—or even murder resulting. The slightest incidents create friction: the way a man uses his knife, chews his food, or scratches his insect bites can create a situation which can become homicidal.

The young voyageurs, too embarrassed to back out with their new-found support, drew up basic rules. They started down the long waterways that could lead to Nome—or nothingness. Despite their good intentions the rules didn't help.

They followed the old routes of the voyageurs into the Mackenzie system. Winter bound them at Fort Smith. They knew they probably could not survive the winter in each other's company. A wise decision was made. Each voyageur found a trapper he could work with during the long winter months ahead.

In the spring they started out. Friendship lasted two weeks. They still carried on. At Great Slave Lake the ice had not yet broken up so they hauled their supply-laden canoe over its icy surface. At breakup they continued down the Mackenzie to Rat River portage and thence through a series of lakes and rivers to the

Yukon. They battled high winds and rough water for more than a thousand miles. After reaching the Bering Sea, they made the final 300 miles along the coast to Nome.

The 7,000 mile voyage included about 150 miles of portages and had taken 18 months including the seven-month winter layover.

20th Century trippers follow the trans-Canada waterways of the voyageurs.

STUNT VOYAGEUR

Chicago adventurer Francis Brenton probably holds the present world record for "stunt" canoeing. He has twice canoed across the Atlantic—once he was rescued 30 miles from the African coast by a Russian merchantman—and made a 12,000-mile voyage from South America to the States. He has also canoed to Haiti.

His favorite trans-Atlantic craft are two canoes rigged as a catamaran.

THE VOYAGE THAT NEVER WAS

Had patriot Benedict Arnold (1741–1801), brilliant combat general and strategist of the Continental Army and "Father of the American Navy," selected light canoes rather than heavy wooded bateaux (rowboats) for his historic and heroic march up the Kennebec and down the Chaudière to Quebec, Canada, today might well be part of the United States.

The earlier arrival that canoes would have occasioned would have effected an earlier junction with Irish-born General Richard Montgomery, and Montreal as well as Quebec City would have been ours. The capture and holding of those two cities would have brought the rest of French Canada into line.

We are fortunate, indeed, to have such a fine neighbor but it is interesting to speculate on the course of North American history—and society today—had Arnold used canoes.

3
Canoe Talk

I've become very fond of this companion of ours, which carries us along so resolutely. All the more so because one is so thwarted in an affection for a canoe.

—Florence Page Jacques, *Canoe Country*

A cold wind swept up Narragansett Bay from the white-capped Atlantic and slammed loudly against the thinly clapboarded "boot" (recruit) barracks at the Naval Training Station in Newport, Rhode Island. It was January 21, 1941. Several hours earlier, before the swearing-in ceremonies, the recruiting officer gave us a bit of ironic encouragement: "Better six years in the Navy than a lifetime with the wrong woman and raising a baby that may not be yours."

It was nearly midnight. We hadn't eaten since noon—we were tired, cold, and thirsty. We began to regret—we still do—having left a potential career in the U.S. Army's (horse) Cavalry. Only there wasn't going to be a horse cavalry anymore. That was why we left the Army. We wouldn't have anything to do with an army that didn't appreciate horses or horse-trained cavalry officers.

A grizzled enlisted man wearing seven hash-marks—that's 28 years' service—came up the stairs. A boot timidly asked, "Where do we sleep, on the floor?" The old salt grimaced, "Listen, son, you're in the Navy now. This here Navy doesn't have floors, only decks."

From that day forward, floors were decks, walls were bulkheads, ceilings were overheads, stairs were ladders, and mealtime was chowtime.

It seemed ridiculous, at the time, to be awarded an extra tour of mess cooking—that's the Navy's K.P.—because we were inadvertently caught calling a "deck" the "floor."

Later, when "General Quarters" sounded on North Atlantic convoy runs, and all hands moved quickly, quietly, and efficiently to battle stations, we began to appreciate our common language. Aboard ship—and at times ashore—there would be no time to interpret your shipmate. When he said "deck" or "ladder" you knew instantly and exactly what he meant.

There are times during canoe voyages when it is important to know immediately and exactly what your shipmate, or fellow voyageur, means when he says or indicates stern or bow.

We've included some basic ship nomenclature. A canoe, much more ancient than the naval vessels of today, uses many of the same nautical terms.

GLOSSARY

Accessories —Basics needed by all canoeists such as paddles, life preservers and lines. See *Luxuries*.

Aft —Toward the *stern* (*which see*).

Ahead —In front of the canoe.

Aluminum	—Durable and light metal used in constructing canoes.
Amidships	—The middle (center) of the canoe.
Astern	. —Behind the canoe.
Bailer	—Any container used to bail, or scoop out, water shipped aboard. Some bailers are designed especially for the purpose.
Bang Plate	—A metal plate permanently fitted to the forward curve of the bow and stern to protect from damage. Sometimes termed "stem band" or "stern band." These can be separate parts designed to be fitted to canoes which do not come equipped with them. Some canoe materials, Royalex, for instance, do not require metal bang plates.

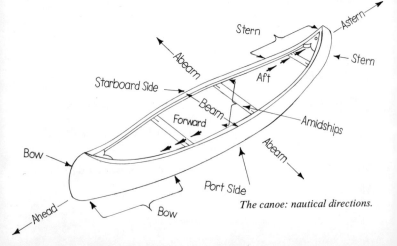

The canoe: nautical directions.

Beam
—Maximum width of canoe, usually at amidships.

Bilge
—Curved portion of the canoe's hull that lies underwater. Also applied, at times, to the regular canoe deck when a wooden removable deck is laid over integral deck.

Bilge strake(s)
—Bottommost planks of a planked canoe.

Bilgewater
—Water sloshing along the canoe's deck that has been shipped, or which comes from leaking water containers.

Bivouac
—An emergency or unplanned overnight campsite.

Blade
—Broad flat portion of a paddle.

Bow
—Forward section of canoe. Also, very forward tip of canoe.

Bow deck
—Small covered portion of bow.

Bowman
—The forward, or front, paddler or passenger.

Bow seat
—Forward (or front) seat.

Bow thwart
—Thwart (*which see*) located nearest bow.

Bracket
—Fixture used to mount outboard motor on canoe, just forward of the stern.

Bulkhead —Wall(s) of the bow and stern flotation compartments.

Carry —Both verb and noun are synonymous with *portage* (*which see*).

Cartop carrier —Rack fitted to automobile top for carrying one or two canoes and setting pole. Special racks can accommodate several canoes.

Centerline —Imaginary line running through center of the canoe from bow to stern.

Center thwart —Thwart (*which see*) located near amidships.

Center strake(s) —Planking on a canoe's side.

Deck —Inside bottom of the canoe. See also *Bow deck* and *Stern deck*.

Depth —Distance between bottom of the keel, or from bottom of hull on keelless canoes, to gunwale. Usually measured amidships. Should never be less than 12 inches.

Disembark —To get out of the canoe.

Ditty bag —Small canvas or nylon bag for carrying small items of gear.

Double-ender —Standard canoe with pointed bow and stern.

Draft —Amount of water displaced

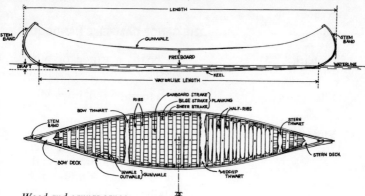

Wood-and-canvas canoe.

by loaded or unloaded canoe. Synonymous, at times, with *draw* (*which see*).

Draw
—Synonymous with *Draft*. Also meaning to pull a paddle toward the canoe (indraw), or to push away from the canoe (out-draw).

Duffel
—Canoeist camping equipment. Synonymous with *gear*. *Duffel* is essentially a landlubber's term. *Gear* is nautical.

Duffel bag
—A canvas, more recently nylon, bag carrying duffel or gear.

Duluth
—Name for classic cavernous canvas pack of Northwest canoe country. Sometimes known as the Poirier pack, after its designer.

Embark   —To board a canoe or other vessel.

Fiberglass   —A material used in modern canoes.

Flotation compartment —A chamber usually located under the bow and stern deck. This feature is usually found only on aluminum or magnesium canoes. Styrofoam has replaced air chambers on better aluminum canoes. The chamber provides increased flotation should the canoe capsize or a hole be rammed in the hull.

Freeboard   —Distance from gunwale to water surface. There should always be a 6-inch minimum between water and gunwale.

Forward   —Toward the *bow (which see).*

Freight canoe   —A canoe usually over 20 feet in length and up to 5 feet wide and nowadays usually with a square stern for mounting an outboard motor. Can carry several tons of equipment and supplies. Usually found in the Canadian bush and used by professionals.

Garboard strake(s)   —Planks next to bilge or bottom planking of planked canoes.

Gunwale(s)   —Originally applied to inner and outer wooden, usually ash, strips extending along both sides of the upper edges (sometimes called *rails*) of the canoe. See *inwale* and *outwale*. Most fiberglass, aluminum and Royalex canoes have solid strips of metal or plastic. In such cases there is a gunwale but no inwale or outwale. Gunwale is always pronounced "gunnel."

Gunwale guard (or cover)   —Rubber or plastic guards to protect paddle and gunwale from excessive wear. Also reduces noise on aluminum canoe. Guards may be short and cover only immediate area of paddle location or can cover both gunwales along entire length.

Half-ribs   —Just what the name implies. A method of reducing weight and production costs or of increasing strength.

Headband   —A wide leather band for the headstrap of a tumpline (*which see*). Attached to Duluth-type packs, head and neck carry much of the burden. Frequently, the headband is miscalled a tumpline.

Height   —Maximum height of canoe

from bottom of keel to top of bow and stern.

Inboard —Inside the canoe (or any craft). Also applied to inboard motors or engines.

Inwale —Inside section of the *gunwale* (*which see*).

Jury rig —A temporary repair.

Keel —A narrow strip fitted to the bottom of the canoe along the centerline. Designed to increase craft's stability. Usually made of wood or molded as in Royalex canoe. Aluminum on aluminum canoes. Shallow keels are designed for river running, deeper ones for lake canoeing.

Leeward —Downwind; the direction the wind is blowing toward. A technique of guiding a canoe through rapids.

Lining —Two lines, one to stern section and one to bow section, are attached to control the canoe from shore and avoid portaging. Also called "tracking."

Magnesium —Light but brittle material used briefly as canoe material and then abandoned.

Montrealer —Huge 30-35-foot-long canoes used in the fur trade to carry trade goods and supplies from Montreal west to Grand Portage, Lake Superior. Canoes returned to Montreal carrying furs.

Oar —This, despite N.Y. *Times* crossword puzzle maker Will Weng, is not the same as a paddle. A paddle is for a canoe, an oar for a rowboat.

Outwale —Outer section of *gunwale* (*which see*).

Packbasket —Beloved uncomfortable basic pack of Adirondack, New England, and Maritime Canada professional, and some amateur, canoeists.

Pack harness —Harness designed for attachment to duffel bags thus converting them into temporary backpack for portaging.

Painter —Line or rope, either permanently or temporarily attached to the bow, stern, or both. The painter, usually a short (10–15-foot) line, is used to secure the canoe to dock or other shore object.

Painter ring —A ring, located on the stem or stern (or both) for attachment of the *painter* (*which see*).

Pemmican —Staple food of the Plains Indians, voyageurs, and explorers. Too often, basic pemmican is corrupted by the addition of unnecessary flavorings or sweets. Basic pemmican is 50 percent melted tallow and 50 percent lean meat. Available today in commercial form.

Peterborough —Our oldest commercial canoe type, named after Peterborough, Ontario. Made of wood planking. Rare sight nowadays.

Planking —Thin narrow boards, usually red or sometimes white cedar, used on wood-canvas or wood canoes. Planking exposed on wood canoes of the Peterborough type or covered with canvas or Dacron on wood-canvas types.

Pole —To propel—or restrain—a canoe by means of a *setting pole* or poles (*which see*).

Pontoon(s) —Detachable cylinders of aluminum or plastic which are supported outboard by a light frame. Designed to stabilize canoe. Sometimes used to alleviate tyro's fear of canoe's mythical instability. Solid balsa blocks are sometimes used.

Port —Left side or to the left (facing forward) side of the canoe. Formerly called *lar-*

	board but changed to avoid confusion with *starboard*.
Portage	—To carry canoe from one body of water to another (verb). "Portage" also is that stretch of ground between two bodies of water, or around obstructions on a river, over which a canoe is portaged or carried.
Portside	—Left side of canoe, facing toward bow.
Prow	—The edge of the bow that slices through the water.
Push pole	—See *Setting pole.*
Ribs	—U-shaped (by steaming) strips of red or white cedar that curve downward from one gunwale to and across the deck and up the other side terminating at the gunwale. Ribs average 2·inches in width. Spacing of ribs varies, but rarely are they more than 4 inches apart. Ultra-lightweight wood-and-canvas canoes are partly created by spacing ribs further apart. Ribs are always found on wood and wood-canvas canoes, rarely on other types.
Rope	—This is a lubberly term. Correct nautical terminology is *line.*

Royalex —A nonporous thermoplastic canoe material.

Seating thwart —Some canoes have seats replaced by slightly wider-than-normal thwarts. As canoeist kneels—they serve as butt-rest.

Setting pole —A pole, usually hardwood, from 10 to 14 feet long, shod with metal point. In mucky bottom or swamp country, an expanding and contracting device is used on the tip to prevent the pole from sinking into the mud. When fitted with this end, the pole is often called, notably in the South, a *push pole.*

Shaft —That section of the paddle, miscalled *handle* by tyros, between grip and blade.

Sheer —The curving upward sweep of the bow and stern seen from the side.

Sponsons —Air chambers built along and below gunwales. Not usually found on most contemporary canoes. Designed to increase floatability of capsized canoes. Most often used on older models of wood-canvas canoes. Sponsons add weight and make for more difficult maneuvering.

Spray cover   —A waterproof canvas or ny-
                           lon cover designed to fit
                           over the canoe. Used to re-
                           duce shipping water while
                           passing through white water
                           (covers are fitted with man-
                           holes).

Spreader   —See *thwart*.

Square stern   —Canoe with square stern de-
                           signed specifically for use
                           with outboard motor.

Starboard   —Right side, or to the right
                           side, of the canoe facing for-
                           ward (toward the bow).

Stern   —After (rear) section of the ca-
                           noe. Also, rearmost part of
                           the canoe.

Stern deck   —Small covered section of the
                           stern.

Sternman   —Stern- or rearmost paddler.

Stern seat   —After, or rear, seat.

Stern thwart   —*Thwart (which see)* located
                           nearest stern.

Strake   —Synonymous with *planking*.
                           Applicable only to plank ca-
                           noes like wood Peter-
                           borough or wood-canvas ca-
                           noes. See also *garboard,
                           bilge* and *center strakes*.

Switch   —Cry from bowman to stern-
                           man or vice versa when pad-
                           dler wishes to change paddl-
                           ing sides.

Throat

—Section of the paddle where *shaft* (*which see*) widens into the *blade* (*which see*).

Thwart

—A narrow (2-inch average) bar extending across canoe from gunwale to gunwale. *Spreaders* as they are sometimes termed keep canoe sides from caving inward. Most canoes have a minimum of three but some fiberglass and molded Royalex craft have only one.

Tie-downs

—Lines or straps designed to secure canoe to cartop carriers.

Trim

—*Verb,* to load a canoe so that it is properly balanced. *Noun,* the balance after loading. A properly balanced canoe is "in trim." An improperly balanced canoe is "out of trim."

Tumblehome

—The convex, inward curve of the hull from waterline to gunwale.

Tumpline

—A wide (2–3 inch) leather band with latigo straps attached. Is worn around the head while gear such as duffel bags, secured with straps, is toted on back. Experienced voyageurs are capable of toting 300 pounds for short distances.

Waterline —The line bounding a canoe's hull where it meets the surface of the water.

Waterline length —The bow-to-stern distance that lies in the water.

Water skiers —A goddam nuisance to canoeists. Nautical version of the skimobiler.

Windward —Upwind, or the direction from which the wind is blowing.

Yaw —Unintentional deviation from plotted or intended course, from one side to the other.

Yoke —Commercial yokes are arched wooden frames, like the water-carrying yokes of yore, designed to fit around the neck and over the shoulders for the purpose of carrying the canoe. Commercial yokes are usually padded with a foam material. A *jury rig* (*which see*) can be fashioned from two paddles.

Canoe with kneeling thwarts in lieu of seats.

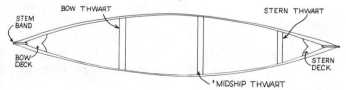

STEM BAND
BOW THWART
STERN THWART
BOW DECK
STERN DECK
MIDSHIP THWART

4
How to Select Your Canoe

Thus the Birch Canoe was builded In the valley, by the river. . . . And it floated on the river Like a yellow leaf in Autumn, Like a yellow water lily.

—H. W. Longfellow, *Hiawatha*

The canoe probably had as its genesis a primitive man straddling a log, drifting downstream. Sometime later, days or centuries, a stick became a primitive paddle.

Centuries later, the dugout canoe, usually a burned or gouged-out single log, came into being.

Even today the dugout is the world's most widely distributed canoe. The Pacific coast of North America, the Louisiana bayous, Florida swamps, the banana republics of Central America, Amazon country, Africa, and Southeast Asia all know the dugout.

The Sandwich Islands, now known as Hawaii, were settled more than 130 generations ago by Boru Boru natives who paddled 5,500 miles to their new home in dugout canoes.

Ancient Britons may have watched that vigorous visitor Julius Caesar from their fragile-framed, hide-covered coracles.

Andean Indians for centuries used reed canoes while American Plains Indians used bullboats—willow frames covered with buffalo hide—along the great rivers of the West like the Upper Missouri and Yellowstone.

Many North Americans picture canoes as the leaf-like but rugged birchbark canoe paddled by a solitary Indian, or a larger birchbark canoe with war-whooping braves in pursuit of the heroic Daniel Boone or his contemporaries.

For centuries, the kayak of the Russian and American Eskimo has helped provide food and clothing for the world's most northerly dwellers.

Call it canoe, kayak, bullboat, coracle or what you will, the canoe is the world's oldest, and to many of us the most significant and romantic form of transportation.

Those of us fortunate to view the far corners of the globe (if a globe can have corners), know that in the Canadian Northwest, from Maine to Madagascar, and from Zanzibar to the Zambesi, canoes are the automobile of the outback. Prospectors, geologists, missionaries, physicians, scientists, Indians, trappers, and headhunters use the canoe as a daily form of transport.

Here are some factors to consider in choosing your own canoe:

Length

Overall canoe lengths shorter than 16 feet, while easier to maneuver, do not make the headway of the 16-to-18-footers. Many authorities condemn even the 16-footer as inadequate for extended voyaging.

Sigurd F. Olson, one of our most knowledgeable voyageurs and a leading ecologist, made a three-week, 500-mile voyage along the Churchill River with five companions. They used three wood-and-canvas 16-foot Peterborough canoes.

We've made four-week voyages in 16-footers with but one resupply depot en route.

There is an advantage in those 18-footers over the 16-footers where the bow is slightly higher, the beam 2 or 3 inches wider, and the freeboard is slightly greater with an equal load. Cubic and weight capacity is also greater.

Length, though it is not the sole criterion, has a direct relationship to capacity.

A major factor among many canoeists, in determining their canoe's length, is weight.

Many small-car owners choose 15- or 16-footers over 17-footers because this reduces the amount of overhang. But we've known small-car owners who tote 17-footers atop their cars and have no trouble.

Those voyageurs who are lucky enough to be able to cruise three or four weeks long (this includes many college faculty members) often select a 17- or 18-footer because of the capacity. Sigurd Olson, as noted before, made a three-week wilderness cruise, with only one resupply point, in a 16-footer.

Weight is a major factor in determining ultimate length. Few recreational canoeists want to tote a canoe weighing more than 75 pounds. Many of us prefer lighter weights.

The 17-footer is an excellent compromise. Then, too, canoeists in Canada who fly into or out of the bush in float-equipped planes are restricted by law to a maximum canoe length of 17 feet.

Alumacraft's recently marketed "Quetico," partly

designed by our friend and outfitter, Jon Marshall Waters, is 17 feet long and weighs 69 pounds. For an extended voyage we prefer this canoe to our 16-foot Royalex.

The 15-footer (we once owned a Grumman in this length), being relatively short for its beam, is somewhat more difficult to handle and its load capacity is more limited. Due to its light weight, particularly in the lightweight Grumman version, it is quite practical for voyages of about a week provided your outfit is compact. The somewhat greater difficulty in handling is noticeable only to more expert canoeists.

Weight

Weight alone should not form the basis for your canoe selection. The advantages and disadvantages of each type of material, structural features, and type of canoeing contemplated should bear on your selection.

Leisurely cruising along placid waterways in rural areas or semi-wilderness doesn't require the most rugged construction, the widest beam, maximum bow/stern depth, nor the greatest depth amidships.

Portages are a factor. Few portages or short ones mean that you can select a heavier, or longer, canoe than if you plan voyages with numerous portages.

Physical condition is a factor. I could carry more weight at 20 than I can at 53. At least I no longer attempt to carry the heaviest canoes, unless assisted, and on solo voyages assistance does not exist. Solo voyages, however, do not require a heavy canoe.

You may prefer the classic wood-canvas canoe, but if weight is a major factor then you may have to get an aluminum canoe, or settle for a shorter lightweight wood-and-canvas model.

Some comparative weights and materials:

	16-foot	*18-foot*
Old Town Royalex	58 pounds	68 pounds
Old Town Fibreglass	77 pounds	89 pounds
Old Town Wood/Canvas	85 pounds	100 pounds
Chestnut Wood/Canvas	76 pounds	88 pounds
Chestnut Fibreglass	75 pounds	NA
Chestnut Aluminum	79 pounds	NA
Grumman Standard	NA	85 pounds
Grumman Lightweight	NA	67 pounds

The above figures are not an exact comparison, because of differences in bow/stern depth, depth amidships, beam, and number of thwarts. For example, the 18-foot Old Town "Guide" model in wood and canvas has a 37-inch beam, and a 23-inch bow/stern depth and is 12 inches deep amidships whereas the Chestnut "Prospector" in the 18-foot "Voyageur" model has a 38-inch beam and a 24-inch bow/stern depth and is 15 inches amidships.

Beam

Avoid any voyaging canoe with an amidship width less than 36 inches. Most canoes with a length of 16 feet have at least that much beam. The wider the beam the more stable the canoe (provided hull design is identical). A flat-bottom canoe with a 36-inch beam will be more stable than a rounded-bottom canoe of slightly greater beam. Rounded bottoms are not usually selected for a voyaging canoe.

Beam should have a direct ratio to length. Chestnut "Prospector" model canoes increase their beam by 1 inch for every additional foot of length between 15 and 18 feet.

Some very short canoes like the Mansfield 13-footer have a wide beam, but this is not designed for cruising. It is a one-man, cartop fishing canoe.

Depth

Reject for voyaging canoes with an amidship depth less than 12 inches. A canoe carrying two people and one or more weeks of supplies and equipment may well weigh up to one-half the actual—as differentiated from advertised—load capacity of the canoe. When a canoe, regardless of its amidship depth, has less than 6 inches of freeboard, then it is overloaded and becomes hazardous in running seas or in white water.

Well-designed canoes built by reliable and knowledgeable manufacturers have a standard ratio of depth-to-beam-to-length. As the length increases, so does the beam and the depth. Some manufacturers practice deception by advertising the bow depth (height) as canoe "depth." Anyone conversant with canoes would recognize that no 17-foot canoe would have a 22-inch depth amidships.

A well-designed 16-footer will have at least a 12-inch depth amidships, while an 18-foot "Prospector" will have a minimum of 15 inches.

"Prospector" models will have a greater depth by as much as 2 or 3 inches than a model designed for childrens' camps or Sunday-afternoon courting.

Bow/Stern Depth (Height)

Bow and stern are usually the same depth. The

bow depth of a canoe designed for both river and lake voyaging is of necessity a compromise. The bow must be deep enough to knife through a lake's running seas or through heavy white water. Bow and stern ends should not be so high that they act as sails. Any up-curved bow or stern is affected somewhat but on certain canoes the upsweep is excessive.

Here again, first-rate manufacturers, like Old Town and Chestnut, have a ratio between length, depth, and bow/stern depth. A 15-footer has a bow depth of 19 inches, the 16-footer, 23 inches, and an 18-footer, 25 inches.

Wood-and-canvas "Guide" and "Prospector" models, designed for professional use or for recreational voyages to the outback, have deeper bows and sterns than so-called "pleasure" or "camper" models. Here "camper" doesn't mean use by voyageurs. They are intended for summer camps. The "camper" models are not designed to withstand really heavy use.

The bow depth on a typical 16-foot "pleasure" canoe is 20½ inches, while on the same manufacturer's 16-foot "Prospector" model it is 23 inches.

Well-designed aluminum canoes usually have shallower bow/stern depths than wood-and-canvas models.

Chestnut makes four aluminum canoes in 15-to-18-foot lengths. Three have identical bow/stern depths of 20½ inches. Aluminum canoes have more buoyancy than wood-and-canvas ones. Thus they ride higher in the water. While a 20-inch bow depth is proper for an aluminum canoe, it would be poor design on a less buoyant wood-and-canvas craft.

Keels

Keels prevent sideslipping in fast currents or in the

wave and wind action on lakes. Wood, wood-and-canvas, and some fiberglass canoes usually have wooden keels. Aluminum canoes have aluminum keels. Old Town Royalex has a shallow, tapered, molded keel. Many canoes have a compromise keel—not really deep enough for big lake canoeing nor shallow enough for river running.

General canoe manufacturers like Old Town and Grumman offer special keels and keelless canoes. Chestnut, which makes general-purpose and special-purpose canoes, provides a variety of keels depending on the basic use the canoe is designed for.

The lake keel is usually a hardwood strip, sometimes an inch or more deep, for canoes used on wide rivers and lakes or salt water. This keel can be used for river running but it is too deep for satisfactory or efficient use in shallow water. The shoe (river) keel is a wide flat strip designed for river running.

Some canoes, like the Chestnut "Prospector" models, are keelless. This is fine for rivers. Some sideslip that might be encountered in lake travel is partially counteracted by the basic canoe design.

Hull Design

The flatter the bottom, within reason, the greater the stability and, other factors being equal, the greater the load capacity. This is a desirable feature in a voyaging canoe.

Long, parallel gunwales that taper into the bow/stern are somewhat more stable, provide greater load capacity, and give better overall handling; most desirable in a voyaging canoe.

A sharply curved bow/stern is desirable for canoes primarily used in whitewater competition but not for voyaging canoes.

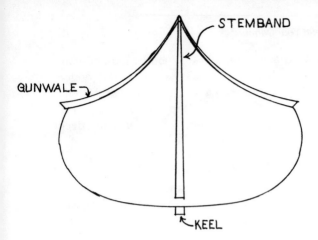

FLAT BOTTOM

Flat bottom provides greater stability and capacity.

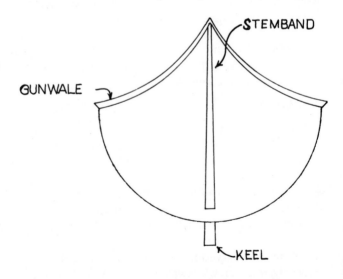

ROUND BOTTOM

Round bottom, while less stable, moves faster through the water than the flat bottom. Designed for racing and whitewater work.

Seats and Thwarts

Our Royalex 16-footer has one wooden thwart amidships. Wood, wood-and-canvas, and most fiberglass canoes have wooden thwarts. Aluminum canoes have aluminum thwarts.

Most 16-footers have two thwarts, and 17- and 18-footers have three. There is no fixed rule and variations will be encountered.

Thwarts provide bracing and strengthen a canoe, but until recent years canoes had no seats. Thwarts were located slightly lower than those of the present day. Paddlers kneeled and rested their backsides against the thwarts. Some Canadian canoes are still made this way.

There are usually two canoe seats in canoes up to 20 feet. They are made of cane in wooden or wood-and-canvas canoes, and we have seen wooden seats in fiberglass craft.

These are features which apply to canoes in general. We will now have a look in more detail at specific types and makes of canoes.

PETERBOROUGH ALL-WOOD CANOES

In the mid-1870s a Peterborough, Ontario firm made what may have been the first successful commercial canoe. The Peterborough was constructed with ribs and planking like the wood-and-canvas canoe which was shortly to follow. The Peterborough did not, however, have a canvas skin over its cedar planking. Planking was so closely fitted that it was watertight.

These were superbly crafted canoes. In 1947 we bought an ancient all-wood Peterborough in Stockholm and used it until we returned to this country four years later. We voyaged in it from Norway to Southern

France. It took us along the Rhine, Rhône, Seine and many other European rivers and streams. No major canoe company that we know of still makes the wooden Peterborough, and it's a shame.

WOOD-AND-CANVAS CANOES

Construction is of thin red or white cedar, or spruce, planks which are closely fitted horizontally to U-shaped cedar cross ribs. The closer the ribs, the stronger and heavier the frame will be. A typical cedar rib is ⅜-inch thick by 3 inches wide. They are usually spaced 2 inches apart. Many freight canoes capable of carrying 3000–5000 pounds have ribs ½ inch thick by 3 inches

*Chestnut wood-and-canvas canoe. This Ogilvy model,
designed for rough use, has closely fitted ribs.*

wide and spaced only 1¼ inches apart. Ultra-light-weight canoes use light canvas such as #10, while wilderness canoes like the "Prospector" models use the more durable and heavier #8 canvas. Freight canoes often use heavy #6 or #4. Dacron, lighter than canvas, reduces the overall weight of the canoe. Gunwales and thwarts are wood. Seats are cane, slats or babiche (varnished rawhide as used in snowshoes).

The precise origin of the wood-and-canvas canoe is lost in obscurity but two companies, Old Town in Maine and Chestnut in the Province of New Brunswick, remain prominent in their respective countries after a near century of first-rate canoe craftsmanship and design.

An Old Town wood-and-canvas canoe in the making.
Close-fitting planking is secured to cedar ribs.

Old Town, to millions of Americans, meant "canoe" until the advent of the aluminum canoe in 1945. Old Town now makes Royalex and fiberglass as well as wood-and-canvas craft. Chestnut makes aluminum and fiberglass along with its famed wilderness wood-and-canvas canoe.

The wood-and-canvas canoe, despite premature obituaries, will be around for many years. It has some important advantages. Aside from esthetic considerations, the wood-and-canvas canoe is a sleek and lovely craft. Further, it is almost silent as it glides through the water. It is an ideal craft for the fisherman and for the wildlife photographer.

This type of canoe, to our way of thinking, being made of wood and canvas, both organic materials, blends into the countryside or wilderness far better than the easier-to-maintain aluminum or synthetic canoe.

We consider finely crafted canoes by Old Town or Chestnut to be as lovely as a fine bamboo fly or spinning rod, or a gold-inlaid engraved shotgun.

The canvas-and-wood wilderness canoe is capable of absorbing considerable punishment. Damage to the canvas is easy to repair, and two or three fractured ribs are not sufficient damage to even beach the craft.

Because wood-canvas canoes are handmade they are available in a wider and more practical range of modifications of beam, depth, and bow/stern depths.

The oft-alleged disadvantage of the wood-and-canvas canoe—that it is fragile—is simply not true. Sigurd F. Olson in *The Lonely Land* substantiates this in his story of his 500-mile Churchill River voyage. So does Eric Sevareid's *Canoeing with the Cree,* which tells of his experiences with an 18-foot Old Town canoe.

However, wood-and-canvas canoes do require more maintenance than any other type. This is why

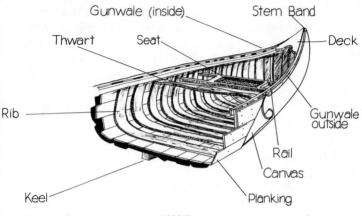

Wood-and-canvas construction (Old Town).

most canoe liveries with fleets of several hundred canoes use aluminum.

Wood-and-canvas canoes are often condemned on the basis of weight. They do weigh more than a lightweight aluminum canoe of the same size or than one of Royalex, but standard-weight aluminum and fiberglass canoes weigh about the same for the same length. Canvas, however, tends to absorb water, and it is reported that an 18-footer can absorb 10 pounds or more of water.

Wood-and-canvas canoes require more work to maintain than any other commercial type. The work consists of scraping and repainting or revarnishing. This should be done whenever needed, but once a year is the average. As much of the old paint as possible should be removed. One coat of paint can add up to 10 pounds of weight. After white water usage, check ribs for cracks and canvas for cuts, tears, or abrasions.

Wood-and-canvas repair kits, available from most manufacturers, usually contain pieces of canvas, nails and Ambroid cement. All canvas rips or tears should be repaired immediately. This arrests further damage. Small breaks in the wood hull can usually be repaired with the items in repair kits. Well-constructed canoes can survive, without immediate repair, the breakage of a few ribs.

ALUMINUM CANOES

Aluminum canoes are usually made of two half-hull sections riveted together. Grumman canoes from 1945 to 1953 had fore and aft air chambers for flotation. Since then, Grumman and most imitators have used styrofoam in the fore and aft compartments.

Seats and thwarts are usually of aluminum. At least one aluminum canoe manufacturer, Grumman, offers section or full gunwale guards or covers. These reduce the noise from paddles hitting the gunwales and also reduce paddle and gunwale wear.

The advantages of aluminum canoes are numerous. They are virtually maintenance-free and almost unsinkable. They are light in weight (in the lightest version), a godsend for portaging. Many used aluminum canoes show innumerable dents and scars but they are rarely punctured during voyaging. Aluminum, with the possible exception of the recently developed Royalex thermoplastic, may be the toughest of canoe materials. The canoes can be used to reflect campfire heat into a tent, or even to heat water for a much-needed bath. In this case, the aluminum canoe serves as both kettle and bath tub.

As to disadvantages, aluminum canoes have a high degree of buoyancy (this has its obvious advantages) so

Grumman aluminum canoe. Aluminum canoes should always have flat rivets on hull bottom. They are less apt to shear off on rocky river bottoms than round-headed rivets.

that the canoe can drift away more readily from you should you capsize. Buoyancy means that the canoe rides higher in the water than wooden, wood-and-canvas and some fiberglass models, and that the bows must be several inches shallower than identical-length models made from other materials.

Aluminum is noisier than nonmetallic materials like wood-and-canvas or Royalex. This is of greater concern to wildlife photographers and fishermen than to canoe voyageurs. This drawback is tempered by the fact that some, including this writer, find that aluminum sounds a louder warning when scraping over rocks or very shallow bottoms. Aluminum canoes long in the sunshine can get uncomfortably warm but not unendurably hot—and the bottom also transmits cold.

Some dislike aluminum because of its metallic, anti-wilderness appearance. This can partially be overcome by having it factory-painted, a good idea on two counts: it reduces glare and prevents salt-water corrosion. Our last Grumman was painted marsh-brown for more effective camouflage while hunting waterfowl.

Despite these drawbacks, aluminum canoes require almost no maintenance. This is why it is the most popular type used by canoe rental services. Canoe liveries owning hundreds of canoes could not afford to maintain wood-and-canvas canoes.

Factory-painted canoes rarely require full paint jobs. Post-voyage touch-ups can be easily done with the special spray paint often available from manufacturers like Grumman; the price is $3.95 per quart.

Small punctures can be repaired by pounding both sides of the puncture with small round stones until the edges are flat. The hole is covered inside and out with waterproof adhesive tape (a 2 x 180-inch roll of waterproof adhesive tape is one of a canoeist's most useful repair items). Large holes, up to 4 inches, should be flattened in the above manner. Stuff an unfilled hole with cloth (we once used a shirt tail), and then cover it with waterproof adhesive tape on both sides.

Back home, locate a shop with aluminum riveting facilities and have an aluminum plate riveted over the rupture.

ROYALEX CANOES

Royalex construction consists of an eight-ply laminated sheet of thermoplastic heated and positioned over a hull mold. A vacuum sucks the sheet into place. After cooling, the hull is removed and rough edges are trimmed. Seats, a wooden thwart or thwarts, and a vinyl gunwale trim are fitted.

Royalex ABS, a relatively new thermoplastic, has

been extensively tested in the factory and afloat by companies like Old Town but it is, in our belief, too early to render a judgment as to its merits in comparison with other materials.

It is virtually maintenance-free, it is the lightest of current commercially available canoe materials, and it is extremely rugged. After minor blows, the material, like rubber, springs back into its original shape. Major dents are removed by heating.

This year, from June into November, we deliberately left our 16-foot "Chippewayan" atop the station wagon when it was not in use. The sun had no apparent effect on the craft.

My 16-foot Old Town Royalex canoe.

This past spring we acquired an Old Town "Chippewayan" canoe. An 18-footer was not immediately available, so we settled for a 16-footer. It has seen considerable use on rivers and on Lake Champlain, one of our largest and most treacherous freshwater lakes outside of the Great Lakes. It has been satisfactory to date.

We talked with several Royalex owners and users and did not encounter among them a rumored criticism that the canoe tends to bend or flex (it has no ribs). This might be true of an 18-footer, but we have not found this fault in our craft.

Punctures are repaired by heating (a candle or cigarette lighter will do) the area surrounding the hole and then molding the flowing material into the breach. This is what Old Town's president, Deane Gray, told us. Being a conservative Yankee, the spirit did not move us to drive a hole deliberately through the canoe to test Gray's advice. He assured us that this medication for wounded Royalex canoes has been successful in factory and field tests.

The Old Town Canoe Company is at present the only major manufacturer of Royalex canoes. There may be small manufacturers unknown to us. We understand that several, mostly shoestring operators, abandoned sporadic attempts to use Royalex as a constuction material. The retail price in 1973 of a 16-foot Chippewayan was $345. An 18-footer was $375.

FIBERGLASS CANOES

Each manufacturer seems to use his own particular method of construction in using fiberglass.

Fiberglass is a relative newcomer (although not as new as Royalex) as a canoe material. Early models were mostly made by companies new to canoe making. The oldliners like Grumman, Old Town, and Chestnut, preferred to remain with their particular materials until the material had proven itself. Awkward and sometimes dangerous designs characterized the first few years.

Newcomers either quit or improved design and workmanship. Ultimately, Old Town and Chestnut entered the field. Their fiberglass canoes are characterized by the same high standards as their wood-and-canvas models.

Durability and freedom from maintenance chores are the chief advantages of this material. On the debit side, fiberglass canoes are just about as heavy, sometimes heavier, than their wood-and-canvas counterparts. Unlike the latter type, however, fiberglass will not absorb water unless the outer skin is ripped away.

We prefer the lovelier and more versatile wood-and-canvas models to fiberglass, but it is virtually maintenance free. Repairs usually can be effected with fiberglass patching kits.

A 17-foot-2-inch Old Town "Carleton Voyageur" is $320 compared to $385 for the same length in Royalex or $680 for a wood-and-canvas "Guide" model (17-footers are not available).

Chestnut's 16-foot (they don't make 18-footers) fiberglass "Camper" model is $251 compared to $245 for their same length aluminum "Mink" model or to $374 for their same length "Fawn" model in the "Prospector" series.

Chicagoland Canoe Base makes a well designed "Canadien" fiberglass canoe in several lengths.

THE NE'ER-DO-WELLS

Two canoe materials that flitted briefly about our waterways were Dow Chemical Company's magnesium

and plywood. Magnesium, while lighter than aluminum, is not as rugged. Plywood was just too heavy.

5
Outfitting your Canoe

*"I could carry, paddle, walk and sing with any
man I ever saw. I have been twenty-four years
a canoe man, and forty years in the service: no
portage was ever too long for me. Fifty songs
could I sing. I have saved the lives of ten voyageurs. Have had twelve wives and six running
dogs. I spent all my money in pleasure. Were I
young again, I should spend my life the same
way over. There is no life so happy as a voyageur's life."*
—Dr. Grace Lee Nute, *The Voyageur*

Canadians, past and present, have more experience
with canoes and voyaging than any other people in the
world. That is appropriate, as our friendly neighbor has
about one-half of the world's freshwater area in lakes
and rivers. Canadian law requires that all canoes carry
an approved life preserver for each occupant plus a
spare paddle. Despite the lack of such legislation in this
country, common prudence dictates that it is rash to
fare forth even for a Sunday-afternoon pond cruise
without this safety equipment.

WHAT IS OUTFITTING?

This chapter is concerned only with equipment designed to make the canoe a more efficient mode of travel. Outfitting for canoe camping is covered in Chapters 6–15.

Gear for canoe outfitting may be divided into three categories:

1. *Basic necessities* like paddles, poles, tracking lines, and life preservers (a legal necessity in some areas).

2. *Conveniences* like jury-rig decks, gunwale guards, seat packs, carrying yokes.

3. *Sunday-afternoon trip items* which have no place in canoe camping and cruising. Examples: seat backs, seats, sponsons, pontoons, seat cushions (as opposed to functional life preserver cushions).

PADDLE MATERIALS, DESIGNS, AND CONSTRUCTION

Hardwoods are heavier and more durable than softwoods but are more prone to warpage. Softwoods, easier to paddle with because they are lighter, are less prone to warpage but are far more easily damaged on rocks and rough river bottoms.

Maple is probably the most durable of the several paddle woods but is very heavy. It is rarely seen these days.

Many professionals have switched to white ash. This hardwood, while heavier than spruce, will withstand considerable battering. There is a wide variation

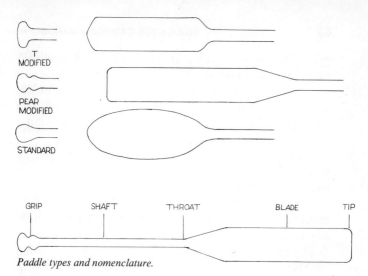

T
MODIFIED

PEAR
MODIFIED

STANDARD

GRIP   SHAFT   THROAT   BLADE   TIP

Paddle types and nomenclature.

in the density of ash. This means that two ash paddles of the same size and design may have different weights. Weight is a matter of personal preference. Avoid ash with knots.

Spruce is a relatively light wood and favored by many women. It is the best softwood material.

Well-made laminated paddles may outlast the non-laminates but our limited experience with them has not been reassuring. We know several experienced paddlers who swear by them.

Fiberglass kayak paddles have been around for several years. It is inevitable that standard single canoe paddles will be made of this widely used material.

Spruce is favored by some professionals for lake work where high winds and running waves make paddling difficult.

Blade widths vary between 5¾ and 8 inches, although extremes exist. Narrow blades offer less resistance to the water and so are less tiring. Wide blades are more tiring because of increased resistance but they also propel the canoe farther at one stroke than narrower blades. We use Old Town's widest white-ash blade (7¾ inches); price, $13. We've long since used wide blades and find their use not particularly difficult. Janet uses an Old Town spruce paddle with a 6½-inch blade; price, $12.50.

Blades should not be more than ⅛ inch thick so that they will knife through the water with minimum resistance. Thicker blades should be sanded down.

There is no necessity for varnishing blades but makers varnish them because the vast majority of holiday canoeists, as opposed to canoe voyageurs, seem to think that varnish is an improvement.

No varnish should be on the grip where you hold it by the shaft. Our paddles have no grip varnish. We sanded off the varnish along the lower section of the shaft.

Our personal preference in blade shapes is for the basic Maine Guide, or Maine, or Guide (different names for the same type blade) with round or curved blade bottom. Many voyageurs, notably Midwesterners, prefer the flat or square blade bottom, usually in conjunction with the T-shaped grip.

The classic paddle grip is pear-shaped. We find this far more comfortable than the T-shaped grip. Most users of the T-grip that we have interviewed have never used the pear grip. Some of those who switched to the latter type have been surprised at its comfort. Don't take our word for it—try both.

Paddle Length

Bowman's paddle should reach from the ground to his chin or nose. Sternman's paddle should reach from the ground to his eyes or the top of his head.

This is one of the several traditional methods used to determine the approximate length of your paddle. The only method that works is experimentation. Borrow or rent paddles before you purchase one. If you do make an error, the cost of a new paddle is not prohibitive. You can probably sell your mistake.

Outfitters usually stock paddles ranging from 5 to 6 feet in 3-inch or 6-inch increments.

Janet is 5 feet 4 inches tall, but a 5-foot-6-inch paddle is her best fit. I am 6 feet 7 inches tall and use a 6-foot paddle with no problems, but a custom-made one a few inches longer might be a better fit.

In theory the spare paddle length should be a little short for the sternman and a little long for the bowman. However, Janet originally used a 5-foot paddle and we used the 5-foot-6-inch paddle for a spare. She accidentally discovered the spare was a better fit so we swapped off the 5-footer and secured another 5-foot-6-inch spare.

Plastic Blade/Aluminum Shaft

I have not tried this space-age paddle. An Iliad Classic paddle used by a friend, whitewater canoe designer and manufacturer Jim Henry, has a hollow aluminum shaft covered with a knit stretch nylon sleeve that is saturated with epoxy resin. Jim says this provides a firm grip under the wettest conditions. The standard shaft has neoprene rubber grips. Blades of both Standard and Classic models are molded from high-density fiberglass cloth and epoxy resin.

These paddles are widely used by whitewater canoemen and are undoubtedly lighter, more efficient and more rugged than the classic wood paddle, but I prefer the more esthetic look and tradition of the latter.

Iliad paddles are made by Iliad, Inc., 168 Circuit St., Norwell, Mass. 02061, or can be ordered from Mad River Canoes, Waitsfield, Vt. 05673. Write for catalog. Prices start at about $30.

PADDLE CARE

Paddles should not be left on the ground where they can get damaged. Keep them out of the sun to prevent warpage. Don't use paddles as setting poles. Don't stand paddles with the blade on the floor, either in camp or at home. Suspend paddles with a piece of nylon parachute cord from a tree branch out of the sun, or from a nail in the wall at home.

There's only so much that can be done with a badly damaged paddle. Immediately when damage occurs, switch to your spare and then undertake emergency repairs at camp.

Split or cracked blades are probably the most common damage. Edges can be repaired with epoxy glue or with a fiberglass filler. More permanent repairs can be effected at home by using a thin copper strip around the paddle bottom. Fiberglass may be used instead of a copper strip.

Never start a voyage with a paddle that has obvious defects with the idea that it will hold out. A broken paddle can lead to disaster. Avoid such situations by starting with paddles in faultless condition. Keep that good spare where it can be readily reached by the bowman or stern paddler.

SETTING POLE

Setting poles are indispensable for getting a canoe

upstream through shallow water. One or two poles can be used. Our 14-foot Old Town ash pole is shod with a slightly blunted, iron tip so that it won't slip so readily on wet rocks. We've heard about aluminum poles, but have never seen one. They may be lighter, but we're sure that they aren't as flexible or as durable as ash.

Our pole may be too long, as references in canoeing literature mention only 12-or 10-foot poles. However, with my exceptional height and long arms, the 14-footer is about right. It creates no major stowage problems in a 17-foot canoe.

Push Pole

This is the Dixie version of the Yankee and Canadian setting pole. Mud bottoms require a clam-shell type of head that opens and closes. Home-made push poles are often used by folk like those of the Okefenokee Swamp who led us to the headwaters of the Suwannee River, made famous by Stephen Foster, although he never saw it. These poles, with a foot-long strip of wood nailed to the pole's bottom end, don't readily sink into the muck.

Some greenhorns call setting poles "push poles." This is technically the wrong term, though an apt description of their use.

FLOTATION VESTS

Every canoeist who cannot swim should always wear a flotation vest when he is afloat.

Every canoeist, *regardless* of his swimming ability, should wear a flotation vest when running white water or when cruising wind-whipped lakes.

Flotation vests should be immediately at hand.

Mine is carried just under the flap of my personal pack which always sits directly in front of my stern seat. Janet (she is usually in the bow) also carries her vest in her personal pack, which is located just behind the bow seat.

The cheapest, least comfortable, and least reliable flotation vest is the so-called Mae West type worn by fliers in World War II. These air vests, inflated orally or by CO^2 cartridges, are subject to puncture. The voluptuous actress' bosom may be comfortable but her namesake isn't. Vests should be as comfortable to wear as possible. One tends to avoid donning an uncomfortable rig.

Comfortable and reliable flotation vests cost $25 to $36. This is expensive, but so are other types of life insurance. Our Flotherchoc ICF (International Canoe Federation) approved vest is collarless. Its slim bulk with PVC air cells allows unrestricted arm and body

Flotation jackets.

movement. Covered with brilliant international orange nylon, it weighs 26 ounces and costs $36. The zipper is rustproof.

Vests sold by marine supply stores or marinas may not be safe or comfortable for voyaging purposes. Neither are all so-called racing vests.

CUSHIONS

We use these as kneeling pads in those rough-water conditions where paddling in the kneeling position is safer—it lowers the center of gravity, reduces wind resistance, and is more efficient. Coast Guard-approved flotation cushions like ours are 15 x 15 inches and cost $6. You can use your flotation vest for a knee pad, but the times you kneel will be the times you should be wearing your vest.

CARRYING YOKE

Major canoe manufacturers like Old Town and Chestnut make their own carrying yokes. Each yoke is adapted to a particular size and model of canoe. Old Town's standard yoke is padded with foam blocks designed to ease the load on the shoulders.

Many experienced canoeists don't want to be bothered toting another piece of gear. However, the center, and sole, wooden thwart of my Old Town Royalex "Chippewayan" canoe is designed for easy removal. It is then replaced with a padded carrying yoke; price, $22.50. Unpadded yokes usually cost a few dollars less. Some yokes fit over or alongside the center thwart.

Fiberglass and aluminum are used in combination with wood in the construction of some yokes.

Commerical yoke on my canoe.

TRACKING LINE

The line used for "tracking" or "lining" a canoe through rapids or shallows as an alternative to portaging or running is usually ⅜-inch manila or ¼-inch nylon.

Lengths commonly used are 50-foot, 100-foot, or in some cases 150-foot lines. We generally have a 50-foot nylon line mounted fore and aft. In unknown country or where we know extra lengths will be required, two 50-foot spares are carried.

Synthetic lines or nylon or Dacron are mildew- and rot-resistant but they are more difficult to knot securely. A bowline is the best knot to use.

Some voyageurs use inexpensive sash cord. This should be checked frequently. It should be replaced at regular intervals. All lines, regardless of material, should be kept dry and coiled when not in use.

FLOOR RACKS

Removable floor racks raise gear above the deck and keep it drier. These come in sections and are made by canoe manufacturers for specific canoe sizes and models. Old Town's sectional floor rack costs $30. Racks can also be made of wooden slats with cross bottom pieces or an arrangement of slats connected by rust-proof metal links. These can be rolled when not in use.

Racks can be very useful but they're an additional nuisance on a portage.

Along with many other voyageurs we use racks cut from dead saplings along the waterways.

A waterproof pocket beneath canoe seat is a handy item.

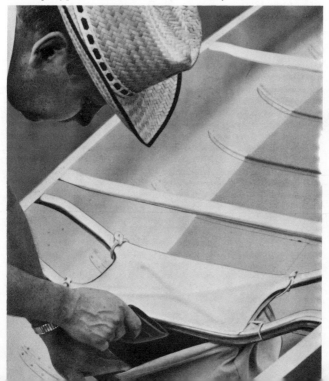

SPRAY OR SPLASH COVERS

These waterproof covers fit over the entire canoe. There is a spray and splash skirt for each paddler. The rig is made for particular canoe lengths and models. I have never bought one. It may be the $285 price tag or the feeling that if the canoe capsized I might never wiggle my long legs out from under the skirt in time to catch my breath again.

There are times in running white water when this cover would be useful to keep the canoe from shipping water and to keep the packs and other gear dry. Gear can be kept fairly dry by the judicious use of waterproof sacks and then wrapping all gear in a waterproof nylon or canvas tarp.

I know of no other spray-cover maker than Old Town. There may be some custom makers.

An Old Town wood-and-canvas Guide Model canoe, surging through whitewater on the Yukon River, is fitted with a spray cover.

Part II
The Camp

6
Packs and Sacks

The canoe voyageur, unlike the backpacker, has a plenitude of pack and sack types available. The problem is which one to select. Voyageurs rarely confine packs and sacks to a particular type. Experienced voyageurs may have several packs and sacks: Duluth, packbasket, Gerry Tote Box, duffel bags, and sometimes a plywood grub or kitchen box. Rarely are all packs or sacks used on a single cruise. Some packs or combination thereof are more suitable for long voyages than for short ones.

Canoe packs and sacks should be the largest you can find. A full-length mattress, either air or foam, occupies considerable space but weighs little (5 pounds or less).

Nylon, waterproofed or water-repellent, and canvas duck are principal pack, sack, and tent materials.

The Gerry Tote Box is molded plastic. The packbasket, made of woven ash strips, requires an outside canvas cover (old style) or an inner polybag (new style).

Waterproofed nylon duck (5–6 ounces), the preferred pack material, is lighter than canvas duck and is rotproof.

Some packsack manufacturers like Kelty do not use waterproofed nylon in their sacks. They offer, at additional cost, a pack raincoat, or rain cover. This waterproofed nylon cover fits the top, bottom and sides of the packsack. The inside back of the pack, that portion nearest your back or closest to a canoe deck, is not protected. If you have such a pack, line the inside of the pack with a large durable polysack. (Polyethylene garbage bags are not sufficiently durable.)

Waterproof nylon packs ultimately lose their waterproofing. However, our Camp Trail Horizon bags have seen four seasons of hard use and they have not as yet lost their waterproofing. These bags, too, can be fitted with polysacks once the factory waterproofing loses its effectiveness.

Canvas Duluth packs can be re-waterproofed by treating them with one of the various waterproofing compounds available through camp outfitters. The waterproofing effect of water-repellent or waterproof packsacks should be increased by stowing sleeping bag and

Duluth-type packsack (Woods #1 Special).

Writer's Duluth-type kitchen pack (Woods #200).
Note headband.

clothes in waterproof stuffsacks. Packs may be made of waterproof material but the pack design is rarely watertight. Water, in case of total immersion, can pour in under the main pack flap and elsewhere. All gear including food should be in watertight, waterproof stuffsacks, or polybags.

THE DULUTH PACK

Northwestern and Canadian professional and many amateur canoeists swear by the huge canvas Duluth packsack and swear at the woven packbasket of the Maine woods and Adirondack canoe country. But

Maine and Adirondack canoeists swear by the woven packbasket and will have nothing to do with a Northwestern Duluth packsack.

This is largely a matter of ignorance of the other groups' favored toting method. Both sides have common ground in the duffel bag.

The situation is not quite as parochial as it was. Many Northeasterners travel to central Canada and Minnesota where they can hire entire outfits including grub and canoe. The outfit invariably includes Duluth packsacks. A smaller number of Midwesterners and Canadians visit the Adirondacks and the Maine woods.

The Duluth pack is sometimes called the Northwestern or Poirier pack. It was formerly made in three basic sizes ranging from 24x24 to 28x28 inches. These had no bellows sides because the front and back joined each other like the front and back sides of a pillowcase.

The present standard Duluth pack measures 28x30 inches. The front and back join like the sides of a pillow or envelope. The 2¼-inch-wide leather shoulder straps are adjustable. The large backflap is secured by three equally-spaced 1-inch-wide leather straps. The shoulder straps at the top are securely anchored to the canvas by rugged rivets. The 3-inch-wide headband is made of canvas webbing or leather. The pack is made of waterproofed 18-ounce canvas. There is a double thickness of canvas on the pack's bottom. The price is $29.95 with head band or $25.95 without the band.

We own four of these packs, though all four are rarely in use at one time. Each pack holds one week's food supply. Each day's rations is in its own polybag. Each meal is in its own smaller polybag. An eighth bag holds general basic items like flour, fish fry mix, sugar, and coffee.

The biggest Duluth pack, the so-called Paul Bunyan, is identical to the above pack except that it has a 6-inch set-out (sides). We use one of these packs for our personal gear: foam pad, sleeping bag, personal gear bag and clothing stuffsack. These bags, complete with headband, cost $39.95.

The Duluth Tent and Awning Company, manufacturers of the above packs, offer a less expensive series of packs, some of which have 6-inch set-outs, in several sizes. These packs are made of lighter (15-ounce) canvas and have web shoulder straps—and they are rugged.

Food, clothing, and sleeping gear are carried in waterproof sacks, as is most of our other gear or supplies. You can always use polybags for those odds and ends of gear for which one doesn't have regular waterproof stuffsacks or bags. We use color-coded polyurethane-coated nylon bags that are toted inside the pack.

This pack has no frame to hold it away from your back, so it is necessary to pad that part of the pack which rests against your back with wide, soft items such as sleeping bags or mattress pad stuffsacks.

Adirondack packbasket.

THE PACKBASKET

The packbasket, sometimes known as the Adirondack pack, is a longtime favorite of Northeastern professional and recreational canoeists. It is useful afloat but uncomfortable to tote on long portages. Professional canoeists like guides, trappers, prospectors, and Boy Scout counselors get paid for their suffering. We are out to enjoy ourselves. We see no need to suffer needlessly.

The packbasket, usually made of ash strips, is best used for toting fragile items like eggs and lanterns. With the advent of durable, rugged, padded lantern cases, foam-padded, watertight camera cases, palatable powdered eggs, or suitable fresh-egg carrying containers, the need for the packbasket is diminishing.

Our large packbasket is about 21x16x12 inches. Complete with carrying harness, padded shoulder straps added, it weighs 48 ounces. There are smaller

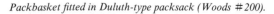

Packbasket fitted in Duluth-type packsack (Woods #200).

baskets and larger ones. Most baskets are available with canvas covers. If you decide on a packbasket, do not get the canvas cover. Line the pack with a polybag.

L. L. Bean, a major packbasket distributor, offers three packbasket sizes which are sized in pecks. Prices range from the 2-peck (15 inches deep) at $8.25, through the 3-peck (18 inches deep) at $11.25, to the 4-peck (21 inches deep) at $15.50, postage free. Current packs are fitted with web shoulder straps and harness. Sponge rubber shoulder pads are included. Bags are fitted with a leather carrying handle.

We use our packbasket for toting kitchen gear: cook pots, frypan, stove, coffee pot, fuel bottles, kitchen roll, and lantern.

DUFFEL BAGS

The duffel bag, sometimes called a cargo bag, has long been a canoe voyaging staple. A duffel bag should be commodious, waterproof, rotproof, durable, and designed so that contents are protected but easy to get at. This means a full-length nylon zipper.

Two modern duffel bags with which we are familiar are the Cargo Bag by Alpine Designs and the Dufflebag by Camp Trails.

Cargo Bag (#435) measures 12x12x30 inches. Its nylon zipper has a storm cover. Weight, 12 ounces; cost, $10.

Camp Trails' Dufflebag (#298) measuring 36x13x13-inches was dropped from the 1972 catalog and we regret this because it was the best and largest-sized duffel bag we have used.

Conventional suppliers like L. L. Bean still offer rubberized water-repellent canvas-duck zippered duffel bags. These bags are heavier but no more durable than our lighter, waterproof nylon bags. Our Alpine Designs Cargo Bag weighs 12 ounces, while a conventional bag of comparable size weighs 44½ ounces, or three and one-half times as much.

Some war-surplus stores carry Navy or Marine Corps seabags, or Army barracks bags. The former two are better in that they are more water-repellent. These bags, however, are too bulky for most canoe voyaging. They all can be made more waterproof by treating with one of the various canvas waterproofing compounds available through most sporting-goods stores.

These bags, however, have the disadvantage of a draw string top opening. They are nowhere near as convenient or as waterproof as the water-repellent nylon bags with zipper closures.

In terms of price, there is not much difference between war-surplus bags and Alpine Designs' smaller, lighter, and more efficient Cargo Bag.

Fanny pack (Alpine Sports).

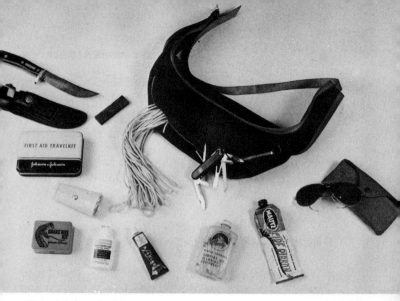

Writer's belt pack with emergency gear.

BELT PACKS, POCKETS, AND POUCHES

Normally, while voyaging, our packs, duffel bags, and other gear, excepting axe, setting pole, and spare paddle, are securely lashed within a nylon waterproof tarp. Each morning we decide what we need for cameras, filters and other camera gear (unless we are carrying a special waterproof camera case), pipe tobacco, lunch and snacks. These items are placed in one of our belt or fanny packs. The pack may be worn or lashed by its belt to the canoe seat or center thwart.

Our fanny pack, the one we use most, is by Camp Trails (#404). It measures 16x7½x4 inches. Made of waterproof nylon, it has an inside pocket and is mounted on a ½-inch nylon belt. Similar packs are made by several other manufacturers. Price: $9.95. This fanny pack has many uses. It carries lunches on day treks and it will hold basic survival gear.

Belt pouches are useful, though less commodious. Our Camp Trails Belt Pouch (#275) of waterproof nylon measures 7x3½x3 inches and weighs 2 ounces. Price: $5. Alpine Designs offers a waterproof nylon Pocket (#44) measuring 9x5x2¾ inches. Its full length zipper has a storm flap. Ours is orange, to match our packs, etc., but it is also available in yellow, red, navy, and turf. Price: $6.

PACKFRAME AND PACKSACK

Oldtime professional canoeists, like Calvin Rutstrom who dipped his first paddle long before World War I, look with disdain on canoe campers who use the packframe with attached packsack. They believe the frame is unnecessary.

We know from extended experience that the frame is useful. It keeps the pack up off the deck. The packsack can be quickly detached and the frame readily used for the portage of motors or other cumbersome gear.

The packsack, usually made from water-repellent or waterproof nylon duck, has at least six outside pockets for keeping gear accessible. This is especially handy when the same gear is always stowed in the same pockets.

Many backpackers wishing to avoid increasingly overcrowded trails or in search of new experiences are switching to canoe camping and voyaging. Having already invested $50 to $70 in a frame and packsack, they understandably loath to invest in another pack. Ultimately, however, they will find that two frame packsacks cannot carry enough gear for two people for much more than a weekend. This is partially due to the con-

Pack frame (Gerry).

siderable increase in comfort afforded the canoeist over the backpacker. Much of the appreciable increase is in bulk rather than in weight. Our sleeping bag stuffs inside a rolled 20x36-inch (18-ounce) poly-foam sleeping pad but our 72x20-inch (60-ounce) poly-foam sleeping pad requires its own stuffsack or bag. Larger stoves require more fuel bottles. The more comfortable canoe tent is bulkier than the backpacker's scanty backpack tent.

The modern welded or bolted contoured aluminum packframe is entirely different from the oldtime Yukon or Trapper Nelson wood frame and canvas bands.

Quality packframes, depending on size and construction methods, cost from $18.75 to $30.

Most frames are aluminum though some manufacturers offer the slightly lighter magnesium frames. We prefer the less brittle and far more durable aluminum frame.

PACKSACKS

The best packsacks are made of substantial nylon duck. Zippers should be nylon and not metal. Rusted zippers are a nuisance. The pack will have two upper exterior side pockets and two somewhat smaller lower exterior side pockets. There will be one large flap pocket and one further down on the center of the pack. Most two-thirds frame packs are divided into two horizontal compartments. The upper, or main compartment, reached by opening the storm flap, is usually two or three times the size of the lower compartment. The latter has its own horizontal zipper.

The flap should extend at least halfway down the pack and over the sides of the top. Some packs have light aluminum stays which hold the pack's main compartment open as a convenience while loading or unloading.

Two-thirds Packsacks

These packsacks occupy about two-thirds of the packframe's overall length. The remaining one-third of the frame is occupied by the lashed-on stuffsack with sleeping bag and foam pad.

Two-thirds-type pack and frame (Camp and Trail).

There are two basic methods of fitting two-thirds packs to the packframe. The top-mounted packsack occupies the upper portion of the frame; the bottom-mounted packsack carries a sleeping-bag stuffsack above the packsack.

Most packers prefer the top-mounted pack as it is not necessary to unlash the sleeping bag stuffsack to get into the main upper compartment. Two-thirds frame length or full frame length packsacks can have added capacity by adding a packframe extension or by purchasing a frame like our Alpine Sports Expedition pack with an attached packframe extension that can be telescoped in or out of the frame as the need arises. The price for pack and attached frame is $69.75.

Full-Frame Packsacks

Some packers prefer the packsack which occupies the full length of the packframe. One advantage is the additional protection afforded the sleeping bag stuff-sack. The disadvantage is that one has to dig out more gear while getting to the bottom of the bag. Of course, rarely-used items, or spare food bags, can be placed at the bottom of the pack. The full-frame pack usually has more commodious bottom exterior side pockets than does the two-thirds frame packsack.

A typical full-length frame packsack is Camp Trails Timberline bag. This measures 31x14½ inches. Depth tapers from 8¼ inches at the top to 7 at the bottom. There are six exterior pockets. This bag has one feature that we do not like—the zippers are metal rather than the more durable and rustless nylon. The zippers are, however, covered with storm flaps. Weight, 23¾ ounces; capacity, 4230 cubic inches; price, $28.95.

Full-length frame pack (Camp and Trail).

Extra-Large Packsacks

Full-length frame packsacks have expansion tops. These are "sleeves" which, when fully extended, add 9 to 11 inches to the packsack's normal height. They can be folded down into the upper compartment when not needed, or as the number of daily food bags dwindles.

My personal pack is a Camp Trails Horizon Bag (#560), large size, mounted on a Camp Trails Skyline Cruiser Frame (#501) with a padded hip belt. The 22x14½-inch-wide pack tapers from a 10-inch top to an 8¼-inch bottom. There are two upper side pockets, two lower side pockets, and a center pocket. These have plastic zippers with a storm flap. The map pocket (center of flap) is Velcro-flapped. Aluminum spreader bars hold the pack open for loading or unloading.

The pack weighs 26½ ounces and the frame, complete with hip belt, weighs 37 ounces. The frame measures 31½ inches high and is 14½ inches wide. The bag is fitted to the frame with clevis pins. Pack material is 6-ounce waterproofed nylon duck.

This is a two-thirds top mounted pack. The lower portion of the frame, beneath the packsack, holds a sleeping bag and foam pad in a stuffsack.

We also have an Alpine Sports Expedition pack and frame.

Janet uses a large Horizon bag almost identical to mine. It is 18 inches high by 15 inches wide. The depth tapers from a 10-inch top to a 7-inch bottom. It weighs 22 ounces. Side pockets are slightly smaller.

Our bags are made by Camp Trails, Phoenix, Arizona, but there are several other first-rate frame and packsack makers.

We would not purchase packframes and packsacks strictly for canoe camping. Ours were bought primarily for backpacking in the mountains, but we occasionally use them for weekend canoe trips. Economy-minded campers who both backpack and canoe will be better served with frame packsacks. They are adaptable to canoeing, but Duluth packs and packbaskets are not readily adaptable—nor comfortable—for backpacking in the mountains.

Pack Care and Maintenance

Canvas packs should always be dried out after a drenching by rain or waves. Mildew and rot are the great enemies of pack longevity.

Leather pack straps should be cleaned occasionally with saddle soap, and made water-resistant by applying a silicone spray or paste like Sno-Seal. Nylon packs should not be washed with a detergent.

Writer's personal pack (Woods Nessmuck).

Always check your packs upon returning home. Have zippers repaired and straps resewn whenever necessary.

Packs should be stored in a dry place. We store our packs in footlockers. This keeps them from collecting dirt and we always know where they are.

The canvas Duluth pack when properly cared for lasts about ten years in the outfitting service. A pack used only a few weeks a year should last a lifetime.

Under less demanding canoeing conditions, our packs and sacks are wrapped in a waterproof nylon tarp lashed to the gunwales or thwarts. The tarp doubles as a groundcloth or shelter. In the rare case of capsizing, the canoe will float with the gear lashed to it. It is infuriating to watch unsecured packs float downstream.

7
A Good Night's Sleep

Nor ghosts, nor Rattlesnakes, nor Spiders, nothing can prevent the fatigued Voyageur from sleeping.

—Nicholas Garry

There's more truth than fiction in the voyageur's adage that "a good night's sleep is the best thing you can tote in your pack."

A long, bright day at the paddle with gentle touches of light breezes and slaps by high winds topped with a satisfying dinner requires at least eight hours of undisturbed sleep. This means a down-insulated sleeping bag that is roomy enough to stretch out and roll over in. Beneath the sleeping bag is a comfortable full-length air mattress or foam sleeping pad. Your head rests on an air-filled pillow or a clothing stuffsack.

Your bed roll is carried in a waterproof sack to ensure that you will always have a clean, dry place to sleep.

Canoe campers who confine their voyaging to the warmer months or to Florida winters can purchase suitable sleeping bags for as little as $35, or less if they purchase surplus Army or Marine Corps bags.

Although the less expensive bags can be used for canoe camping we suggest that you buy a good goose-down bag if you can afford it. Goose down is lighter than its synthetic or chicken-feather counterpart and, pound for pound, compresses into a smaller space.

Voyageurs can tote somewhat greater bulk and weight (lighter bags cost more) than can the back-packer. The latter, at high altitudes, requires protection from colder temperatures than those encountered by voyageurs, who usually confine their camping to the mild temperatures of late spring through early fall, or to Florida winters.

INSULATION MATERIALS

The type of insulation is the basic factor in determining the price of a sleeping bag. The most expensive bags are better made and of better materials, and are of a superior design. The cheapest types of insulation—cotton batting and kapok—are worthless.

Goose Down

This is the best insulating material. Down has the great advantage of extreme compressibility. Such bags, costing $95 and up, are not required for canoe camping. I use such a bag because I bought it originally for backpacking but it fits my canoeing needs as well. I would not purchase one for canoe voyaging alone because the insulation factor, a minimum temperature recommendation of 0° F., would not be needed.

The best of these bags, with very few exceptions, are made by manufacturers specializing in backpack hiking and mountaineering equipment such as bags, packs, down jackets, and tents. Exceptions include Eddie Bauer and the Alaska Sleeping Bag Company.

Duck Down

This material, while light and possessing many of the fine qualities of goose down, is usually supplied in the medium-price range, $58 to $75. Craftsmanship may be nearly as good as in the higher-priced goose-down bags but because of its use at more moderate temperatures, it is not necessary to provide the features required in minimum-temperature bags. Duck down might well be my personal choice were I purchasing a bag strictly for canoe camping. It could also be used for mild-weather camping.

Chicken-Feather-and-Duck-Down Mixture

This is found in many U.S. Army and Marine Corps sleeping bags and in some low-cost commercial bags. The surplus bags we're familiar with have workmanship and design much superior to new commercial bags of the same material.

A U.S. Army mummy bag weighs about 7 pounds and the surplus rectangular bag nearly 10 pounds. If economy is your watchword consider a surplus bag. The heavier rectangular bag is more comfortable.

Dacron

This is the best synthetic material yet used in sleeping bags. There is, however, a difference in workmanship and design. A well-made and properly designed Dacron bag costs about $35. It takes more of the bulkier Dacron filament to keep you warm and comfortable. A good Dacron bag such as Gerry's Quetico Sleeper is superior to a chicken-feather-and-duck-down mixture.

The Quetico weighs about 4 pounds and costs $35. This taper bag measures 78x30 inches and has a rugged zipper that runs down the side and across the bottom. Paired with a second bag, it makes a comfortable double sleeping unit. This bag is the standard sleeping bag furnished by most outfitters in the Quetico-Superior canoe country. L. L. Bean offers a Dacron bag for about $20, but it is not as good as the Gerry Quetico.

If we were to purchase a bag strictly for mild-weather canoe—or car—camping, we'd buy a Gerry Quetico. Dacron has the advantage—besides price—of drying much faster than down.

TYPES OF SLEEPING BAGS

Mummy Bag

This type, so-called from its resemblance to ancient Egyptian mummies, is the lightest and most compact type of bag. Essentially a backpacker's bag, it is also the

Writer's Gerry Wilderness sleeping bag and shorty foam pad.

least comfortable in that one cannot turn over inside the bag. The entire bag turns when you roll over.

Today, the better mummy bags have zippers down the side and across the bottom. Two bags can be fastened together to make a double bag.

Mummy bags are the warmest because the body has less inside area to heat. This is not a major factor in the late spring through fall canoe season. Canoe voyageurs should not select this type of bag.

Rectangular Bag

This type of bag is designed particularly for travelers using motor vehicles, aircraft, horses, or dog teams. Canoeists can use them but in our personal belief, based on considerable experience with all bag types, the tapered or semi-rectangular bag is the one to select for canoe camping. It weighs slightly less and is not so bulky.

The rectangular bag is the commonest and the cheapest bag—in price and usually quality. Backpackers, and experienced canoe voyageurs, are too discriminating in matters of practicality and quality to use inferior bags. Some rectangular bags, like Eddie Bauer's, are intended for mechanized transport.
anized transport.

Rectangular bags are also the coldest because they require more body heat to warm them up, although this is not a prime factor in canoe camping. A typical rectangular bag measures 36x78 inches.

Taper Bag

The taper bag was developed by Gerry Cunningham to meet a growing demand for a bag that is more

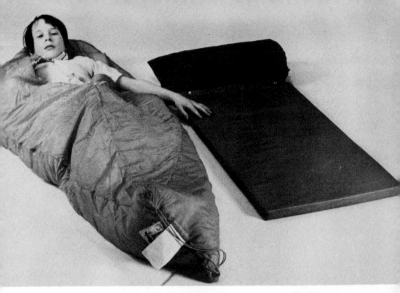

Fifteen-year-old Dean uses his classic mummy-type Dacron-filled bag for backpacking and canoe camping. Beside him is a full-length foam pad.

comfortable than a mummy but not as bulky as a rectangular bag. Gerry, until recently, was the only manufacturer of this type. Black's also makes first-rate taper bags.

The standard Gerry bag, closed, is 78 inches long. Width tapers from a 30-inch top to a 20-inch bottom. Since 1972, his two most expensive bags, the Wilderness and Yosemite Sleepers, have been available in an 86-inch length.

The bags have a full-length zipper that runs down the side and across the bottom. The bag may be completely opened for drying and airing. In warm or hot weather the bag can be spread open for maximum air circulation. Our bags double at home as comforters for the guest room.

Gerry recommends his regular (78x30 inches) bag for persons up to 6 feet tall. His extra-large bag (86x30 inches) was not on the market when I purchased my Wilderness bags several years ago. I am 6 feet, 7 inches tall and have been perfectly comfortable in the standard bag. Both the standard and extra-large bags can be extended by a detachable snap-on down hood. I have never had occasion to use the hood on voyages.

My only criticism of the Gerry bag was the too-delicate plastic zipper. It has now been replaced with a much more rugged zipper.

A major criticism by some of open-mouth bags is that they cannot be closed, and thus let in cold air. This is not true of the Gerry bag which has drawstrings. Besides, there is always the hood.

The estimated minimum temperature for the Wilderness Sleeper is 0° F. My experience with this bag has been in temperatures ranging from -5° F. to 87° F. At the lower temperatures I used the snap-on-hood. In mild temperatures, the bag is left partly open and in higher temperatures, I zip open the entire bag.

I have slept in this bag more than 200 nights under conditions ranging from cold nights at more than 14,000 feet to humid Florida summer nights, from cool evenings in the desert to nights in the Appalachian Highlands. It is my favorite all-purpose sleeping bag.

It is not necessary to purchase this type or quality bag if you confine your camping to canoe voyages. However, if you also backpack, you will find this, or similar bags by other manufacturers, a first-rate outfit.

MATTRESSES AND SLEEPING PADS

Air Mattresses

Full-length air mattresses have long been standard in voyageurs' bedrolls. Today, many canoe campers are switching to foam sleeping pads. Air mattresses are less bulky than foam and are more flexible for stowage. They are also subject to puncture and provide no insulation because the temperature of the air inside the mattress is about the same as that outside the sleeping bag. This, however, is not a major deterrent for mild-weather canoe campers.

Some air mattresses can be inflated only by lung power, others only by foot pumps. Other mattresses can be inflated either way. This is probably the best, since foot pumps have a lamentable tendency to malfunction. It requires some time to inflate these mattresses but this can be done after dinner around the campfire, or while the cook is preparing dinner.

The best air mattresses are probably the rubberized nylon type. Air mattresses are tufted or tubed. Tufted mattresses seem more comfortable than the tube type, but are usually designed so that a leak lets out the entire air supply. Some mattresses have a separate valve for each tube.

Air mattresses, except mummy-shaped G.I's, are rectangular. Standard lengths are 72 to 75 inches while widths vary from 26 to 32 inches. Weights run about 4 to 5 pounds.

The Super Royal Crown offered by outfitters like Camp & Trail measures 74x32 inches. This tufted mattress is about 5 inches high when inflated and weighs 5 pounds. Price: $16.95. A typical foot pump weighs 8 ounces. Price: $2.50.

Some Army & Navy stores and outfitters carry G.I. rubberized nylon mattresses. This mummy-shaped affair is 29 inches broad at the widest point, and 72 inches long, and weighs 2½ pounds. Outside tubes are larger than the inside ones. This feature is intended to prevent one from rolling off the mattress. Price: $17.70.

It is important not to overinflate air mattresses to avoid straining seams, fittings, and fabric. You should be able to poke a finger in the top surface and touch the bottom surface. A repair kit with patches and cement is an essential item for air-mattress users.

Foam and Open-Cell Sleeping Pads

For the past five voyaging seasons we have used Gerry foam sleeping pads. This pad (#N610), covered with a waterproof nylon shell, measures 72x24x1½ inches, and weighs 50 ounces. The pad has its own tie straps but it can be rolled more compactly with nylon web straps. It is almost as comfortable as the best air mattresses and much less apt to let you down. Should water seep inside the waterproof cover, remove the shell and kneel on it to squeeze the water out. Price: $13.50.

Black's Kampamat, carried by many outfitters as well as by Black's themselves, is made of water-resistant polyether foam. This requires no waterproof cover and is quite compact because of the continuous convolutions on the underside.

Super size measures 75x27x2½ inches and weighs 3 pounds, 9 ounces. It rolls into a 27x8-inch pack. Price: $13.50.

Standard size measures 75x22x2½ inches and weighs 2 pounds, 14 ounces. Packed size is 22x8 inches. Price: $7.

A carrying cover and tie straps are available.

We have used none of Black's popular items but several friends and acquaintances report that they are quite comfortable.

Ensolite Pads

These are designed for insulation and not for comfort other than the comfort provided by insulation. They are light and compact but there is no need for a canoe camper to purchase one when comfortable pads and mattresses are available at reasonable cost. Backpackers taking up canoeing should leave their Ensolite pads at home and secure an air mattress or foam pad.

Sleeping-Bag Shells

Manufacturers who presumably neither know nor care anything about camping offer waterproof shells for sleeping bags. They retain body moisture, and on a dry night, by morning you're almost as soaked as though you had slept in the rain without a waterproof cover.

Windproof shells are a different matter. We frequently use Gerry's so-called "Winter Shells." These single shells—they hold one sleeping bag and either a shorty or full length mattress—are made of closely woven windproof nylon. Weight, 11 ounces; price, $15.

Gerry no longer offers his double-bag (21-ounce) shell, but some outfitters still have a stock. We own one and it is very comfortable.

These shells, while designed for high altitude or winter camping, are useful in all seasons. Slick nylon sleeping bags tend to slide off even slicker nylon-covered foam pads. Shells prevent slippage. Shells have a side zipper.

Bough Beds

The mattress made from evergreen boughs has long been a wilderness camping tradition. Today the bough bed is passing from the backpacking and canoe-ing scene. It is illegal to cut live boughs (or trees) in most state, provincial, and national parks and forests. Even in the outback where bough cutting is permitted the bough bed has given way to the more comfortable air mattress or foam pad.

It takes 30 to 60 minutes to cut sufficient boughs for a comfortable bed. It takes us no more than 20 seconds to unroll either our short or full-length foam pads. These are comfortable and they don't punch holes in the nylon tent floor. We don't have to spend time removing needles from the tent deck before stowing it into the pack.

Bag Liners

Some canoe campers demand a liner in their sleeping bags for additional warmth. Manufacturers provide liners in a variety of materials and prices. Some users of nylon taffeta liners find them unpleasantly slippery. Cotton flannel is about the most popular and least expensive material.

Nylon taffeta lining material allows one to turn over inside the bag with a minimum of friction. We like the material and wouldn't have a sleeping bag lined with anything else. We had twenty years of experience with other materials before nylon taffeta became available.

Nylon taffeta costs money. It doesn't make sense to pay additional money for a nylon-taffeta-lined bag and then go out and spend money for a liner to counteract nylon taffeta.

Gerry, who uses nylon taffeta linings in all his bags (including his Dacron-filled Quetico Sleeper), makes no provision for tying in liners. Some bag makers provide inside tie strings. If you insist on using bag liners then get one which has inside tie strings to secure the liner. Otherwise, you'll get snarled up in the liner.

Outfitters who rent sleeping bags often provide liners. This obviates the necessity for dry cleaning or washing the bag after every client. Some people don't like the idea of sleeping in a bag that has been used by a previous voyageur.

CARE AND REPAIR OF SLEEPING BAGS

• Immediately upon returning home from your voyage, check the bag for down leakage (you may have noticed it before). Check the zippers. The manufacturer is usually the best place to repair damaged zippers. Most local zipper "hospitals" lack materials and know-how to repair bag zippers. Zippers on first-rate bags rarely require repair if they are treated with care.

• Dry-clean or launder bag when needed. Dirt-encrusted bags lose some of their insulating capability.

Dry-cleaned bags should be thoroughly aired before using. Sleeping-bag users have inhaled dry-cleaning agents—toxic fumes—with fatal effect.

Home-launder bags—do not trust commercial laundries. They should be hung up to air and dry out of doors. Apartment dwellers can hang bags over the shower curtain rod.

• Bags should not be compressed when stored at home. Hang in a clothes closet or fold loosely on a closet shelf. Keep away dust by covering with a light plastic sheet or dry cleaner's clothes bag. Bags can be used as comforters on beds in rarely used guest rooms.

THE BED IN ACTION

Immediately after the tent is pitched, the foam

pads are unrolled along the tent floor. Where the tent is on a slight slant, your head should be on the uphill side. When your head is lower than your feet, blood rushing to the head can cause headaches or dizziness.

Sleeping bags are removed from their stuffsacks, zipped wide open, and then hung up or laid out to air. When spread on the ground, they should be secured by rocks at the corners. Sleeping bags that have blown into the water will not add to sleeping comfort. Return bags to the tent before dew forms.

Prior to bedtime we place flashlight, toilet paper (known as teepee in more genteel circles), pipe and to-bacco, or cigarettes and lighter, inside a shoe. Moccasins are placed at the foot of the bag near the door. This is in the event of a nocturnal visit to the latrine.

We sleep nude. It is handier, more comfortable, and practical. Body moisture passes from a nude body into and mostly through a bag. When clothing, includ-ing pajamas and underwear, is worn, some moisture is retained in the clothing. You wake up with a soggy, un-comfortable sensation.

On cool evenings the bag is zipped closed. On warm evenings it is left partially zipped open, and on hot evenings it is left completely open.

Stove, coffee canister, and cups are close at hand for coffee in the sleeping bag before rising. After that first cup, we slip into net undershirt and shirt while still in the bag. If it is really cool we slide into undershorts, or long johns, shorts or trousers before getting out to commence breakfast.

Once out of bed, both sleeping bags are unzipped, taken outside and strung up to air. This airing process removes some of the body moisture absorbed by the bag during the night. Some moisture, up to one pint per person, passes through the bag and through the unwaterproofed nylon inner wall. It is then condensed on the inside of the waterproof tent fly. This is the theory, and it seems to work.

Sleeping bags are the last items to be packed away before loading the canoe.

The daily drying process has to be postponed during stormy weather.

If the bag does get wet during a prolonged rainy spell, spend a sunny day in camp to dry wet gear, including packs and clothing. This is also a good time to wash clothes and to fish.

8
Tenting Tonight?

*You should be prompt in embarking and dis-
embarking. Do not carry either sand or water
into the canoe. It is not wise to ask too many
questions nor should you yield to the itch for
making comments about the journey, a habit
which may be cultivated to an excess. Silence
is a safe and discreet plenishing. Should there
be need of criticism, let it be conducted modestly.*

—Father Le Jeune, advice to
young missionaries in 1650

Canoe country is sometimes bug, snake, and rainy
country. Except in spring and fall, this means a tent—
and a tent that has a sewn-in floor and mosquito netting, and that is reasonably water-repellent.

Most tents used by canoe campers we've encountered—as compared to experienced voyageurs—are either too small, or too big and heavy.

Backpacking weight is not a reliable guide—tents
are with one notable exception too small. Voyageurs
tote more gear than backpackers and it won't all fit into

The Sandpiper tent, from Trailblazer by Winchester, measures 10x8 feet, sleeps four comfortably, and weighs 32 pounds—a good deal heavier than my favorite tent, the Gerry Fortnight, but still portageable.

a backpack tent. True, one can stow gear under an up-turned canoe but this leaves it vulnerable to porcupines or other hungry critters.

Canoe campers using tents too big, or too heavy for portaging, are usually outfitted (overfitted might be more properly descriptive) with tents designed for car camping or for fixed-base camps.

The latter category includes umbrella tents, pup-tents, wall tents, and the drawing-board nightmares of deskbound dudes. These tents have their proper place in camping but not for voyaging involving portages. They are suitable for car camping or for the canoeist operating from a fixed base. The cheaper the tent the heavier it is apt to be. An umbrella tent made of heavy duck canvas will cost less than one of the same design made from Egyptian cotton or pima cloth.

TENT MAKERS

A small number of tent manufacturers—they usually make packframes, packbags, and sleeping bags too—make tents of first-rate quality and craftsmanship. These firms specialize in backpacking and mountaineering tents. A few like Gerry make tents suitable for canoeing.

Large-scale manufacturers produce low- and medium-priced tents for car camping. Sometimes they make tents designed for backpacking and canoeing. These are usually too heavy, poorly designed for their intended use, and of mediocre workmanship.

Such tents are adequate for car camping where, if something happens to the tent, the campers can get in their car and drive to a nearby motel. There are no motels in the mountain wilderness or along outback canoe trails. A tent defect that is simply an inconvenience to a car camper can be a serious matter for a mountaineer or a voyageur. Can you imagine being without protection in a mosquito-infested area?

Few production-line tent makers offer custom-made tents. With the passing of David T. Abercrombie & Co. and of Walter Stern we lost two of the best custom tentmakers. They offered a variety of styles. There were several sizes in each style. Each design was available in several fabrics ranging from the expensive but light Egyptian cotton to the least expensive but heaviest material. The workmanship on tents in all price ranges was excellent.

TENT MATERIALS

Unwaterproofed Nylon

Nylon is the best voyaging tent material when used in a well-made, properly designed tent. It is light, durable, strong, makes up into a compact roll, and is rot- and mildew-proof. It is also the most expensive but we strongly believe that its virtues outweigh price; nylon will last longer and thus prove less expensive.

Tents made of unwaterproofed nylon must be of such a design that they can be covered with a waterproof nylon fly. This can be readily done. Our present voyaging tent is designed this way and we have no complaints about its effectiveness.

Waterproof Nylon

Several tents, mostly for backpacking, are made of waterproof nylon. Tents utilizing this material have to be designed with considerable ventilation, more than one might want during a wind-driven rain, to keep condensation from collecting inside walls and roof.

Canvas

The best canvas for canoe tents is the very light and strong Egyptian cotton. It is used by only a very few good tent makers like Black's and Camp & Trail. The latter uses pima cloth, which is almost identical to Egyptian cotton.

Canvas must be treated with a compound which both waterproofs the material and makes it rot- and mildew-resistant.

There are times when you must move on before

giving the canvas a chance to dry out. After the voyage, dry the tent completely before stowing it. Do this at the earliest opportunity.

DESIRABLE CHARACTERISTICS IN TENTS

Weight: Not exceeding 15 pounds.

Size (two people): A 6x8-foot or 7x7-foot minimum and 8x9-foot maximum. It is not always easy to locate a flat piece of ground larger than our recommended maximum. Sometimes an apparently level spot develops a slant once the tent has been erected and the beds are in place.

Height: A 5-foot minimum allows dressing or undressing in relative comfort. Tents higher than 6 feet can create problems when high winds blow off the lake.

Poles: Exterior sectional inverted-V aluminum poles are best. Forget this business of leaving poles at home to save weight. A set rarely weighs more than 1½ pounds and are well worth the time and effort saved in locating, chopping, and limbing shear poles from the woods. Chopping live trees is forbidden in many places.

Floor: A sewn-in waterproof floor keeps seep water, bugs, and snakes outside. Floors are easy to clean. Tents with sewn-in floors are easier to stake out.

Stakes: Avoid tent designs (they are usually for car camping) like the poptent or draw-tight type—they have no provisions for stakes. We once saw an unoccupied and unstaked tent blow into a lake and float away. If you imagine that such a tent has some advantages, then sew on stake loops.

Quality tents usually have stakes of proper design

and length. Cheap tents, or even expensive ones designed by those who have never used them, usually have poor-quality or poorly designed stakes.

Mosquito netting: Good-quality tents have good-quality netting. Be careful not to burn holes with matches or campfire sparks. The entire front of the tent should have mosquito netting fitted with a rugged nylon zipper. There should be adequate-size tapes for tying back netting when it is not being used. The rear wall should also have netting.

Ventilation: It should be possible to open the front all the way, and the back wall should open at least halfway. Whenever a cookstove or lantern is burning in the tent, always leave some ventilation. People have died from cooking in sealed tents.

Fly: A waterproof fly is most desirable on unwaterproofed nylon tents and is useful on waterproofed canvas (cotton) tents. The fly keeps the tent 5 to 10 degrees warmer in cool weather, and about the same number of degrees cooler in warm weather. Flies on unwaterproofed tents should extend about 2 feet beyond the front and rear walls.

Bulk: The smaller the bulk, the less space the tent occupies in pack and canoe.

Erection ease: Two of us, under ideal conditions, can erect our fortnight tent in 5 to 7 minutes. It may take several times as long in a high wind.

Rot- and mildew-proof material: Basically, this means nylon or Egyptian cotton treated as are Thomas Black's tents, with an effective anti-rot compound.

Cook hole: This is a small circular or semi-circular section of the floor that can be zipped open so that the cookstove rests directly on the ground rather than on the canvas or nylon floor. This feature is usually found only in mountain or high-altitude tents but it should be included in all tents with sewn-in floors.

Our current voyaging tent meets the above requirements. This is Gerry's Fortnight Tent. Staked out, it measures 8x9 feet and has a maximum height of 6 feet in the center. It is fitted front and back with high-quality nylon mosquito netting.

The tent is light, but as heavy as we care to tote over portages. It is the lightest tent for its size that we know of.

Weight, including tent, fly, poles, stakes, lines, stake bag, and tent bag is 10½ pounds.

The tent is large enough to accommodate two people comfortably, their sleeping bags, full-length foam pads or air mattresses, packs, packbaskets, tote boxes, paddles, and other gear including rifles, shotguns, or fishing tackle. There is still enough room to dress, cook, eat, or loll about on a rainy day.

On cool evenings, the Coleman lantern not only provides a cheery light for reading and checking gear, but enough warmth for comfort.

The tent is designed for three or four people. Two adults and two children have lived in it. However, when kids are along, we prefer that they have their own sleeping quarters. A backpacker's tent suffices for them. Our tent is used for personal sleeping and living quarters and as a community galley, messhall, and living room.

This tent (and we've tried many) is the most practical, pleasant, and comfortable home away from home we've ever owned or used.

It is also the most expensive standard voyageur's tent on the market. Considering its virtues as a canoe or car camping tent, the $195 price tag is not excessive—

about the equivalent of 10 to 12 days' motel accommodations.

We suggest two improvements. A zippered cookhole should be provided as a place to set the stove while cooking indoors. A nylon loop sewn into the peak would provide a place to suspend the lantern.

Prior to adopting our present tent we used a Gerry Camponaire that is identical, except for size and price, to our present tent. The Camponaire measures 6x8x5 feet, weighs 7½ pounds, and costs $140. We wanted more room but this tent would be adequate for most couples.

CLASSIC CANOE TENTS

A-Tent

The "A" (wedge) tent has long been the basic tent design for voyageurs.

The traditional size for two voyageurs is 7x7 feet, height is 6 feet. Nowadays, the tents usually have sewn-

A-tent is popular canoe-country model.

in floors and built-in mosquito netting. Weight varies with the type of canvas, but it can weigh up to 20-odd pounds. An 8x10-foot A-tent will sleep four.

The seams on the sewn-in floors are at the floor line as opposed to the bathtub construction of Gerry-type tents where the roof joins the wall several inches above the floor line. We prefer the latter construction.

Outfitters usually supply A-tents with no poles. Voyageurs are expected to follow canoe-country tradition and cut shear poles. This is a nuisance. Finding, cutting, and lashing poles together takes 30 minutes or more.

Shear poles are usually cut from live saplings—trees no more than 2 to 3 inches in diameter. The shear-pole tradition is so strong that even in some national forests where regulations specifically prohibit cutting live trees, the rangers look the other way when they see freshly chopped shear poles supporting a tent.

Sometimes, in areas like Quetico-Superior, newly arrived voyageurs find freshly cut poles stacked upright against a tree. This inhibits rotting. If you do use shear poles, please follow this practice so that the next camper won't have to cut a new set of poles.

Outfitters follow tradition (and save money) by not supplying jointed aluminum tent poles.

Wall Tent

Generally unsuitable for recreational voyaging because of weight and bulk. Useful size: 8x10 feet. An 8x10-foot Stormhaven by Black's, one of our better makers, weighs 40 pounds complete with alloy poles, lines, and stakes, or pegs as our British friends call them.

This is a good basic tent for fall canoe and hunting

Wall tents are usually too heavy for portaging but make excellent fixed base camp shelter.

trips where a woodburning stove is required. This type of tent can be fitted with windows and an asbestos-rimmed stovepipe hole for the woodburning sheepherder's stove.

Baker Tent

This tent resembles one-half of a wall tent plus an attached awning or fly to provide protection from sun, rain (although not wind-driven rain), and light snow. It provides a very pleasant shelter in the bug-free season or in areas where there is no privacy problem and is our favorite under these conditions.

These tents are lighter than one might think. A 7½x7½x6-foot tent complete with aluminum poles, stakes, and lines can weigh as little as 12 pounds when made from Egyptian cotton or a similar lightweight material.

When a hardwood fire is built against a rock or green log reflector, the heat is reflected back into the tent. The fly or awning can be closed during wind-driven rains or a separate front flap can be attached.

Prices vary with size and material; $100 is about the minimum.

Whelen Lean-to Tent

This is a pocket-size, one-man version of the Baker tent. It has a minuscule fly and no rear wall. It can be fitted with an attached or detachable mosquito netting. This useful little tent was designed by the noted out-doorsman Colonel Townsend Whelen. Today, the better Whelens are essentially made to order. Minimum price about $75.

Adirondack Tent

This lean-to type tent was adapted to tent form from the classic Adirondack log three-sided shelter by Walter Stern. It is an excellent compromise between the weight and bulk of the Baker tent and the lighter, less commodious Whelen tent. Since Stern's demise, this is a custom tent.

Our borrowed Adirondack tent measured 7x9x6 feet and weighed 10¼ pounds, complete with four 6-foot sectional aluminum poles and pegs. It was fitted with nylon-zippered mosquito netting.

Miners' Tent

This pyramidal tent, and its improved modifica-tions for cold-weather or high-altitude work, resists wind better than any tent we know. It is lightweight for its size. Its sizable floor area compensates for its lack of vertical side walls. Our old David Abercrombie Miners' was 9 feet square and was 6½ feet high at the peak. It was fitted with a sewn-in floor and mosquito netting. Weight: 10¼ pounds.

A disadvantage of this tent is its center pole. An outside peak loop should be provided so that it can be suspended from a tree or shear poles.

Explorer Tent

None of our immediate acquaintances at the Explorers' Club has ever used one of these tents while exploring but that doesn't mean it couldn't be done. The romance of the name has probably accounted for much of its sales. It comes in a wide variety of sizes, and weight also depends on the material used. Some versions are fitted with a T-bar center pole, although outside shear poles can be used. Smaller versions like the 4½x6½-foot model of this tent are often called canoe tents.

Explorer tent (various sizes) is old-time canoe camper's favorite.

A typical tent is 7x8x6 feet and weighs 15 pounds, complete with poles and stakes. Most Explorers are fitted with mosquito netting on door and vents. A sewn-in floor is traditional.

BACKPACKING TENTS

Backpacking tents, to our way of thinking, are too small for most voyaging. These tents are essentially emergency shelters and thus are not designed to be comfortable quarters.

Some experienced voyageurs prefer backpacking tents. Eric Morse, probably Canada's best-known recreational voyageur, and his wife use one of Thomas Black's first-rate backpacking tents.

The most spacious backpacking tent we know is the one we use. It is Gerry's Fireside (4½ pounds) and its floor space of 6x8 feet is the same as our old Camponaire, but the headroom (5 feet) is less. We know of no other tent that is so light and rugged in this floor size. Price, $90.

If you cannot afford to spend $100 or more on a canoe tent, then this is an excellent compromise. You can use it for backpacking, too.

TENT CARE TIPS

If you purchase your tent directly from a store, examine it carefully before leaving the premises. Count the poles, stakes, etc., and then check the seams to see if any stitches have been missed.

If you purchase through the mail, examine the tent as soon as you get it. If anything is missing or askew, notify the supplier immediately. We once departed for a voyage without checking a new tent and discovered that the waterproof fly was missing.

Set up and take down your tent in the backyard before departing.

Gently spray water—not a full blast—from a garden hose on the tent or sleep in it during a rain before shoving off.

Keep poles and stakes in a separate bag (good makers provide them) from tent and fly. This reduces the likelihood of punctures.

Don't camp on gravel bars, if they can be avoided, with a sewn-in bottom tent. We always place a floor-size 4-mil poly tarp beneath the tent floor. Examine the ground carefully before staking out the tent.

Don't camp under a tree with dead limbs. A breeze might drop one through the tent.

Avoid placing nylon tents under evergreen trees that can drop sap or gum onto tent fabric. This can affect waterproofing adversely.

Wash in plain water but do not use chemical cleaners on nylon tents or packs. This may harm the waterproofing.

Be careful not to let sparks hit tent fabrics. Holes can be repaired with ripstop tape. Prevention is better than cure. Observe safety precautions for gasoline and gas stoves and lanterns.

Check tent upon return home. Repair or replace anything damaged or missing.

Make sure tent and fly are dry before stowing them away in closet. Damp canvas tents may mildew and rot.

Tent or Camp Sites

- Avoid sandy beaches, at least during the early stages of the trip, otherwise sand will be in your bed, food, and other gear for the remainder of your cruise.
- Avoid gravel bars. Gravel punches holes in both tent and human bottoms.
- Avoid swampy areas. Very few swampy or wet areas are free of bugs, even during the time that is normally bugfree between the last of spring and the first fall frosts.
- Avoid rock. Obviously, this makes pitching a tent difficult.

Campsites during the bug season—usually in June through mid-July—should be located on points or other areas exposed to breezes. A light breeze tends to reduce the bug population.

During prolonged rainy spells or in areas subject to high winds, avoid unsheltered sites; a site sheltered by trees on three sides is ideal.

A campsite should provide an area large enough to pitch your tent. The cookfire should be no closer than 12 feet to the tent. There should be a place large enough to beach your canoe (always invert it). We try to have a few trees between the canoe and the water. High winds have been known to tumble a canoe more than 50 feet from the beach into a lake or river. This points up one advantage to the noisiness of the aluminum canoe. You may hear it banging over the rocks, intent on a crewless voyage.

It is not always possible to select an ideal site. Your chances of locating a desirable site, or in some instances any site at all, are substantially enhanced if you commence looking in midafternoon.

Topographical maps—canoeist maps are even better—are useful in selecting a general, if not specific, area for a site.

In some areas like Maine's Allagash River or the Boundary Waters Canoe Area of Superior National Forest (Quetico-Superior), camping is allowed at designated sites only.

Suitable sites are sometimes located at one or both ends of a portage.

Leave your campsite clean but don't destroy your fireplace. Leave it for the next voyageur. He will appreciate it as you will when you find a ready-made fireplace. Burn all burnable trash and take away your tops, aluminum foil, and bottles. Thoroughly drench your fire with water.

9
Camp and Trail Gear

In brief, it is well to be cheerful, or at any rate to appear so. Everyone at the portage should try to carry something according to his strength, be it only a kettle. For example do not begin paddling if you are not prepared to continue paddling. Stick to your place in the canoe. Be assured that if once you are set down as a trouble maker and a difficult person, you will not easily get rid of such a reputation.

—Father Le Jeune, advice to
young missionaries in 1650

The time has come to decide what gear goes into your packs and pockets and what remains at home—or unpurchased.

Dozens of items can be useful on a canoe trip. We must decide between "useful" and "essential." Most items discussed in this chapter come within the "essential" category.

Every voyageur—and backpacker too—should always have on or about his person the following essentials:

Maps in map case (one set maps per canoe).
Orienteering-type compass.
Matches in waterproof safe and reliable lighter,
  spare flints, and fluid.
Pocket flashlight with spare batteries and bulb.
Two-inch roll waterproof adhesive tape.
Personal medicine kit.
Anti-sunburn cream.
Anti-bug dope.
Sheath knife.
Sun or shooting glasses.

Writer's personal gear.
(A Mallory flashlight should have been included.)

You may think anti-bug dope and anti-sunburn cream are frills, but in my opinion they are not. The most effective—and expensive—anti-bug dope we've used is Cutter Insect Repellent. Fortunately, a small amount goes a long way. This works for us on mosquitoes, gnats, "no-seeums," horseflies, and blackflies. Apply lightly to exposed parts of the body. Price: $1.50 (1 ounce in plastic dispenser). An old standby of the pre-Cutter era is 6-12, a commercial version of the G.I.'s anti-bug dope. Remove from glass bottle and pour into polyethylene screw-top flask. Price: $1.00 per 2-ounce bottle. You will also need an aerosol bomb of anti-bug spray for your tent and for spraying the area.

Anti-sunburn lotion is a necessity. Many voyageurs, including this one, frequently travel stripped to the waist during non-bug time. Most any standard drugstore lotion seems to be effective.

AXE

The axe is the supreme survival tool—for those unfortunates who find the occasion to survive when voyaging. You can build deadfalls for trapping game to provide food and clothing or build a log cabin or raft. Its steel head struck against stone produces sparks to light tinder for the fire that provides warmth and protection against wild animals. Its nobility remains untarnished while cutting humble firewood.

Except for firewood—and this can be done faster and more efficiently with a saw—and for cutting tent poles there is little need for an axe today, except for those who fare forth into the true wilderness country of northern Canada.

Just about every American—even though he's

never touched an axe before—who ventures into the woods and mountains believes he's the reincarnation of Daniel Boone and hence is an expert with the axe. Give a man (the unecologically minded one) a spot of trees and the damage begins. This type slashes away at both live trees and deadwood without discrimination.

Occasionally the axe slips and causes severe wounds. A serious axe wound means a fatality unless bleeding is stopped immediately. Sometimes this requires suturing arteries or veins. This repair can only be done by a doctor. Evacuation by air—if such is possible—may be imperative.

Many outfitters in the Quetico-Superior area supply saws with their client's outfit. Axes are furnished only upon request. One outfitter supplies both hatchet and saw. The hatchet—popular belief to the contrary—is more dangerous to the user than an axe. It can also damage live trees. One outfitter who had been supplying saws says the demand by his clients for axes is so great that as of the summer of 1974 he will again include axes with all outfits.

The demand for axes would be sharply reduced if outfitters would supply tent poles instead of compelling voyageurs to cut their own poles.

I use a 2½-pound-head cruising axe with a 28-inch handle. Made by Snow and Nealley of Bangor, Maine (they supply Maine's loggers), it is distributed by L. L. Bean. Cost, $9 including blade shield.

We've never seen an axe blade shield that couldn't stand improvement. A sharp axe will ultimately cut through the shield's forward edge. Insert copper rivets along that edge or rivet a piece of soft copper along it.

Hypercautious mothers have been responsible for many serious accidents because they warn their sons to keep clear of sharp knives and axes. This disastrous warning stems from ignorance. A dull knife or axe is far more apt to slip than a sharp blade.

Before you depart for the bush, sharpen your axe and knife on soft and hard Arkansas oilstones. Don't ever sharpen your axe or knife on an electric power grinder. The high speed removes the temper. The best sharpener we've seen for axes, knives, scythes, and other cutting tools is the old hand-powered or foot-treadled grindstone that was once an important tool in every rural, and many small-town, homes.

Take a 6-inch mill file and a Carborundum stone to keep an edge on your axe. The file will take out major nicks.

To prevent rust, keep the axe blade lightly oiled when not in use. Wipe the oil off (your pocket bandana handerchief will do) before using it.

Avoid hatchets—their function is to extract money from Boy Scouts and innocent car campers. Shun, too, the double-bitted (two-bladed) axe. This is a tool of the professional woodchopper and logger. Be careful with your axe. Always keep it in its sheath when traveling. When the axe is in occasional use around camp, sink the blade into a log. When lopping branches from a dead tree or fallen log, hold the axe so that the blade cuts away from you. Before splitting chunks into firewood, cut a notch in the log that serves as your chopping block. Always check the axe head to make sure it is secure before using it. And I repeat: Remember that a dull axe is more apt to slip and cut you than a sharp axe.

BINOCULARS AND MONOCULARS

Good binoculars or monoculars are not indispensable for canoe voyaging but they are very useful and add to the enjoyment of the trip. We always take them.

Select individual-focus binoculars. This gives you adjustment for the peculiarities (if you have any) of each eye. Fit both objective lenses and eyepieces with plastic dust caps. Hard leather or plastic carrying cases provide better protection than soft plastic or leather cases. Avoid zipper-closure cases.

The 7 x 35 binocular has replaced the pre-World War II standard 6 x 30 glass. If you are going to get only one glass—either binocular or monocular—secure the 7 x 35 as your all-round glass. The 8 x 30, more popular in Europe than in America, is also an excellent all-round glass.

The 7 x 50 glasses, designed for marine use, are too heavy if you are a backpacker as well as a canoe cruiser. Avoid glasses above 9x. They are too powerful to hold steady unless you have a tripod or bipod support for them. Then they lose a great deal of their portability and are clumsy. They'll rarely be ready when you want them.

Fine binoculars, like a fine rifle or first-rate sleeping robe, should last through your voyaging days. Use only camera-lens tissue to wipe lenses. Keep glasses and carrying cases free from dirt and moisture. Carrying cases and the leather on the binocular should be cleaned occasionally with saddle soap. Waterproof with a silicone wax.

A monocular is one-half of a pair of binoculars, less the connecting bridge. Monoculars, after a half hour's use, are slightly more tiring to the eye. This disadvantage can be modified for those with normal distance vision, by shifting the eyepiece from eye to eye every five or ten minutes.

The monocular, easily carried in a shirt pocket, is

less cumbersome and less subject to breakage than neck-dangling binoculars. Binoculars are subject to a 10 percent federal tax but for reasons known only to God and Washington bureaucrats, monoculars are federal-tax-free.

Our 8 x 30B Zeiss monocular (8 ounces) cost $174.50 complete with leather case and carrying strap. This monocular has a focusing device similar to that of a camera lens. With an adapter it is used as a 400mm telephoto lens on either of our Zeiss Icarex S 35mm cameras. With supplementary lens it can be used for closeup (macro) photography. Its major disadvantage compared to our standard 400mm lens is the low basic f-16 lens stop. However, many telephoto shots—notably scenic ones—can be readily photographed.

It is not necessary to purchase such an expensive monocular. Some cost as little as $10, but we would not recommend them. Dave Bushnell offers 7x and 8x monoculars from $39.50 to $45 that are quite good.

If you already own adequate binoculars, you can obtain photo adapters for using the twin-barreled instrument from Bushnell Optical Company, Division of Bausch & Lomb, 2828 East Foothill Blvd., Pasadena, Calif. 91107. Write for their catalog.

Do not expect to get the same fine optical quality from $25 binoculars that you would from a $375 pair. Many of us, however, do not really utilize the more expensive optics. If you plan to use either your binocular or monocular for photographic purposes, get the best you can afford. Remember, you'll get better optics in a $100 monocular than in a $100 binocular.

If you don't want to risk dunking your Zeiss, Leitz, or Bausch & Lomb glasses you might be interested in Bushnell's 8 x 30 Expos. Painted a brilliant, international safety orange, they float. Weight, 12 ounces; price, $29.95.

Glasses are not essential but they may save you many weary miles of paddling because they can help you locate a portage landing or a campsite. They also will furnish you with many delightful moments of wild-life observation.

NYLON CORD

A 4-ounce, 50-foot hank of 550-pound-test para-chute cord has many uses. We carry two such hanks, one of which has been cut, as necessity demanded, into varying segments. These serve as emergency shoelaces, belt, and other useful functions. My full-length piece is used to lash tarps, rig a clothesline, and haul packs up banks and cliffs. After cutting a piece from the cord, bind both ends by melting in the flame of a match or lighter. Price, $1.25.

FIRE-LIGHTING MATERIALS

These can be penny box matches, paper book matches, wooden kitchen matches, waterproof matches, or a pipe lighter.

Take your choice, but there should always be a spare supply of matches in a waterproof container somewhere on your person, and in the pockets of each of your fellow voyageurs.

We've used a U.S. Army surplus watertight match-box for nearly twenty years to carry our emergency sup-ply of matches. These, in theory, are not to be used save in an emergency. For most purposes, like fire or stove lighting, we use a Zippo lighter. Take enough fluid and flints. Evenings around the campfire are hard on match, lighter, and pipe tobacco supply.

A Gerry poly bottle (1 ounce) holds about 60 kitchen matches. This watertight container fits into the Optimus 111B stove box.

Metal Match

This is only 3⅓ inches long and weighs only ⅕ ounce. Shave off a few scrapings of the space-age oxides that this flint stick match is made from. Combine with a small amount of dry tinder. Use striker or a knife blade to create sparks. The shavings and tinder ignite first. This flame ignites kindling wood. Experiment before leaving on your voyage. Price, $2.50.

I carry spare cigarette lighter flints beneath the fabric padding in the base of my lighter.

Coghlan of Australia offers windproof and waterproof matches. They come in "penny" sized matchboxes. Windproof matches cost 10 cents per box of 25. Water and windproof matches cost 75 cents for two boxes.

Pipe lighters are safer than matches. They are less likely to cause fires because they are not carelessly thrown away.

Nonsmokers seem to be more careless with matches than smokers who are accustomed to igniting a daily round of coffin nails.

Fire Starters

The need for artificial fire-building aids has somewhat diminished since the advent of the trail stove but there may well be times when only a campfire will bring warmth to your shivering body and dryness to your soaked clothing. Here, a fire starter can be a godsend.

Candles were long the traditional emergency fire starter. They still serve the purpose, but even better is Mautz Fire Ribbon. A 5-ounce tube should see you through a two-week voyage with some to spare. Price, 80 cents. You may not use it once, but if you need it, you won't begrudge weight or price.

Don't expect to ignite a 12-inch-diameter damp—or dry—log by squirting a gob of Fire Ribbon on it and then touching a match or lighter flame to it. You have to observe the usual drill for fire building: tinder, kindling, thin sticks, and then larger pieces. The Fire Ribbon, or other igniter, will help damp wood catch fire.

FLASHLIGHTS

The days of toting a 1-pound, two-cell flashlight are gone. The Mallory plastic pocket flashlight weighs 3½ ounces, complete with two AA (penlight size) Mallory Duracell alkaline batteries and bulb. Price, $1.95 with bulb and batteries.

This torch just about lights up to its advertised 250-foot range.

A pair of alkaline AA batteries (1½ ounces) lasts, at continuous usage, about four hours, or eight times as long as two AA zinc-carbon batteries.

We sometimes tote a third or community flashlight. This is a plastic case-plastic lens Mallory C light. It weighs 7½ ounces complete with two Mallory Duracell (alkaline) C batteries. The batteries weigh 4½ ounces per pair. Continuous-use life is about 15 hours compared with standard C batteries (3 ounces) that last less than two hours. Price, $1.75 per pair. Effective range on this light is 500 feet plus. Price, $2.49. Mallory lights are available from most outfitters.

Flashlights get accidentally switched on while in the pack. Each morning reverse one battery. Upon arrival at your campsite switch the battery to normal position. Keep the light in your pocket until bedtime and then switch it to the open end of your pillow-clothing stuffsack, or shove it into your shoe. The flashlight is flat-sided so that it will not roll when laid down.

Carry spare bulbs and batteries—allow two per week. Batteries give fair warning of their decline by fading light, but bulbs go suddenly.

GLASSES

Carry spare eyeglasses in a hardcover case in an accessible place but where they are not apt to get lost. We never fire a handgun, rifle, or shotgun unless we wear shooting glasses. Bausch & Lomb shooting glasses have hardened lenses. They come in green for bright, sunny days and yellow (Kalichrome) for foggy ones. Price, about $25. Shooting glasses can be made to your prescription.

Sun glare from large expanses of sunlit water can be painful to the eyes. It temporarily reduces your night vision. Polaroid glasses protect one's eyes and because of their polarizing capability, it is possible to see through the surface of the water. This is useful in fishing and while scouting out new waters. Get a clip-on elastic cord from your optician. This will keep your glasses from falling overboard.

JACKKNIVES AND SHEATH KNIVES

There was a time when every able-bodied American boy and man toted a jackknife. Today, few men other than some outdoorsmen, farmers, or ranchers even own a jackknife. Some cities, we understand, have laws against carrying them; not just the switchblade but the plain, everyday jackknife.

A good jackknife with a carbon-steel blade is hard to find. Most companies have switched to stainless steel. This material doesn't take or retain an edge the way carbon steel does.

Avoid the tiny penknife as well as the mammoth jackknife, sometimes referred to as the "toad stabber." A 4-inch-long bone-handled knife with two blades is adequate for most chores. We use one blade for cutting food and the other for general use.

I tote, and always have, a jackknife in my left hip pocket beneath a red bandanna. This goes for country or city, wilderness or saloon. My present jackknife—a Case—cost about $9. My first one—purchased without my parents' knowledge—cost 9 cents. That was about 1926. Utterly lacking in knife knowhow, I folded the blade on my thumb and ran bleeding to my father. He took me to the doctor (office calls were 75 cents in those days), who sewed me up. Father took the knife away and gave me one of his old ones, but not before instructing me in the use and care of jackknives.

A jackknife is a tool—and a fine one. It deserves proper care and respect. Never wash any knife blade. Wipe it clean and dry after using. Oil the joints occasionally. Remove the debris that creeps into blade pockets. Sharpen on hard and soft oil stones. On the trail, use a Carborundum stone.

Swiss Army knives are popular. Many of the gadgets are useful, others are useless. One major criticism: They should be made—at least the knife blades—of carbon steel instead of attractive-looking but inferior stainless steel.

My Swiss knife has two knife blades, metal saw, wood saw, screwdriver, Phillips screwdriver, nail file, leather punch, magnifying glass, ivory toothpick, tweezers, can opener, bottle opener, and scissors. The only item we need that's missing is a corkscrew for wine bottles. Some Swiss knives have them but they lack the fancy gadgets of our model.

Several years ago when I gave one of these knives to Janet she thought I was crazy. Whoever heard of a woman with a jackknife? She has long since admitted that a day rarely goes by without her using at least one gadget—and sometimes even a knife blade.

Prices for these knives range from about $10 to $20. At least one per party is useful. The more elaborate ones soon wear a hole in the pants pocket so a belt case is often furnished. Janet totes hers in her handbag or fanny pack.

Every canoeist should also carry a good all-purpose sheath knife. I used my 4½-inch-blade Randall knife for seventeen years. It cost $15, but it would take nearly $50 to duplicate today. The knife, complete with sharpening stone (in a pocket on the sheath), and the very durable Heiser sheath weighs 11 ounces.

This knife's overall length is 9½ inches. Maximum blade width is 1 inch. The handle is shaped to fit a large hand comfortably. The handle design ensures a secure, safe grip. The forefinger groove is comfortable and provides additional security.

Avoid two-edged "dagger" knives like the "Arkansas Toothpick" or the big Bowie knives. These are for fighting and not for fun. Avoid blades beyond 4½ or 5 inches.

I have yet to see a stainless-steel knife, advertising to the contrary, that will take or hold as fine an edge as does carbon steel. Carbon will discolor and it rusts. There is no excuse for rusting if you wipe it clean after use.

Sheath knife handles are made from leather washers (the longtime standard), ivory, stag (bone), plastics, and other materials. The trend is toward plastics, but our leather-washer-handled Randall, as noted above, has given us excellent service under a wide variety of conditions. We ask no more. Leather handles should not be washed, but cleaned with saddle soap.

There are whole series of don'ts for knives including not using them as can openers. However, if you own a knife long enough and use it often, some of the don'ts will surely be violated.

LANTERNS

Candle lanterns—long a voyaging standby—have been largely replaced by gasoline pressure lanterns. Candle lanterns, however, are still useful, provided you don't want to read on rainy nights.

The gasoline lantern widely used throughout the North Country does a surprisingly good job of warming up a tent on chilly or damp nights.

There are also butane and propane lanterns.

Gasoline

The Coleman lantern has been a world-wide camp lighter for many years. The single-mantle lantern (Model 200A195)—you don't need a double mantle for voyaging—is the best light source we know for all camping, save backpacking. I have owned several over the past quarter century and when I followed instructions, they have given hundreds of hours of safe, trouble-free illumination. The glass globes break occasionally, of course, and the expendable mantles and generators are replaced when needed.

My lantern weighs about 3½ pounds empty. It is 12 inches high and the maximum diameter is 6 inches. The 1⅞-pint fuel tank provides up to four hours of illumination.

Coleman supplies an "Accessory Safe." This moisture-proof container holds two spare mantles and a replacement generator. The safe clips onto the lantern base so mantles are handy. Price, $4.95.

Stowing a lantern safely can be a problem. Coleman now offers a lantern case (Model 200-567). Weight empty, 4½ pounds. Price, $4.95. The case also holds the Accessory Safe and a Coleman No. 0 filter funnel.

Coleman recommends using only white (unleaded) gasoline or Coleman stove and lantern fuel. Average price, 90 cents per gallon. Amoco is a readily available gasoline that contains no lead.

Regular and "low lead" gasoline can be used with safety and efficiency, but after several weeks, lanterns and stoves require a thorough cleaning.

Fuel should be filtered before using in stoves or lanterns. Coleman filter funnels are available in two sizes at hardware stores.

Butane and Propane Lanterns

These lanterns are slightly easier to operate than the Coleman. Just turn the valve—no pumping is required.

Some women campers who are afraid of gasoline

appliances prefer the supposedly safer and more convenient Bleuet (butane) or Primus (propane) gas cartridges. Neither Bleuet nor Primus is as rugged as the
Coleman. This is probably a small matter on short voyages. Precautions for lantern usage are similar to those
for stoves using identical fuels.

The Primus Minilantern (weight with full cartridge, 20 ounces) operates on an 11-ounce butane cartridge. You can read by this 75-watt-equivalent light.
Lantern price, $12.95. Fuel price, four cartridges for
$3.95.

Bear in mind that butane fuel cartridges and propane cylinders are difficult to obtain in the back country. Because empty containers are disposable, they are
not allowed in the Boundary Waters Canoe Area of the
Superior National Forest.

WORK-CUTTING AND DIGGING EQUIPMENT

The machete, combination tool and weapon, is
usually available in war surplus stores. Mine has an 18-
inch blade and a 5-inch handle. It has been most useful
on Florida canoe trips to clear away high grass and
brush from the campsite as an anti-snake precaution.
Weight averages 2 pounds. Prices vary. About $2.50 is a
good average.

Canoeists would do well to follow the example set
by most canoe-country outfitters and tote along a shovel
for digging latrines. Tents are rarely ditched nowadays
inasmuch as most tents now have sewn-in floors. Tent
ditching, particularly along popular canoe trails, is a
poor ecological practice.

Many war-surplus and some sporting-goods stores
carry G.I. folding shovels (36 ounces). Price, $2.50 (av-
erage).

There is considerable truth in the woodsman's adage that "A tenderfoot can cut wood faster with a sharp saw than an experienced woodsman with an axe."

There are two basic folding saws used by voyageurs, triangular and rectangular. The Sven saw (16 ounces) forms a triangle when it is opened. This type will not cut through such large logs as the rectangular type, but it is more readily available and will handle nine out of ten logs encountered by campers. The saw when folded is 24 inches long. Price, $8.95. Extra blades, $2.25. The rectangular saw (20 ounces) will cut somewhat larger logs than the Sven saw but either will handle most camp cutting chores. Price, $9.95.

TOILET ARTICLES

Stainless-steel mirrors weigh 2 ounces and come in a plastic or canvas case. Available at most outfitters, these are sometimes called signal mirrors. Price, 50 cents to $1.

A trail razor (1¾ ounces) is available from Gillette in a collapsible model with a five-blade packet in a foam-lined zipper case. Price, $1.25.

A toothpaste brush (⅔-ounce) from Denmark holds a 10-day supply of toothpaste in the hollow handle. A turn of the screw dispenses it. Price, $2.25. One handle with extra heads (60 cents each) can service several.

Remove the cardboard core in rolls of toilet paper so that it will stow more compactly. The average need is about 7 to 9 feet daily. Carry paper in plastic watertight bag. Wet toilet paper is messy and worthless.

WATER CONTAINERS

Voyageurs normally are surrounded by water, but it's not always drinkable. Witness the Upper Ammonoosuc where the Groveton pulp mills make the stream water undrinkable. A $5,000,000 plant to remove stream pollutants is now being built.

At least one canteen per voyageur is advisable. We use a French-made Klerplast (3 ounces) poly canteen. A screw-top cover is attached to the bottle's neck. Price, $1.

Collapsible plastic jugs of 1-gallon, 2½-gallon, and 5-gallon capacities are available. They provide a useful water supply for the cook. When traveling through country where the water is known to be polluted (usually by paper mills in canoe country), we carry one or two 2½-gallon jugs filled with drinkable water. Two 2½-gallon jugs are easier to handle than one 5-gallon jug.

10
Boots, Breeches, and Bandannas

Backpackers who take up canoeing or canoeists who take up backpacking will find the switch requires very few additional clothes. The major difference is in footwear. The voyageur requires less rugged and less expensive footwear. Most of us canoe in seasons requiring no down-filled garments. Most everyone who participates in some form of outdoor activity, except winter sports, will have in hand the basic clothing and footwear.

UNDERWEAR AND SOCKS

Scandinavian fisher folk, for many centuries, have worn fishnet underwear. Modern fishnet underwear is ideal for most weather. Air pockets provide insulation from heat or cold. We wear fishnet T-shirts and shorts for outdoor and city use. In winter, we switch from shorts to net longjohns. Women no longer have to look unattractive in white net underwear. Dark blue or black net T-shirts, publicly worn under a blouse, are attractive. A net T-shirt worn under any summer shirt is cool and comfortable on most summer days.

Whether we are canoeing, cross-country skiing, snowshoeing, fishing, shooting, hunting, backpacking, or mountaineering, we wear only woolen stockings or socks. These are usually Norwegian Rag (wool) socks or stockings. They are 85 percent wool and 15 percent nylon reinforced toes and heels.

Recently "stocking" and "sock" have become interchangeable. Socks reach above the ankle. Stockings reach mid-calf or to just below the knee. Stockings are preferred when wearing shorts in bug country or in cold weather.

From late spring through early fall we usually paddle barefoot. Exceptions are in bug time and when running white water. We prefer some protection should we have to wade through rocky or pebbly bottom to shore or if the canoe is lost, footgear is needed to hike in. Heavy socks or stockings cushion your weight when toting a heavy pack. Wet wool socks are warm and not uncomfortable. Wet cotton socks are cold, clammy, and uncomfortable. Two pair of socks or stockings are usually adequate for most voyages, particularly if you canoe barefoot.

SHORTS

I abhor trousers, except in cold weather, and wear shorts whenever possible. I even wear shorts for spring cross-country skiing.

Shorts can be worn in moderate bug time when exposed knees are liberally coated with an effective anti-bug dope. They can be worn in most North American canoe country from late spring through early fall.

In warm weather, shorts are cooler because the air

strikes the exposed knees and legs. Wet clinging trouser legs are uncomfortable. Trousers made from the same material as shorts take longer to dry. Trousers, even the most amply sized, bind at the knees.

My Duxbak shorts of cotton-polyester take about an hour to dry after using them as swimming trunks. You don't have to take them off. In warm weather they dry while you wear them.

TROUSERS

"The West Grew up in Levis" say billboards that desecrate the scenery west of the 100th meridian where the West begins. Levis, though legally a trademark of Levi Strauss-made pants, have become so popular that it is now a generic term for all tight-fitting, blue denim trousers.

Anyone wearing Levi-type trousers for active recreational purposes, except the horseback riding for which they were designed, is foolish. Levis chafe the crotch, bind the knees, restrict leg action, are hot and uncomfortable when dry, and are cold, clammy, and uncomfortable when wet. Avoid them.

Tan or light-green slacks of cotton-polyester (the same as my Duxbak shorts) with slightly tapered legs are comfortable voyaging trousers. Take a pair for use in bad bug country.

Cuffs are useless and a nuisance and can be dangerous. I almost fell 2,000 feet into Wyoming's Ten Sleep Canyon when my boot heel caught in the cuff of my hunting trousers and tripped me.

All trousers and shorts, country or town wear, should have button-down flaps on the hip pockets. One

pair of spare shorts is adequate for just about any
length canoe voyage, a weekend to a month.

FOOTWEAR AFLOAT

The backpacker has little choice among footwear
types. There is no basic canoe boot as there is a hiking
or mountaineering boot.

Canoe travel, as differentiated from portaging, requires soft, pliable shoes with non-skid soles. Tennis
shoes, either oxford or ankle high, are inexpensive and
practical. Nylon is superior to canvas. It is rot-resistant,
dries faster, and is cooler than canvas. Sperry Topsider
shoes have the best-gripping soles of any tennis style
shoes we know. They are designed for use afloat. Price,
about $10.

Soleless Indian moccasins made by outfits like
Quoddy are probably the most comfortable. The soled
Indian moccasin is next in comfort. I wear soleless moccasins afloat, when I'm not barefooted, and ashore I pad
them against stones and pebbles with mesh innersoles.

Moccasins are the only leather footgear I wear in a
canoe. Water ultimately ruins leather. My Quoddy soleless moccasins, because I wear them so much ashore,
only last a season, but they are inexpensive; about $10.

Leather hiking boots have no place in a canoe.
They are too stiff-soled and are hard on fragile canoe
materials.

PORTAGE FOOTWEAR

Footwear for portages is a different matter. Many
portage trails are damp and marshy, or rocky and slip-

pery. Both conditions may be encountered on the same portage.

A man toting a heavy pack or a canoe and light pack needs a stout pair of shoes. The favorite footwear of many professionals is the L. L. Bean Maine Hunting Shoe with leather tops and replaceable rubber bottoms. They are hot in the summer. Steel arch innersoles should be worn to provide additional support to your weight. Wear wool stockings to provide additional cushioning. Get the 8-inch featherweight version of the Bean boot.

Leather hiking—not mountaineering—boots like L. L. Bean's Maine Guide Shoe, or a similar boot by Bass, are justly popular along canoe trails.

There is no ideal one-purpose boot for use afloat and on portage. The best portage footwear is a compromise. The soleless moccasin or tennis shoe and a Maine Guide type boot will cover most recreational canoe camping situations.

Leather footgear and leather packstraps of the Duluth packsack should be frequently treated with Sno-Seal, a water-resisting compound.

L. L. Bean's shoepacs, tennis shoes, and soled moccasins.

PULLOVERS

When the pullover sweater is worn as an outer garment a fine machine-knit one, like the Cortina, which is a closer-knit sweater than a handmade one, has superior wind resistance. When worn under a windbreaker, the hand-knit ones are adequate. It is only during early spring and late fall canoeing that a heavy pullover is desirable, especially for hunting and wildfowling.

Light sweaters are inefficient as insulation, but they are one of man's most comfortable garments. While rarely ever toted on backpacking treks, an ancient Shetland pullover, complete with black suede elbow patches, goes along on my voyages. When worn over a Viyella shirt it keeps me warm on the chilliest nights likely to be encountered. The best Shetlands are British-made. Price, $15 to $17.50.

SHIRTS

The most comfortable shirt material I have found is Viyella or a similar flannel. Viyella is 55 percent Egyptian cotton and 45 percent Australian wool. The wool is from Australia, but the Egyptian cotton comes from somewhere south of Cairo, Illinois. Men's shops like Brooks Brothers carry Viyella shirts but most of them are designed for ski or hunting lodge lounging rather than for active sports. The best I've seen or used came from Abercrombie & Fitch. They have longer than usual tails, and have two commodious chest pockets with button-down flaps.

My three shirts cost $16.50 each in 1961 and there is mileage left in the two remaining ones. Viyella shirts today cost $17.50 to $25. As I have remarked earlier, I usually travel stripped to the waist. When it is cool enough to warrant a shirt I usually slip into a Viyella. There are times, however, when it is warm and I've not yet acquired a sufficiently deep tan, and something else is needed. I wear a light short-sleeved Sea Island cotton polo shirt. There are many similar types on the market, usually made from a synthetic. Any of these types should be serviceable.

RAIN AND WIND GEAR

Wear waterproof clothing and you get almost as wet from perspiration as from the rain. Water-repellent clothing leaves one at least slightly damp. Sometimes, I prefer to get wet from the rain (it's rather pleasant in warm rain) rather than to be restricted by cumbersome rain gear.

Rain-gear types include jackets with a front zipper and an optional hood; pullover parkas that come to about halfway between the waist and knees; and the cagoule (monk's hood) that ends between the knees and ankles. This provides the greatest protection but is the most cumbersome to wear. It is a favorite of canoeists who are wet-weather fishermen.

Rubberwear is largely a material of the past. Most of today's rainwear is lightweight waterproof or water-repellent nylon.

Prices for standard brands range from $12.50 to $25 and depend on type, material, and quality.

Light windproof (not waterproof) shirts or parkas are very comfortable garments when crossing wind-whipped lakes or wide rivers (the Mackenzie is five miles wide).

We've tried parkas and shirts but we don't have a particular choice between the two. Windshirts are shorter, lighter, and less expensive. A decent windshirt costs $12 to $15. Parkas cost about twice as much.

To save weight, bulk, and to reduce the number of garments toted we've been wearing for three seasons a combination rain and wind parka. Made by Camp Trails, it costs $27.50 which is below the price of two separate garments.

The parka has two parts. The jacket has a body of international orange, waterproof nylon. The chest and shoulders are dark-brown nonwaterproof nylon. This is worn as a windproof garment. When the waterproof nylon parka with attached shoulder and chest cape is worn, the outfit becomes a foul-weather parka.

No compromise is ideal but this outfit (12 ounces) works very well. When worn as raingear the front zipper is zipped down to allow maximum air circulation.

MISCELLANEOUS CLOTHING

My investment in the men's hat industry has been microscopic for many years. My 3X Beaver Stetson, my only hat, has been battered by weather for more than fifteen years. I fitted it with a cavalry-style chin strap for windy days. It cost me $25 in 1958.

Your head should have protection against the sun. A wide-brimmed hat provides a hanger for a mosquito headnet as well.

The red vagabond crusher felt that can be rolled up and fitted into a pocket is a favorite along today's canoe trails. The old voyageurs usually wore colorful stocking caps. These had no brim. My Stetson, despite the great affection I have for it, is more often absent than present. This is wrong, because all the great outdoors writers from Kephart to Colin Fletcher recommend hats.

A stout, simple, rugged leather belt has far more uses than simply keeping your pants up. A spare pack lashing, an emergency packstrap, a short clothesline are but a few of the things a belt could be used for. I've never had occasion to use one in these ways but the possibility exists.

The standard 22x22-inch or 24x24-inch bandanna handkerchief is one of anybody's most useful items. Originally designed as a neckerchief, as the name implies, the bandanna is useful as a hot pot holder, emergency sling or triangular bandage, for wiping blood or dirt from knife blades, as a flashlight, lantern, or automobile headlight cleaner, towel, wash cloth, dish cloth, gun wiping cloth, as a head cooler dipped in water on hot days, or as an aid in removing stubborn wine corks or jar tops.

Even in the summer, some days are cold, wet, raw, and windy. I wear knitted wool cross-country ski gloves beneath cotton workmen's rubber coated gloves. Ski gloves keep hands warm and the rubber gloves keep them dry.

Broadbrim hat is a must for sun protection.

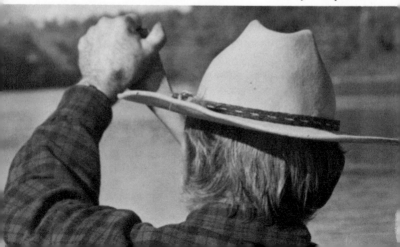

CLOTHES TO TAKE

Below is my personal list for 12 to 14 days. On longer voyages, I take another pair of shorts or trousers and an additional shirt.

1 pr. cotton-polyester trousers (no cuffs)
2 pr. cotton-polyester shorts
2 pr. net undershorts
2 net undershirts
1 pr. red underdrawers
1 Viyella long sleeved shirt
1 Sea Island cotton shortsleeved shirt
3 pr. wool stockings
1 2-inch-wide leather belt
1 Stetson, 3-inch brim, fitted with chinstrap
1 light sweater
1 heavy wool sweater or down-filled sweater
1 wind/rain parka
1 pr. knitted wool cross-country ski gloves
1 pr. rubber coated cotton workmen's gloves
1 pr. soleless moccasins
1 pr. tennis shoes (ankle-high)
1 pr. L. L. Bean Guide Shoes or Maine Hunting
    Shoes

Finicky women have no place on a canoe voyage. Most women, however, are more particular about having an adequate supply of clean clothing and underwear along. Let them take what they want as long as it doesn't fill more than two standard clothing stuffsacks—and as long as they understand that they must tote their own wearables.

My clothing travels in a waterproof nylon stuffsack that has snaps for attaching to my Gerry Shorty foam sleeping pad for use as a pillow. This, however, is rarely

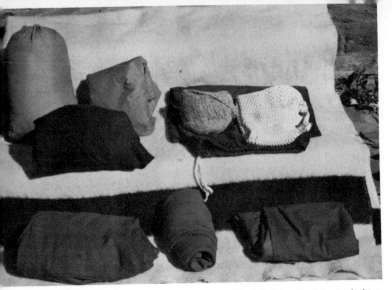

Stuffsack holds writer's basic clothing.

toted on canoe voyages. My 72-inch-long Gerry foam sleeping pad has no provisions for attaching the stuff-sack/pillow. The stuffsack, 12x20 inches, weighs 3 ounces. Price, $2.75.

Weekend or even week-long cruises should require little clothes washing. On voyages of more than a week's duration we usually stay ashore, except for fishing, about one day out of every five or six. On that day, un-less the layover was caused by foul weather, we take a few minutes to wash stockings, underwear, shirts, and shorts.

Woolite is good for washing woolens like stockings, while Trak, a cold water soap, is adequate for the rest.

Clothes can be dried on a temporary clothesline of nylon cord. Sometimes wash can be spread out on the ground. Rocks are a fine drying place because they readily absorb and then radiate the sun's heat. Clothes stretched on the ground should be secured against wind by holding them down with small stones.

11
Kitchen Afloat

There are three schools of canoe kitchen gear toters.

The ultra-go-lighters (many are backpackers) take the lightest foods and equipment.

The canoes-can-carry-anything school totes tables, chairs, stove stands, and plastic sinks. This gear may be all right for a fixed base camp or for camping with a car and using a canoe for daily excursions, but it's poor stuff for the outback and portaging.

The moderates carry light gear when long portages are on the route or carry some light items with a few heavier pieces like cast-iron frypans. This is the school whose tie we wear.

We started with ultra-light gear but soon discovered that canoe voyages allow slightly greater luxuries and also, in many instances, require more durable gear.

In the beginning some canoe campers tote pots, frypans, and other gear from the home kitchen. They discover that the most efficient voyageurs use gear specifically designed for the canoe chef, or gear from car camping and backpacking that can be readily adapted to voyaging.

STOVES

Many voyageurs, like backpackers, now take trail stoves on cruises. Even some old-timers advocate their use. Some canoe campers do all their cooking on trail stoves while others use them for a fast cup of coffee or instant soup. Ed Sturgis, of Charlotte, Vermont, spends several weeks annually on solitary voyages. When Ed takes along companions, he stands by tradition and allows stoves to be used only during rainstorms.

I have used trail stoves on all backpacking and canoe voyages since 1947 when I bought my first Primus in Stockholm.

There are two basic trail stove types. One type weighs 20 ounces or less. These are basically backpacking stoves, but we used three Primuses for many

One-burner lightweight trail stoves:
at left, Primus 7IL gasoline stove;
at right, Bleuet S 200 Butane cartridge stove.

voyages during the past quarter century. The second type is the heavier, faster-heating stove like our Optimus 111B (54 ounces). We consider this too heavy for backpacking but ideal for canoe, horse packtrip, and car camping. There are several considerations in selecting stoves.

Safety

Some fuels are safer to handle, store, and use than others but all stove fuels are safe when proper precautions are taken. We've never worried, or had trouble, with any recognized brand of stove or fuel when we followed operating instructions and handled the fuel with the precautions necessary for that fuel.

Speed

A stove's efficiency is based on the length of time required to boil one quart of water. We have seen stove users cussing because their stove did not boil water as fast as the advertising stated. Stoves are usually rated with the air temperature at 70°F. and at sea level. Some stoves (not gasoline) lose their efficiency at freezing or subzero temperatures. Other stoves, like butane, will not function at subzero temperatures. Low temperature is of no concern to voyageurs. However, many canoeists are also winter camping or cross-country ski buffs. If you are selecting one stove for several types of camping, then the low-temperature factor should enter into your decision.

Reliability

The world's largest and oldest manufacturer of trail

Soup's on: Powerful Optimus 111b gasoline stove boils water in four minutes. This is the writer's favorite canoe-camping stove.

stoves, A. B. Hjorth of Stockholm, makes stoves under the trade names of Primus, Optimus, and Svea. The Primus, formerly made in kerosene, gasoline, and propane models, has been the worldwide standard for explorers for more than 80 years. Better than 90 percent of trail stoves used by backpackers and voyageurs are Hjorth-made. All Primus, Optimus, and Svea stoves are extremely reliable provided you follow their instructions and use them under stated temperature conditions. The Primus pressure kerosene models are still standard for many Arctic expeditions. We purchased several for our 1953 American Trans-Greenland Expedition. However, only propane stoves are currently made under the Primus name (the Primus 2255 is a backpacker model weighing about 24 ounces with cartridge). Optimus still makes gasoline and kerosene stoves of the type everyone still calls "Primus," and also supplies replacement parts for old Primuses.

Convenience

Butane and propane gas stoves are the most con-venient—simply turn a valve and light—but the least ef-ficient, alcohol excepted. They take a long time to bring liquids to the boil. This is no reason to reject them if you enjoy their convenience. Many women are scared of gasoline and prefer what they consider to be the safer and easier-to-operate gas burners.

Weight

This is not a crucial factor is voyaging. The heavi-est trail stove, Optimus 111 (kerosene), or 111B (white gasoline), weighs slightly more than 3 pounds.

All trail stoves are single burners. On those rare oc-casions when we tote a two-burner arrangement, we prefer two single burners to one double—or even triple-burner stove. We use our two Optimus 111B single burners or one Optimus 111B and our trusty Primus.

Our two Optimus 111B stoves weigh just about one-half of what a two-burner Coleman or Thermos gasoline stove weighs. Twin-burner propane stoves like the Primus and the Winchester Trailblazer stoves are usually toted by canoeists who cruise to one location and camp there for an extended period.

FUELS

Alcohol is the least effective of the regular stove fuels. It gives too little heat for too much weight. There is no appreciable weight saving over kerosene or gaso-line. Examples: Optimus III (kerosene) and several Primus models are safe, smelly and not quite as efficient as gasoline.

Kerosene, though somewhat safer than gasoline, should not be handled carelessly. Kerosene is not always available in the outback.

Butane stoves, like propane, are easy to light. A butane stove, like the Bleuet S-200, essentially a backpacking stove, takes 10 to 12 minutes to boil one quart of water. Butane functions poorly at 6° below freezing. Propane is similar.

Gasoline is fast, most efficient, and most dangerous if handled carelessly. It is available even in the most remote Hudson's Bay Company outposts, where it is used for Coleman lanterns, outboard motors, stoves, and heaters.

White (unleaded) gasoline burns cleanly with no fouling residue. Standard (regular and high-test) gasoline fouls up appliances after several weeks of daily use. If you have to use standard gasoline, clean stoves and lanterns weekly. Unleaded gasoline is often unavailable in the outback.

FUEL CONTAINERS

Since I acquired my first Primus in 1947 I've tried several types of containers but most of the time, a one-liter seamless aluminum bottle (4 ounces) with a leak-proof stopper is the mainstay. The Optimus 111B's fuel tank capacity is 1⅜ pints (the tank is never filled more than ¾ full). Our normal fuel consumption rate for both stove and Coleman lantern has never exceeded one gallon per week. Bottle price, $2.50.

Our fuel bottles fit handily into various parts of our pack but are never put with the food supply. The number depends on the length of the voyage and sources of resupply. Some backpackers and voyageurs use red anodized-aluminum bottles for fuel toting. Fuel tins should be properly labeled and never of the same shape, size, or color as bottles containing drinkables.

Voyageurs using outboard motors often use the same type of 2½-gallon fuel containers as for stove and lantern.

STOVE NOTES

Some stoves, like the Optimus 111B, have built-in, self-cleaning needles. Most smaller stoves have a "pricker." These are easy to lose. I tape a spare onto the side of my Primus.

There are two basic types of gasoline and kerosene trail stove feed systems. Larger models like the Optimus 111 and 111B have pumps like the Coleman lantern. These stoves have more intense flames and will operate in subzero temperatures. Smaller and lighter versions of these models have no pumps, nor do the smaller stoves like the Primus and Svea 123. Turn the valve stem. Place your hands around the tank. In a few seconds gasoline seeps upward into the cup at the burner base. When the cup is filled close the valve and light the fuel in the cup. When it is almost burned out, turn the valve on. The stove will flare and then settle down to a slow, steady flame.

Kerosene stoves, because of the higher ignition point of kerosene, must first be primed with alcohol. This involves carrying a second type of fuel supply.

COOKING WARE

Cook Pots

These are the basis of your kitchen. Standard pot

sizes for a two-member outfit are 1½ quart, 2½ quart, and 4½ quart. A four-member party usually adds a 7-quart pot.

The Smilie Company, San Francisco, has long been a supplier of voyageurs' pots. Smilie's aluminum pots cost more but they last longer than other pots we've tried.

A 1½-quart pot weighs 10 ounces. Price, $5.80. A 2½-quart pot weighs 12 ounces. Price, $6.30. A 4½-quart pot weighs 21 ounces and costs $6.95. A 7-quart pot (36 ounces), costs $7.85; 9- and 14-quart pots are also available.

These heavy-gauge aluminum pots have rugged bales and close-fitting lids with D-ring lifters. These pots, unlike many of those in your home kitchen, are designed for use on campfire grates and have maximum stability for height and width. Pots nest one into another. Most camp outfitters offer plastic or nylon pot-carrying bags.

Frypans

It's foolish to tote groceries or catch fish and then destroy the food beyond palatability because of a too-light frypan.

Cast iron is the best but heaviest frypan material. Most experienced voyageurs compromise by using a heavy sheet steel frypan.

The classic canoe-country frypan has no handle. A socket is provided for the insertion of a handle cut at the campsite. A thumbscrew secures the temporary handle in position. A 2-inch-diameter ring is welded onto the pan on the side opposite the handle socket. This allows a pan to be supported on fireplace rocks.

Our classic pan (44 ounces) measures 10 inches

wide by 2½ inches deep. Price, $8.95. This is adequate on most occasions for a couple. A larger pan measuring 14 x 3 inches costs $10.95 and is adequate for four. These pans are made by Greenfield Products, Greenfield, Ohio, and are available through Waters, Inc., Ely, Minn.

Prior to our adoption of the above skillet we spent more than 30 years trying everything from 4-ounce pie plates (a pot gripper for a handle) to 6-pound cast-iron frypans. The Greenfield skillet is almost as good as cast iron and weighs considerably less. Current cast-iron frypans have handles that are far too short for campfire or even home cooking. Even ultra-go-lighters should consider using the Greenfield frypan. Its additional weight, over an aluminum pan, will be more than compensated for.

Canoe chef's kitchen gear.

Coffee Pot

Coffee pots, since the advent of instant freeze-dried coffee, are seen in decreasing numbers along waterways. The only readily available coffee pot we're aware of is the 2-quart aluminum pot (10 ounces) sold by L. L. Bean. Price, $2.20. This is fitted with a non-locking bail and folding handles. For heavy coffee drinkers, like ourselves, the 2-quart capacity is inadequate since the pot can only be filled about two-thirds full or the boiling coffee will spill over the pot sides. The drain holes in the lip are inadequate. If anyone knows of a better canoe coffee pot, let us know.

Aluminum is a poor coffee-pot material. Coffee let to stand for an appreciable period has a chemical reaction with aluminum. The old-time "Graniteware" pots were much better.

Plates

The variety is nearly unlimited and the prices are usually reasonable. We use 9-inch-diameter SIGG plates (3 ounces) which double as bowls. Price, $1.25. In the past we've used Army mess kits (which can double as a frypan), pie plates, round cake plates, paper plates (no more), compartmented plates (too shallow to double as bowls), and a variety of vessels of aluminum, tin, stainless steel, and other materials.

Cups

We use 10-ounce-capacity insulated plastic cups. These were purchased in an A & P store several years ago. Price, 35 cents. They are the best cups we've seen or used to date. We've seen similar cups in other stores but never in a camp equipment shop. Metal cups, excepting the Sierra Club model, burn the lips unless cooled off first. Enameled cups, rarely seen nowadays, are the least guilty of lip burning.

Recipes using cup measurements refer to an 8-ounce cup. It might be more convenient to have drinking cups all of 8-ounce capacity or to get a plastic measuring cup (Price, 25 cents) but we measured 8 ounces in our drinking cup and then painted a line at the 8-ounce level.

Plastic Shaker

A 64-ounce shaker (with lid) of flexible, translucent plastic makes an ideal container for mixing powders, milk, or fruit drinks. This large container can be used to store condiments, or basic items like tea bags, sugar, etc.

KITCHEN ROLL

Twenty years ago we bought a kitchen roll from David Abercrombie. Made of light cotton, it has seen much service and keeps basic kitchen items together. When rolled, it occupies little space in pack or totebox. The roll has separate pockets for these items:

Spatula: Measures 4x11 inches (3 ounces). Price, $1.25.

Wood stirring spoon: Measures 10½ inches (1½ ounces). This is also handy for exercising the chef's eternal prerogative—tasting. Wood won't burn your mouth. Price, 60 cents.

Pot lifter: There are several on the market but ours is the best we've seen or used. Made by SIGG it is 4 inches long (1½ ounces). This has saved many a burned finger—and cuss word—as it clamps onto pot lids. It also

Insulated bowl and cup, compartmented plate, and eating tools. Sheath knife (not shown) serves as table knife.

makes an emergency frypan out of a pie or dinner plate. Price, $1.50.

Kitchen fork: A two-tined fork weighs 2½ ounces. Price: $2.50 (ours is World War *One* surplus).

Fish filet knife: Handy for its purpose, weighs 4 ounces. Price, $2.50.

Fire ribbon: This 5-ounce tube will ignite damp wood. Price, 75 cents.

Tuffy: Cleans pots and doesn't scratch Teflon. Price, two for 39 cents.

Grate (grill): Several lightweight grills are available. Our basic 12x24-inch grill has folding legs. Price, $3.75. We prefer this grill to lighter backpack types. Grill should be large enough to hold a frypan, cook pot, and coffee pot. The grate rests on rocks or green logs. It is carried in a plastic bag.

Handy knife: A Swiss Army jackknife has two cutting blades, wood and metal saws, screwdriver, Phillips screwdriver, toothpick, tweezers, scissors, leather punch, file, nail file, bottle opener and corkscrew. This 4-ounce knife costs $16.75. We would prefer carbon steel blades to stainless steel.

Towels: You can tote paper kitchen towels, but we usually use a 2-foot-square red bandanna handkerchief.

COOK SETS

Suppliers like L. L. Bean and many sporting-goods stores carry four- and six-person cooksets. A basic set for four (6½ pounds) includes 10-quart pot, 4-quart pot, 2-quart coffee pot, and two frypans, including one with Teflon coating. The smaller pots have their own lids, each with a ring lifter. The 10-quart pot uses an inverted frypan for a lid. A detachable handle fits each frypan. The foregoing items are all light or medium-weight aluminum.

The set also includes four multi-compartmented plastic circular plates and four open-handle coffee cups (they nest). The entire unit fits into a canvas or plastic carrying case. The six-person outfit has the same pots but includes an additional two plates and cups. Price (4 persons), $12.95; (6 persons) $14.50.

Our Smilie cookpots (see above) are much superior to any pots we've yet seen in "store" nesting outfits.

Buy a cookset if you must but at least purchase a heavy steel skillet. You can still use the kit's frypans as pot lids.

There is available, for about $40, a stainless-steel "Sportsman's" cookset. Stainless steel is a fine material, except for cutlery, but these expensive pots and pans must have been designed by a non-camper. The frypans and pots with detachable plastic handles, not bails, are entirely unsuited for canoe or even car camping. The outfit includes, of all things, a percolator rather than a coffee pot. You can always discard the guts and boil coffee in the percolator but there's still that little glass top and the pot's handle is detachable plastic. (For this writer, it's no bail, no sale!)

AN ULTRA-GO-LIGHTER'S OUTFIT

Voyageurs wishing to forego the extra pleasures and comforts of canoeing, or those whose route covers an extended time with few or no resupply sources and where there are long portages, can use backpacking kitchen gear.

A basic pot set includes two SIGG medium-weight aluminum pots: 2½-quart (11½ ounces), price, $4.75; and a 4-quart (14 ounces), price, $5.50.

The SIGG pots available from most backpack suppliers have deep lids that can double as plates or bowls (also as a frypan with a SIGG potlifter.) The inch-wide bails lock into the upright position. This is a handy feature. These pots are very durable.

Our go-light frypan, made by Groninger of Switzerland, weighs 14 ounces. With it is a useful 4-ounce lid. This medium-weight aluminum pan is Teflon-coated. European companies use a better and heavier layer of Teflon than do companies in America, where Teflon was created. Price, $6.50.

Unless you plan to do all your cooking on a trail stove, a lightweight backpacker's grate is very convenient. Gerry's U-shaped stainless steel rod is open at one end so that it can be adjusted to the unevenness of the stone sides of your cooking fireplace. Size, 15 x 15 inches, weight, 3 ounces; price, $1.75.

A Primus is our favorite white gasoline trail stove. Weight, 17 ounces empty, 23 ounces full. This stove is not made any more, though Optimus has similar stoves. The Primus 2255, a propane model, weighs about the same as my old gasoline Primus.

12
The Instant Canoe Chef

Hunger is the best of all possible sauces.
                                        —Vilhjalmur Stefansson

Bannock and beans and bacon—since the decline of pemmican as the voyageurs' staple ration—have been the basic foods of canoeists' wilderness diet. Many experienced amateurs have, under the influence of the old-timers, adopted this monotonous ration.

The ultra-go-lighters, many bringing their back-packing experience and freeze-dried or dehydrated rations, have an equally monotonous diet.

Having suffered both extremes, I have settled on compromise rations which include bannock, bacon—beans take too much time—dehydrated soups, and fancy freeze-dried dinners like Shrimp Creole, Chili con Carne Ranchero, Beef Stroganoff, and Chicken à la King. We still use proletarian spaghetti, rice, porridge (oatmeal), and flapjacks.

Abundance and variety of diet depends on proximity to resupply sources. On a 400-mile voyage down the Connecticut or along similar village-dotted streams it is not necessary to carry more than one or two days' rations. This makes portaging the numerous power-company dams somewhat easier. However, we prefer to take a somewhat longer supply of groceries. Voyages through Canada's wilderness may require a two-week supply of victuals, or more.

LIVING OFF THE COUNTRY

Forget it. When planning your grub supply, don't reduce the basic amount by planning to shoot game, or land fish. You can probably take fish but don't count on it.

A basic knowledge of what the country provides should you lose your food supply is a different matter. Every outdoorsman or woman should have some survival know-how.

Throughout much of what is considered canoe country, wild fruits like strawberries, blueberries, raspberries, gooseberries, blackberries, currants, cowberries, and cloud berries are found.

Canoe chef Yukon Jake in action.

Cattail and water-lily roots can be roasted over an open fire on the end of a green stick. Stinging nettle, marsh marigold, dandelion, chickweed, and trillium can be boiled into soup.

The puffball, a readily distinguished mushroom, and widely distributed in North America, makes excellent fare.

Don't forget bird and turtle eggs, snails, grubs, and crayfish. Frog's legs are delicious.

Roasted rattlesnakes along with nonpoisonous varieties taste like chicken. Slice off the head, slit lengthwise along the belly, gut, and skin.

Even if you're not a fisherman, take along in a 35mm film canister these items: 8-pound-test nylon spinning line, #12 hooks, salmon eggs, sinkers, and a lure such as a Dardevle.

Given the above fishing tackle, a stout sheath knife, and matches, a man can accomplish what might seem a miracle. Add an axe, and you can live in comfort.

WATER SUPPLY AND PURIFICATION

Probably no freshwater voyageur ever died of thirst. A drinking-water supply is rarely a problem in the outback. But on streams like the sometimes wild and wonderful Androscoggin, near the pulp-mill towns of Berlin, N.H., and Rumford-Mexico, Maine, there is heavy sulfide pollution.

When voyaging through polluted-stream country (this includes some of northern New England's finest canoe country) we tote our own water. Four 1-quart canteens plus one or two 2½-gallon collapsible plastic water jugs are usually more than adequate for 24 hours.

We don't mind stopping by a pulp mill or other polluter's office to ask for water.

Fortunately, the situation is improving. A Groveton, N.H., firm—long a polluter of the Ammonoosuc and the Upper Connecticut—is building, although not of its own free will, a $5,000,000 pollutant-control plant.

Water can be purified by boiling but the sulfide taste and smell is difficult to eliminate.

Halazone tablets are useful for voyageurs. Price, $1.50 per 100 tablets. Most Halazone bottles have an expiration date on the bottle. Respect it. Put one tablet into a 1-quart canteen. Shake and let set for about 30 minutes. When water looks, or you believe it to be, truly dubious, use two tablets.

Halazone gives water the classic chlorine smell. Some brands include another tablet that kills the odor.

Each meal is packed in its own separate polybags.

Frequently, we use crystallized fruit powders like lemon, lime, or pineapple to disguise the Halazone taste and smell. Hudson's Bay Company 151-proof rum should be a delightful way to remove the Halazone-tablet taste and smell from water, though come to think about it, we don't ever remember putting the tablets into water about to be enhanced by rum. Water for coffee, tea, soup, stews, etc. is purified by boiling.

PLANNING MEALS

• Plan basic "one-dish" dinners, plus soup and fruit. This eliminates or reduces the need for a second stove, makes meal preparation simple and quick, and reduces dishwashing chores. Such meals are easier to prepackage.

• Prepackage meals at home. This saves time, weight, and space.

• Plan menus before purchasing food supplies. Plan each meal of the voyage. Allow spare rations in the event you are delayed in finishing the voyage. Allow one day extra rations for a seven-day voyage and two days for a fourteen-day voyage. While voyaging through rainy country or in the rainy season, you may want to allow a further supply.

• Stow all items for each meal in its own durable plastic sack. Then stow the three meals for one day in a larger sack. Adequate markings should indicate date and meal. This way you don't have to take every-

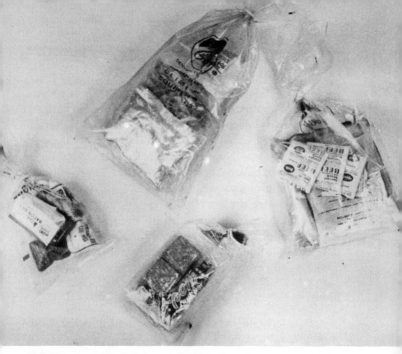

A day's rations include three one-meal bags for two plus high-energy snacks.

thing out of the pack or totebox to find a particular item.

- Divide the chores—while the chef cooks, the partner lays out sleeping bags, collects firewood, and washes dishes.

CLASSIC CANOE COUNTRY FOODSTUFFS

Bacon

Bacon bars, while tasty and no doubt dietetically correct in proper portions, can never replace the wonderful aroma of sizzling bacon mingling with the fragrance of boiling coffee.

The best chunk bacon we know of is the very heavily smoked bacon available at most Hudson's Bay Company posts. We've kept it up to three weeks. Our HBCo. bacon might have remained unspoiled for a considerably longer period but our limited supply tasted so good that it was eaten up before it had a chance to spoil. Sliced bacon spoils too readily. Three days is about the limit in hot weather.

Alas, there are no HBCo. trading posts within the United States. They are colorful, exciting, useful, romantic places. On U.S. voyages lasting more than seven to ten days (about the limit of lightly smoked chunk bacon), tinned Danish bacon is probably your best choice.

Flour

Formerly, this was the bulkiest and heaviest foodstuff toted by canoeists. Two generations ago, classic writers like Horace Kephart recommended 36 pounds as being barely adequate for two men on a thirty-day voyage. Breadstuffs then were a major part of voyageurs' meals. Today, straight flour is rarely toted. It has been replaced by versatile Bisquick for biscuits, bannock, and flapjacks. Add milk (powdered) for the latter. One pound of Bisquick provides two meals of flapjacks and a bannock batch.

Beans

We rarely tote baking beans, not because we deprecate the noble bean (yellow-eyes are the noblest of all), but because when on the move there's no time to bake beans, even precooked ones. To bake bean-hole beans properly, a Dutch oven weighing at least 15 pounds is a prerequisite. That's too much weight to portage.

In the fall, we combine canoe camping with duck shooting or deer hunting, and since no portages are involved, we take along the fixin's for bean-hole beans.

Before departing, 1 pound (minimum) of yellow-eye beans are soaked overnight. The following morning the beans are simmered until medium-soft. They are allowed to cool and packed in a tin or in a plastic bag.

At our permanent tent camp, we dig a hole 2 feet wide and 2 feet deep. A hardwood fire is burned to coals. Beans are placed in the three-legged Dutch oven. About 1 pound of salt pork is sliced into four hunks. Each hunk is sliced several times to the rind but not through it. The pork and two or three doorknob-sized onions are distributed throughout the beans. One cup of molasses and a healthy slug of 151-proof rum are poured into the oven. The final pork piece is snugged into the beans, then water is poured to cover overall. The lid is then popped into place.

Drop the oven onto some coals. Place more coals around the sides and atop the oven. Build a fire atop the bean hole to create a continuing coal supply. Bake eight hours and sit down to a gourmet's feast. Top off with hot buttered biscuits and apple pie baked in a reflector or Winchester Trailblazer stove oven.

Butter

Rich, tasty, melting butter, flowing over hot biscuits or bannock, or inundated by a flood of Vermont maple syrup over a flapjack stack, expands both soul and waistline.

Oleomargarine keeps longer than butter, but as a native and resident of a state that is a major dairy-product producer for the New York–Boston milk market, we cannot admit publicly to using oleo. Privately, too, we prefer the more costly, richer, flavorful, fattening butter.

We tote about 2 pounds of butter on a seven-to-ten-day voyage. That's about as long as butter will keep, and last.

Butter or oleo, were we to use it, is carried in screw-top round aluminum canisters with removable plastic liners. Each canister (3 ounces) holds about ½ pound of butter. SIGG canister price, $1.95.

Butter, or oleo, keeps longer when canisters are placed overnight in water. A spring, lake or stream bottom is a handy cooler. Place canister between and under stones to keep it from washing or rolling away.

Candy

Voyageurs can learn from backpacker's food items. There are times late in the afternoon when one's muscles grow weary and sore. Food is needed that can be quickly absorbed by the bloodstream for immediate energy. Atkinson's Rum-Flavored Candy Bar (6 ounces) has no known equal for this purpose. Price, 50 cents. This bar along with Kendall's Celebrated Mint Candy Bar (we prefer the rum flavor) have long been favorite quick-energy items with British mountaineering and polar expeditions. One bar lasts about three days.

Ordinary chocolate bars melt in warm weather. Hershey Tropical Chocolate Bar (1 ounce) has a high melting point (120°). Price, 15 cents.

Pem-Bars (1¼ ounces) are another high-energy item. Price, 20 cents.

Many folk think of candy as a kid's food. We used to get it for good behavior under trying circumstances. In the outback, be it a mountain peak, jungle, desert, polar regions, or canoe country, candy, of the sort described above, is a basic necessity. These bars are obtained through most backpacking outfitters or through mail-order houses catering to backpackers.

A handful of granulated sugar is an emergency quick-energy item.

Cheese

Grated cheese is not only for spaghetti, but turns freeze-dried eggs into a fairly decent mess of scrambled eggs or omelet. We like the combination of Romano-Parmesan found in supermarkets. A 4-ounce supply, toted in a Gerry poly bottle or reusable squeeze tube, will last about a week.

Solid cheese won't keep so well as grated, but sharp Vermont cheddar will keep up to a week if you can refrain from nibbling. Sometimes we tote Port Salut, Brie, or smaller amounts of Limburger or Camembert.

Cocoa

We use any one of several instant brands which are already mixed with powdered milk and sugar. Roald Amundsen, the first man to make the Northwest Passage and to reach the South Pole, pointed out that neither coffee nor tea provides energy but that cocoa does. Price, 10 cents per serving, one packet per serving. An already mixed Ovaltine is preferred by some voyageurs.

Coffee

The freeze-dried instant type is lighter, more expensive, and quickest to prepare (it saves fuel) but it lacks one of the greatest pleasures of cooking, both indoors and outdoors: the fragrance of boiling coffee.

If you, as we, wish to make that fragrance captive, take one heaping tablespoon of regular-grind coffee for each 12-ounce cup of water. When the water boils, toss in the coffee plus one extra spoonful as a "thank-you-ma'am" for the pot. Boil five minutes and remove from fire or stove. Dash in ½ cup of cold water to settle the grounds (or one raw egg) and cool it slightly.

Boiled coffee, to our way of thinking and drinking, is far superior to percolator, drip, or any other type. Percolators and other fancy gadgets are designed to extract additional money from your wallet and serve only to keep you from the delights of boiled coffee.

Condiments

Spices, herbs, and chili and curry powders give flavor to some of the less-exciting freeze-dried meats and stews.

Garlic in the form of salt, powder, or fresh cloves (the best) is widely used in our stews, soups, eggs, etc. Unless your companion likes garlic, take along a good mouth wash or smell-killer like 151-proof rum.

As for chutney, we select Major Grey's (why doesn't he get promoted?) in preference to Colonel Skinner's. Sun Brand is our preferred brand. This does wonders for eggs.

Oregano enlivens spaghetti sauce while Tabasco sauce is fine for eggs, soups, stews, meat, or just about anything. A little does a lot.

Marmalade, Jam, and Peanut Butter

James Keiller's Dundee Marmalade is our long-time favorite. It comes in crocks and is made from bitter Seville oranges. At home, we use it five days out of seven. This, or apple butter, makes good lunch fare when spread onto leftover flapjacks or Ry-Krisp. We learned the apple butter-flapjack combination from Ernest Hemingway's "The Big Two-Hearted River." Allow 1 pound of apple butter or marmalade per week.

We always tote marmalade, butter, apple butter, and similar items in a SIGG aluminum screw-top container that has a lightweight removable plastic liner with its own inner top. This container holds about 1 pound of butter. Container weight, 6 ounces; price, $2.75.

Peanut butter is high in energy content and filling. It is good for lunch or trail snacks. The smooth type squeezes readily from a Gerry reusable polytube. One pound per week per two persons.

MEAT

Pemmican

Wilson's Meat Bar (3 ounces) is the only readily available commercial pemmican. The bar has 512 calories or about the highest number of calories per ounce of any available food. Price, $1.75.

Pemmican—the word is derived from the Cree word *pimikin*—was originally made from plains animals at hand, like buffalo, elk, deer, and possibly antelope, though the bigger game was preferred.

Squaws separated fat from lean. The lean was cut into thin slices and was sun-dried. The thin slices were then chopped into pieces and put into a skin sack called a *parfleche* which would hold about 90 pounds of pemmican. The fat was melted and mixed with the chopped meat. The ideal ratio is 50 percent fat and 50 percent lean with 80 percent of the calories coming from the fat. Pemmican would last for months. A man can live on a pound a day for several months without the aid of what later became known as antiscorbutics.

Pemmican was the staple ration of the Canadian fur trade. It later became a basic dietary item of white men exploring the polar regions and the tropics. The white man's version is usually beef.

Pemmican is expensive to make and to buy but there is no substitute. It takes 6 pounds of beef, or other meat, to make 1 pound of pemmican.

It was expensive even back in 1953, when the Armour Company, at the request of our friend and mentor Vilhjalmur Stefansson, made up 600 pounds packed in 3-pound tins. One 3-pound tin was the day's ration for three of us. The price was $6 a pound and that was the actual cost of the meat and processing, as it was done as a favor to Dr. Stefansson. At the time I was the organizer and leader of the American Trans-Greenland Expedition—1953. Eating pemmican takes a bit of getting used to. Pemmican can be eaten straight or it can be mixed with water for what our British Antarctic friends call "hoosh." It can be tossed into a stew.

Pemmican's high caloric content per ounce makes it an ideal emergency ration.

Fresh Meat

Our first dinner (it's "supper" in the outback) on a voyage is usually a 3-to-4-pound, 2-inch-thick New York sirloin or T-bone steak (serves two) or a thick ham steak. We may take along a few charcoal briquettes to use under the wire grill (in hardwood country we can use coals, but charcoal is quicker). We have a tossed salad of endive, chicory, romaine, or lettuce. A few potatoes are baked in the coals covered with aluminum foil and served with hunks of butter inserted in a slit. This feast is washed down with a bottle or two of a good dry red California wine. Black coffee, sometimes laced with the old reliable, 151-proof rum, provides the finale.

Voyaging through rural areas like the Upper Connecticut River dotted with an occasional village, we may pick up a steak. On voyages with long stretches between portages, we sometimes tote a lightweight styrofoam ice chest for meat, salad, vegetables, white wine (for our fish), bitter ale, and our most recently caught trout, pike, or bass.

At first, one might think that canoe voyaging is entirely Spartan. We're proud of being able to adapt to the simple, frugal life of the outback, but when the opportunity presents itself, we accept luxuries with gusto.

Dried Meat

Pemmican, not jerky, was the staple voyageur's ration, but jerky, thin strips of dried meat, is light and chewy (that means somewhat tough) and is a good trail snack. Price, 10 cents a strip.

Dried beef makes a first-class meal when served on bannock or over mashed instant potatoes. You can buy cream sauce in packets.

Ham

Small slices from a 2-to-3-pound Daisy ham, partially precooked when purchased, make good trail snacks or can be fried instead of bacon. Served with homemade mustard (add water to mustard powder until it forms a paste), the ham can be served with hot buttered instant potatoes.

MODERN CONVENIENCE FOODS

Powdered Milk

Nonfat, powdered Carnation milk is a voyageur's staple. It can be obtained in 3.2-ounce packets. The nonfat milk is preferred because it is easier to mix than regular powdered milk.

Some voyageurs tote a plastic mixer (you can stuff it with small food items) while others use a mustard or ketchup squirter for squirting powdered milk into water.

Powdered milk is good for mixing with Bisquick or porridge, but some folk prefer the richer Coffee-mate or Pream for coffee.

Spaghetti and Tomato Sauce

Eight ounces will feed two people. Use two tins of tomato paste (add two tins of water to each tin of paste). Toss in garlic, oregano, and if you like it hot, some Tabasco sauce or chili powder. Mushrooms are an excellent addition. They should be sautéed in butter. This presupposes a recognition of poisonous and non-poisonous types. The most common edible mushroom is the "puffball." (Dried mushrooms may be purchased.)

Wilson's dehydrated meatballs complete the Italian touch. Top this all off with a generous shaking of grated cheese.

Sweetenings

We rarely use straight sugar except on porridge. Average consumption seems to be about 1 pound per week per voyageur. Our sugar intake comes mostly from high-energy candy bars and from instant cocoa mixes.

As a Vermont native I swear by Vermont maple syrup as the only fit sweetening for flapjacks, hot rice, and French toast. A pint yields two flapjack breakfasts for two. Molasses and sorghum syrup will serve in the lamented absence of maple syrup but neither can compare with Vermont maple syrup.

Freeze-Dried Dinners

Each trail-food maker has his own specialties. Our favorites are Richmoor's Shrimp Creole and Chili con Carne Ranchero. We add a bit of curry powder and a dash of sherry to the shrimp and chili powder to the chili. Several manufacturers make excellent Chicken à la King.

Many times, notably during storms and when weary from a long, hard day's paddle against the wind, or after a bone-tiring portage, the one-dish dinner comes in handy. In most cases, water is brought to a boil and the dinner is dumped in and stirred occasionally. We stir with one hand and balance our liquid refreshment—that old reliable 151-proof rum—in the other.

Most dinner packets weigh 7 to 10 ounces, and cost from $1.75 to 2.50. When it says, "servings for four" on the box, it means "servings for two" in the bush.

We preface dinner with soup and end with reconstituted dried fruit in syrup and black coffee.

Freeze-Dried Eggs

Today's freeze-dried eggs are a vast improvement over the unpalatable powdered eggs of World War II. Trail-food makers offer a variety for about every taste. There are plain eggs, eggs with bacon bits, French toast mix, and omelet mixes. We frequently add Tabasco sauce and grated cheese. Chutney is a first-rate accompaniment.

We also add bits of Wilson's Bacon Bar to the eggs

or use regular bacon, though by the time we've worked our way through our fresh eggs, the regular bacon is usually gone.

Egg-mix prices average 50 to 75 cents and despite the label's assertion that there is enough for four, you can slice this claim by half—the outdoors doubles your appetite. Weight averages 4 to 6 ounces per packet.

Fruit and Fruit Drinks

Dried apricots and prunes have long been a staple with voyageurs and backpackers. Today, freeze-dried fruits are somewhat more palatable. Our favorite, and that of many other voyageurs, is French Cocktail, also called French Compote or Fruit Compote. This contains several dried fruits.

Apricots now come mixed with sugar, as do several other fruits. Weights average 6 ounces per packet and the cost is about $1. A 6-ounce packet seems a bit too much for two people after dinner, so we finish the remainder at breakfast. Most fruit mixes require 10 to 20 minutes of simmering.

Forget Kool-Aid-type drinks—they are only flavored water—and try fruit-juice crystals that are directly derived from the actual fruit and are not mere flavorings. We prefer lemon, lime, and pineapple but banana, grapefruit, and orange are also available.

Prices range from 75 to 95 cents for packets averaging 4 ounces. Most packets make 1 quart of juice except for lemon or lime, which make about 2½ cups. It is not necessary to make the drink full strength. Sometimes just a few crystals dissolved in your canteen or cup remove the Halazone or bogwater taint.

Freeze-Dried Meat

Freeze-dried pork chops, hamburgers, beefsteaks,

ham cubes, and meatballs are light in weight and when jazzed up with chili, curry, or other condiments are a fairly satisfying meal. (When water is added, the weight is multiplied several-fold.) Two beefsteaks weigh 1 ounce each, contain 144 calories each, and take one cup of water and 10 minutes to prepare. Price, $2.25 (for two). They lack flavor, so add chili powder. Allow two steaks per person.

Two pork chops weigh 1 ounce each, contain 163 calories, and take 1 cup of water, and 10 minutes to prepare. Allow at least two chops per person. Add curry powder for flavor. Price, $1.75 (for two).

A 1-ounce tin of ham cubes takes ½ cup of water and 10 minutes to prepare. Add two eggs or serve with cream sauce and rice. Price, 75 cents (for two). Tabasco helps.

A 1¾-ounce tin of meatballs (about 24 tiny ones) takes 1 minute and about ½ cup of water to prepare. Price, $1.25 (for two). Add to highly seasoned tomato paste.

A 2-ounce tin of three precooked beef patties takes ½ cup of water and 1 minute to prepare. Price, $1.25 (for one). Curry or chili powder and Tabasco sauce in brown gravy makes a great improvement.

Three hamburgers weigh 3¼ ounces and take 1 cup of water and 10 minutes to prepare. Add chili powder in brown gravy mix. Price, $2.00. Allow three per person.

Instant Potatoes

Fresh potatoes are no longer a staple on voyageurs' menus. Instant potatoes are our choice, and we rarely have them more than once a week. Excellent brands include Carnation and French. Get the individual packets.

Dehydrated slices or chunk potatoes provide bulk for stews. Dehydrated potatoes, onion flakes, a combination vegetable packet, and a Wilson Meat Bar (pemmican) make a first-rate stew. Season with garlic, Tabasco and possibly a dash of curry.

Hash-brown potatoes and O'Brien potatoes come in packets from trail-food manufacturers.

Soups

Instant soups made by Stow-a-Way Products are handy and fuel-saving for lunches and a quick burst of energy after unloading the canoe but before setting up camp. Bring water to a boil, dump in the soup packet, stir, turn off heat, cool and spoon or drink.

Standard dehydrated or freeze-dried soups usually require simmering for several minutes after the water

Poly bottles contain some basic condiments and seasonings.

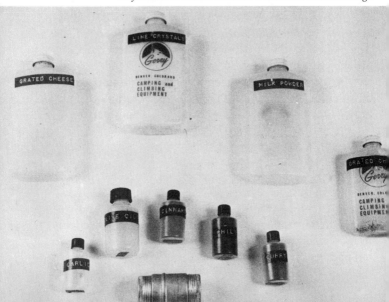

has boiled. They provide more bulk than do the thinner, instant soups. These soups can be obtained in regular trail packets.

Well-known Swiss brands like Maggi and Swiss-Knorr can be purchased at supermarkets. The latter usually require repacking in polybags.

Vegetables

Peas, carrots, corn, and beans are among vegetables currently available in freeze-dried or dehydrated form. Packets weigh 2 to 6 ounces and cost runs from 50 cents to $1. Some varieties require soaking before cooking. We usually avoid this type. Combination vegetable packets are useful in stews.

FOOD CONTAINERS

Unbreakable polyethylene bottles, bags, tubes, and jars are indispensable for toting voyageurs' miscellaneous foods.

The polyethylene containers we use most:

Semi-flat-sided, 4-ounce-capacity screw-top bottles (1 ounce); $1 for four.

Semi-flat-sided, 8-ounce-capacity screw-top bottles (2 ounces); $1 for two.

Polytubes hold up to about 1 pound of peanut butter, jam, etc. The screw-top tubes are filled from the bottom, which is then closed with a rugged clip. They are washable in hot water and can be used many times. Price, $1.25 for three.

Polybags in three sizes take care of most of our bag needs. A 6-inch-long polybag usually holds most of *the items required for one meal; $1 for ten. An 8-inch-long polybag holds three one-meal foodbags; $1 for six. The 18-inch-long polybags are useful for storing numerous items in unwaterproofed packs like the Duluth; $1 for four.*

The above bottles, bags, and tubes are available from Gerry dealers.

Small quantities of foods like garlic powder, Tabasco sauce, etc., are toted in small Austrian-made poly bottles (¼ ounce). Price, 10 cents each.

Also handy are the Austrian-made wide-mouth, screw-top polyjars with ribbed sides for a better grip. These come in various sizes and are used to hold jams, powdered milk, coffee, sugar, etc. Price for largest size, $1.

For many years we've used SIGG screw-top aluminum canisters. Some of these, like the ones we use for butter, have removable plastic liners. These come in a variety of sizes. Price range, $1-$2.50.

Part III
Canoe Techniques

13
Canoe Safety and Rescue

No Indian ever drowned on a portage.
                              —Old voyageur's adage

We swung the canoe alongside the dock. The 140-odd-mile voyage was over. We had survived wind, waves, rain, rapids, 34 portages ranging from 12 to 1,200 yards, bugs, brambles, and black bear forages on our food supply, but not once had we capsized. There had been some close calls, though. An acquaintance ran toward the dock to greet us. I stood up. The canoe, my partner, all the gear, and the empty food packs flipped into the lake.

I received an entirely unexpected and unnecessary bath. I had violated a cardinal rule: I had rocked the boat.

> *Rule 1: Never make a sudden or jerky movement. Slow and deliberate motions are the mode of behavior in a canoe.*

> *Other important rules for canoe safety are:*

> *2. Know how to embark and disembark under a variety of conditions: dock, beach, steep river bank. Practice.*

3. Never overload your canoe. There must always be at least 6 inches of freeboard. Overloading a canoe (with gear, but not with people) rarely happens. With bulky gear, you run out of space before you reach the limit.

4. Always trim your load—both crew and gear. When loading gear, keep the center of gravity as low as possible.

5. Never travel after dark. Rise early and make camp 2 to 3 hours before dark.

6. Never overestimate your ability to handle a canoe under difficult conditions.

7. We've been voyaging for forty years and have never swopped positions with our partner while underway. If you wish to switch positions, do it before you get underway.

8. Don't stand up in a canoe unless you are poling, paddling, or casting. Standing to paddle provides a restful change sometimes or you may need to see farther ahead than a sitting position allows. Experienced New Brunswick salmon guides let only experienced hands cast from a standing position.

CANOE SAFETY—PERSONAL

The American White Water Affiliate, basically concerned with whitewater canoeing rather than with canoe voyaging, has evolved a safety code for whitewater canoeing. Some of these safety rules apply to voyaging which may or may not include whitewater running. This writer's comments, as they apply to voyaging, follow the recommendations of the AWWA safety code.

1. Never canoe alone. The preferred minimum is three craft.

> *Comment:* While valid for whitewater competition or training events this doesn't necessarily hold true for voyaging. Many contemporary voyageurs including myself usually prefer cruising with one companion in one canoe, family voyaging excepted. I even take an occasional solitary voyage. However, if you are afflicted with the great American disease of togetherness, then by all means cruise with other canoes and companions. Throughout much of North America's canoe country there is considerable voyaging in solitary canoes.

2. Be a competent swimmer with ability to handle yourself underwater.

> *Comment:* No disagreement here. Anyone who doesn't swim probably won't be interested in voyaging.

3. Wear your lifejacket wherever upsets may occur. The lifejacket must be capable of supporting you face up if unconscious. A crash helmet is recommended in rivers of Grade IV and over.

> *Comment:* We don't know any voyageurs who wear helmets, but if wearing one makes you feel better, then by all means wear an approved model. Canoes which normally carry life preserver cushions or life preservers should have them secured to thwarts by a light line that can be be cut in a hurry with the sheath knife you should always tote when voyaging.

4. Have a frank knowledge of your canoeing ability, and don't attempt waters beyond your ability.

> *Comment:* Reasonable enough, but you will never progress from Grade I rapids to Grade IV or

Stepping aboard.

more unless you actually run rapids. This should be done in an empty canoe and with an experienced companion.

5. Know and respect river classifications.

   Comment: No disagreement here, but most rivers in the outback have no classifications. When map or lay of land indicates possible rapids ahead, beach your canoe and scout the rapids. If they seem impassable, then portage or track.

6. Beware of cold water and of weather extremes: dress accordingly. Rubber wet suits or long woolen underwear may be essential for safety as well as comfort.

   Comment: Voyageurs usually don't tote wet

suits but we've seen times—notably on windy lakes—when a wet suit would have been welcome. This particular safety rule is, however, primarily aimed at whitewater buffs who of necessity must have protection against cold water because most whitewater running is done in the high-water levels of early spring.

7. Be suitably prepared and equipped: carry a knife, secure your glasses, and equip yourself with special footgear, skin protection, raincoat, etc., as the situation requires.

Comment: Always wear on your belt a well-designed, sharp sheath knife. Even if you're a non-smoker, always carry on your person a supply of matches in a waterproof container. A considerable number of canoeing fatalities have resulted from hypothermia (exposure). Always have dry clothes in a waterproof bag.

8. Be practiced in escape from spray cover, in rescue and self-rescue and in first aid.

Comment: Bravo! As I have already explained, I prefer not to use a spray cover because I am afraid of getting trapped by it.

BOAT PREPARATION AND EQUIPMENT

1. Test new and unfamiliar equipment before undertaking hazardous situations.

Comment: We suggest testing all equipment including new camping gear before taking to the waterways.

2. Be sure craft is in good repair before starting trip.

Comment: Check ribs and planking on canoes that have them. Check rivets in aluminum craft.

Check all seams and hull covering. Check paddles for cracks and blade edge for roughness.

3. Have a spare paddle, affixed for immediate use.

> *Comment:* The paddle should be lashed so that it is accessible to either bowman or sternman. It should be affixed so that it will come loose when you grab it (as with a piece of light string) but it should be sufficiently secured so that it will not come free if the canoe capsizes.

4. Install flotation devices designed to displace from the craft as much water as possible. Check that they are securely fixed. A minimum of one cubic foot at each end is recommended.

> *Comment:* Most current craft have built-in flotation. This is true of the better aluminum craft and fiberglass. Royalex, a closed-cell material, has flotation throughout the craft. Canvas-and-wood canoes have no built-in flotation, their materials are lighter than water and they rarely sink. If your canoe doesn't have built-in flotation, then you can install it. Request suggestions from the manufacturer.

5. Have bow and stern lines . . . use ¼-inch or ⅜-inch diameter and 8- to 15-foot-long rope. Fasten securely to the canoe at one end, and other end must release only if tugged. Floats and knots at the ends are not recommended.

> *Comment:* Voyageurs experienced with tracking—something many competitive whitewater folk aren't—rarely use tracking lines of less than 30 feet and the average seems about 50 feet. There are times when 100-foot tracking lines come in handy.

6. Use spray cover whenever required: cover release must be instant and foolproof.

> *Comment:* Very few voyageurs use spray cov-

ers. If rapids are such that a spray cover is required, you should consider portaging or tracking.

ON THE RIVER

The following procedures are strongly recommended when several canoes travel together.

1. All personnel must know group plans, on river organization, hazards expected, location of special equipment, signals to be used.

2. Lead canoe knows the river, sets the course, and is never passed.

> *Comment:* In new country, and this is what most voyageurs are after, no one in the party may know the waters ahead. If maps or local information indicate rapids, it is best to beach the canoes and scout the water before deciding to portage, track, or paddle.

3. Rear-guard canoe is equipped and trained for rescue; always remains in rear of formation. Each canoe is responsible for canoe behind; passes on signals, indicates obstacles, sees it through bad spots.

> *Comment:* These points are reasonable, but more applicable to whitewater work than to voyaging.

LAKE OR OCEAN VOYAGING

1. Do not travel beyond a returnable distance from shore.

> *Comment:* This is not always possible when crossing a big lake.

2. Know the weather. Conditions on lakes can change drastically within a few minutes. Beware of offshore winds.

Comment: Better to remain windbound ashore than to attempt crossings during dangerously high wind and waves.

3. Lead, rear-guard and side-guard canoes are strongly recommended to prevent large groups from spreading out.

Comment: Large groups are not desirable anyway—at least not to me.

4. Secure complete tide information for voyages involving tidal currents.

5. Canoeist should learn to right, empty water, board a swamped canoe.

THE LEADER'S RESPONSIBILITY

The following section of the AWWA safety code is designed for the leader of a multi-canoe brigade. However, even in a two-member crew, one crewman must make the ultimate decisions. There is no time for debate when falls or a dam lie just ahead. Normally the leader is the most experienced crewman. He is usually the sternman but in whitewater situations he moves into the bow. This swapping of position is not done afloat. The leader, having secured all available route data, will have a good idea of what lies ahead on the day's run. He positions himself in the bow prior to starting the day's run.

1. He must have full knowledge of the river. He determines the river classification on the spot and adapts plans to suit.

Comment: It is not always possible to have full knowledge of a wilderness river, but some data can be secured before departure or from Indians or other residents along the route.

2. He doesn't allow anyone to participate beyond his

proven ability. Exceptions: (a) When the trip is an adequately supported training trip, or (b) when difficult stretches can be portaged.

> *Comment:* We would add tracking as a technique for difficult stretches. This excellent rule is obviously for multi-canoe brigades.

3. He must know what conditions in weather, visibility, and water to expect: he should instruct the group relative to these conditions and must make decisions on the basis of related dangers.

> *Comment:* While designed for groups, a basic knowledge of weather signs is important to single-canoe crews.

4. His decisions in the interest of safety are final.

> *Comment:* Amen!

5. He designates the necessary support personnel, and, if appropriate, the order and spacing of canoes.

WHAT TO DO IF YOU CAPSIZE

1. Be aware of your responsibility to assist your partner.
2. Hold onto your canoe: it has much flotation and is easy for rescuers to spot. Get to the upstream side of the canoe so it cannot crush you against the rocks. Follow rescuers' instructions.

> *Comment:* There may be no rescuers, if you and your partner are alone. This is no cause for undue alarm. Analyze the situation. Make your way to the nearest shore.

3. Leave your canoe if this improves your safety; your personal safety must come first. If rescue is not imminent and water is numbing cold—or worse rapids follow—then strike for the nearest shore.

> *Comment:* Rescue other than by yourself or by your partner is rarely imminent in the wilderness.

Returning aboard an upset canoe.

4. Stay on the upstream end of your canoe; otherwise you risk being pinned against obstacles, or in waves, may swallow water.

> *Comment:* Agreed.

5. If canoeist in accompanying craft capsizes, go after the canoeist. Rescue his canoe only if it can be done safely. It usually can be salvaged at the bottom of the rapids.

> *Comment:* Salvage your canoe and outfit. Light gasoline stove or fire. Prepare hot soup immediately. A healthy slug of 151-proof rum and hot water is comforting. Strip off wet clothing and dress in warm clothes from your clothing stuffsack.

AFTERTHOUGHTS

Two key, and possibly lifesaving, words have been deliberately omitted from the above advice. AWWA advice is designed not for canoe voyageurs, but for whitewater buffs interested in navigating the most difficult rapids within their expertise. To them the words "Portage" and "Tracking" are evidence of failure. To the canoe voyageur who wants to bring his canoe, outfit, and his own hide through rapids with minimal danger, there are times when it is prudent to track or portage.

It must be remembered that much whitewater canoeing is practiced in almost full view of highways or villages. The annual Eastern Slalom Championships are held on Vermont's West River in Jamaica Town. If canoe or kayak capsizes, assistance, safety, warmth, and comfort are at hand.

Whitewater running on outback voyages is an entirely different matter. Experienced whitewater canoeists would be ill-advised to attempt making Grade V or VI runs in semi-wilderness or wilderness where the nearest food and aid might be 100 miles or more away.

It is wildly exciting to run white water, but don't expose your food and equipment to unnecessary danger. If you feel capable of making a difficult whitewater run, then beach and portage your outfit, and make the whitewater run in an empty canoe. The canoe may capsize and you may get wet, but you'll have hot drinks, warm food, and a comfortable, dry sleeping bag that night.

We don't use spray decks on Grades I through III. It is probably advisable to use one on Grade IV rapids. However, we lash our outfit into a waterproof nylon tarp and secure it to the thwarts. There are those who prefer to let their outfit float downstream. We prefer to keep it in the canoe which will almost invariably be recovered at the foot of the rapids, battered perhaps, but usually dry and intact.

Don't attempt to use spray decks unless they have an instant and infallible release. Know how to escape from them. Practice escapes.

When in doubt of your ability to make the whitewater run that lies ahead, always track or portage. This is one reason you meet old professional canoemen.

A canoe with built-in flotation will float even though nearly full of water.

They don't take unnecessary risks. One reads occasionally about the death of a whitewater buff. He, or she,
took unnecessary chances.

Remember—no Indian ever drowned on a portage!

14
Paddle and Pole

Paddling, according to many oldtime professional canoemen, is an ancient and mysterious craft whose techniques can only be learned after years of apprenticeship.

Hogwash! A beginner need know only a few basic strokes. Rudiments can be acquired in an afternoon's session on a quiet pond or placid lake. These are good places to learn because you don't have to worry about currents.

It would be ideal if you have a friend or acquaintance who can take time to show you the basics. Should you live in or near a city or sizable community, your local American Red Cross chapter, the YMCA or YWCA may hold canoe technique courses. Winter courses are held at indoor swimming pools. A pool is an ideal place to learn canoe basics. Many colleges and universities offer canoe courses through their athletic facilities.

Every summer thousands of would-be voyageurs arrive in the Quetico-Superior canoe country with little or no knowledge of canoeing. Many arrive at Ely around midday, spend a few hours in the afternoon with a competent instructor, and the next morning they are on their way for a week or two of backcountry voyaging.

Such neophytes do not tackle white water on their first cruise. If you're overpowered by such ambition then pick a mild section of rapids, stow your gear on the beach and indulge in your first taste—or bath—of white water. It is probably better to do this in the vicinity of other voyageurs so that help is handy.

Lacking experienced friends, canoe training courses, or an outfitter's competent instructor, then hie yourself to a placid pond and take this book along with your companion. Assuming you're both neophytes, take turns at bow and stern paddling positions.

You only need to know a few strokes to accomplish the basic moves: (1) forward or propelling, (2) combined forward and steering, (3) instant stop, (4) sideways, (5) backup, and (6) turning. A knowledge of numbers (4) and (5) helps to accomplish number (6).

Now spend your remaining canoeing years adapting, modifying, and improving these basic techniques.

Switching paddling sides: Oldtime professionals like Calvin Rutstrom and Bill Riviere take pride, and justly so, in their ability to paddle for hours without switching sides. Most recreational canoeists are not that paddle-hardened. There is no set time span for switching sides—we switch every hour or two. This allows the muscles on one side to relax and rest while the other side is exercising. After several days of paddling you'll be able to paddle longer without switching, but don't overdo it. Many tyros switch every five minutes or so. There is no necessity for this excessive action.

Sometimes—usually in shallow water or narrow channels—it is necessary for the bowman to switch momentarily to avoid hitting an obstruction with his paddle.

Bowman: The basic function of the bow paddle is to propel the canoe forward. The bowman, however, has the responsibility for "reading" the water. In the fur-trade days the bowman was paid higher wages than other paddlers because of his water-reading know-how. When both bowman and sternman are equally able in canoe handling, then the paddler with the best water-reading judgment should be the bowman. This is particularly true when voyaging through unfamiliar waters.

The bowman sets the paddling pace, always aware that the sternman's more complex stroke takes slightly longer to execute. He acts jointly with the sternman in executing the jam (stop), backwater, turning, push, and pull strokes.

Sternman: The stern paddle both propels and steers the canoe.

Joint operations: The sternman and bowman dip their blades on opposite sides of the canoe. Exceptions to this are when in crosswinds on a wide river or lake and when executing a turn.

Both paddlers dip their blades simultaneously. Few actions are so nerve-wracking as having your partner break the rhythm by using irregular strokes.

PADDLING POSITION

Old-time canoes were made with wide thwarts—paddling thwarts—rather than seats. The paddler kneeled and rested his backside against the paddling thwart. Some publications like the American Red Cross Canoeing Manual imply that skilled paddlers only use thwarts. This is not true. Many skilled canoeists prefer to use a seat for hour-in and hour-out paddling. It's more comfortable although less efficient.

You should resort to kneeling only when maximum paddle power is needed: paddling upstream against a stiff current or paddling into the wind. Kneeling also reduces wind resistance. It is a somewhat safer position because the center of gravity is lower, but for most, paddling seats are preferred. Ignore the jibes of the snobs who loudly declare that a real canoeman only uses paddling thwarts. If you must join this obnoxious group, specify paddling thwarts when you order your canoe. Most makers will supply them.

Paddling thwarts are slightly wider than regular thwarts so that bone-weary kneeling paddlers can use them in lieu of a regular seat.

Kneeling on unupholstered decks is uncomfortable. Even Cree Indians, some of our best canoeists, use a jacket or shirt as a kneeling pad. We use our life-preserver cushions. Tennis shoes provide an adequate jury rig.

THE STROKES

Bow or Cruising Stroke

This is the basic forward propelling stroke. The paddle is dipped and drawn backward. While drawing backward the paddle is turned so the blade parallels the keel or centerline. Tyros usually—and mistakenly—draw the blade parallel to the curved gunwale.

The bowman uses this basic stroke for one purpose only—to drive the canoe forward. Steering is the sternman's responsibility.

Canadian or Guide Stroke

Sometimes mistaken for the less efficient J-stroke, the Canadian or Guide stroke, though more difficult to master, is less tiring and more effective.

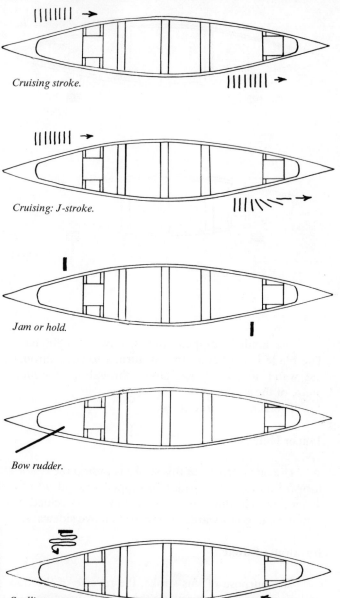

Cruising stroke.

Cruising: J-stroke.

Jam or hold.

Bow rudder.

Sculling.

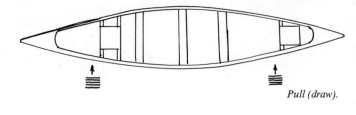

Pull (draw).

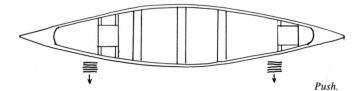

Push.

The blade is dipped, and is drawn straight back. The blade is feathered, that is, turned to edge through the water to reduce resistance, throughout the final phase of the stroke.

This is my favorite stroke.

Jam or Hold Stroke

The one purpose of this stroke is to stop the canoe's forward motion. The paddle is dipped straight into the water and held there until the next move is decided on. It may be to go forward, reverse, or to move sideways.

Backwater Stroke

The purpose of this stroke, the reverse of the bow or cruising stroke, is to reverse the canoe's direction.

Draw Stroke

Push the paddle away from the gunwale with blade paralleling the centerline or keel. Dip blade and draw it toward the canoe.

This stroke moves the canoe sideways. If applied on opposite sides, it can turn the canoe about within its own length.

Push Stroke

This stroke, the reverse of the draw stroke, is more difficult to accomplish. In it, the blade is dipped close to the canoe and the water pushed away from it. This stroke is sometimes used when there is insufficient time to switch blades for the draw stroke.

Sculling, Fishtail, and Zigzag Stroke

This zigzag stroke (there are several versions) can be accomplished without withdrawing the blade from the water. With blade parallel to the keel or centerline, reach out from the gunwale and dip blade as in the draw stroke.

The blade, however, is not drawn directly toward the canoe in a straight line. It is accomplished with a series of continuous S-curves or zigzags. Apply continual pressure while leading first one blade edge and then the other.

This stroke can stop the canoe, pull it to one side, reverse direction, or turn the craft.

SOLITARY PADDLING

Canoe manufacturers, who should know better,

sometimes illustrate a solitary paddler located in the stern position without weight forward. The forward section of the canoe is entirely out of water.

Solitary paddlers should sit just aft of amidships unless the bow section is loaded with gear or some other weight that compensates for the stern paddler's weight.

I prefer the stern position, and when camp gear is not aboard to compensate for weight difference, I use filled 5-gallon plastic water jugs. It takes about five jugs to compensate for my 250 pounds. Some canoe authorities advise against weighing down the forward section but only because it is a nuisance to stow and unload the weight. I prefer a few minutes' extra work and the comfort of stern paddling to the less comfortable (to my way of thinking) amidship position.

The Canadian stroke is suitable for lone paddlers.

POLING

Poling can save weary miles of portaging, and once you master the art you have a skill to be proud of.

North Country polers use setting poles for pushing their way up shallow streams or for snubbing (slowing down) on downstream runs.

Deep South polers use poles—usually called "push poles"—for working their way through the shallow muddy streams and swamps. Some of them use poles almost to the exclusion of paddles.

The best and safest place to practice poling is just off a sandy beach in a placid cove or bay. It takes only a few lessons to acquire the basic techniques, but mastery takes practice.

Once you have acquired the basics, try improving your skill on some shallow, slow-moving stream.

Poling is not difficult. Several years ago, Ronald

Kloepper entered the National Poling Championships with only two months' experience. He won!

Poles are probably adequate 10 to 12 feet long and one of these days I may lop off 2 to 4 feet from my 14-foot ash setting pole.

Some New Brunswick guide friends (they are among the world's most expert polers) often don't want to be bothered with a pole at all times in the canoe. They take along an iron point which they fit onto a young sapling that is chopped when a pole is needed. Other guides always carry a pole.

"Climbing-the-pole" has long been the traditional North Woods poling technique. The advent of competition poling—many use fiberglass poles—has introduced the "jab" and "change-over" technique. We prefer "climbing-the-pole," but sometimes we may use all three methods. The latter two produce the most speed but they also are the most tiring and cannot be used for more than a few minutes at a stretch, at least by me.

Competition distances are short. High-speed poling can be used in these instances. In the outback where it may be necessary to pole for several miles through unknown waters, the climbing-the-pole method is slower but less tiring. The slower tempo allows a more detailed scrutiny of the unknown waters ahead.

Climbing-the-Pole

Stand up in a very slight crouch. Grab the pole in its midsection. Place the right hand 18 to 24 inches (depending on arm length) above the left hand. Jab the shoe end of the pole into the water at right angles to the canoe. The pole should be no more than 3 or 4 inches from the gunwale. Thrust the pole lightly but firmly backward. The canoe is shoved forward.

Continue your thrust, meanwhile climbing the pole by placing one hand above the other and then repeating the process. When you reach the top of the pole, give a final firm thrust. During this process the pole is, of course, inclining increasingly toward the horizontal.

Repeat the process. You'll be surprised at how fast the pole moves the canoe forward.

Don't watch the pole. Inspect the waters ahead for the best possible route.

Jab Poling

This usually calls for a 10-to-12-foot pole, but I get along fairly well with my 14-footer. The pole is jabbed into the water. It is then picked up and the jabs repeated.

Change-over Poling

My 14-footer is ideal for this technique. Jab the end of the pole into the water just slightly behind your body. Now climb-the-pole, hand over hand, in the same manner as for the climb-the-pole technique.

Continue this process until your hands are about 4 feet from the top end of the pole. Now flip the pole out of the water and jab its top end into the water on the opposite side of the canoe. This powerful method, however, cannot be maintained for many minutes.

Ideally a pole to be used for this technique should have a shoe at either end. We get along—as do most others—with a pole shod on one end.

Opposite: Hand-over-hand poling, steps 1, 2, and 3.
Practice in calm water.

15
Outboards: Yes or No?

Outboard motors make river and lake travel easier and portages more difficult.

Many purists among voyageurs resent the intrusion of outboards into their country. We, too, dislike areas dominated by speedboats and water skiers. Fortunately, many canoe-country rivers and lakes have to be portaged into and here we are free of the obnoxious smells and whine of motors.

There have been times, bucking a current or paddling against wind-driven waves, when we wished for a small outboard. Once through the current or beached at the far end of the lake we take pride in having come through on sheer muscle power.

We rarely use an outboard on voyages but we occasionally use one on day-long fishing trips when trolling. We might consider taking along a motor for a trip on the broad Yukon or Mackenzie. It would rest in its canvas case on the deck to be used only in the event of heavy headwinds.

We rather enjoy seeing an occasional Cree, or other Indian, purring along in his freight canoe powered by an outboard. Other outback residents are to be seen as well—the Men of God, trappers, Mounties, Hudson's Bay Company people, and prospectors.

PURCHASING A MOTOR

The lightest motor that will handle your heaviest demand on it is the ideal solution. For some years we used the lightest motor we know of. That is Neptune's 1.7 hp. Mighty Mite. It weighs 16 pounds and has a 1-quart fuel tank. We got ours through L. L. Bean, Freeport, Maine. Current price is $105.

Another superb lightweight motor is the world-famed British-made Seagull. It is slightly less than 2 hp. and weighs 26 pounds. It costs about the same as the Mighty Mite.

Most major American outboard motor makers like Johnson, Evinrude, and Mercury make at least one motor suitable for canoes. Johnson, for instance, makes 2-

Lightweight motor clamped to detachable Grumman motor mount.

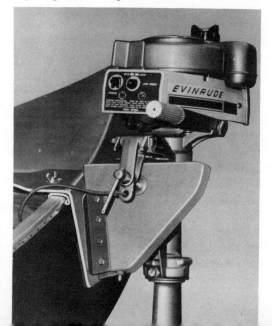

hp. and 4-hp. motors. The 2-hp. weighs 24 pounds and the 4-hp. weighs 32 pounds. The 2-hp. has a 1-quart-capacity integral fuel tank. The 4-hp. has a separate 3-gallon tank.

Four horsepower is about the maximum needed by most recreational canoeists. The big, flat-sterned freight canoes with wide beams (up to 5 feet) and with a load capacity of up to 5500 pounds can handle motors up to 25 hp.

Reliable canoe manufacturers like Old Town, Grumman, and Chestnut have horsepower recommendations that should not be exceeded in the interest of fuel economy, weight, and safety.

Experienced outfitters like those in the Quetico-Superior country will not rent motors in excess of 5 hp. for recreational canoes.

Stern Types

Recreational conoeists should always purchase a double-ended canoe, even though they intend to make occasional use of a motor.

Vee-stern canoes, which have a pointed bow, are difficult to paddle and are much noisier when paddled than a double-ender. This also applies to the big flat-sterned freight canoes.

The offset position of motors on double-ender canoes provides a much more comfortable position for steering than the stern location.

Mounting the Motor

Major canoe manufacturers offer outboard-motor mounting brackets designed for specific models of their canoes. While some brackets can be adapted, it is prob-

Side mount is most convenient method for mounting, steering, and operating double-end canoe.

ably best to use a bracket made or recommended by your canoe maker.

In ordering, state whether you wish a right- or left-hand motor bracket. Most brackets cost between $12.50 and $20.

Repair Kit

This should be toted in a waterproof case. A spare propeller is a must for wilderness travel. Kit should include:

Spare propeller
Spare shear pins
Spare spark plugs (2)
Plug gauge
Wirecutting pliers
Screwdriver(s)—enough to fit all motor screws
Adjustable crescent wrench
Waterproof electricians' tape
Small roll copper wire

Fuel

Most outboard users mix their oil and gasoline before leaving on a cruise. This is convenient, but if you run short of fuel for your lantern and stove, you will not be able to borrow from the premixed motor fuel. Tote a separate plastic container of outboard oil and mix motor fuel as you need it.

Portage

A packframe is the most comfortable method of toting an outboard motor, though I have carried a Mighty Mite under the flap of my Duluth. This was more weight, but it saved an extra trip over a long portage. Spare fuel tins can be carried by hand.

Care and Repair

Learn how to operate your motor and how to make basic repairs before you leave for the outback. Too many outboard purchasers leave for the wilderness before learning the simple rudiments of operation and repair.

Most outboard makers supply, for a modest fee, a protective cover and carrying case for motors. Get one. It keeps out dirt and dust when the motor is not in use. Keep the motor in this case while it is resting in the bottom of your canoe. Some cases have a pocket for spare parts and basic tools. After returning home, check your

Square-stern canoe—more difficult to paddle—should be purchased only when motor is to be used more than paddle power.

Square-stern freighter-type canoe is designed for motor use only.

motor. Is the propeller badly nicked? If it needs replacement, don't use your spare prop. Order a new one. It is easy to use a handy replacement part and then forget to replace the replacement.

Always check your motor before leaving home.

THE GOVERNMENT AND YOUR CANOE

The instant you attach a motor—no matter how small the canoe or how light the motor—you become involved, and with good reason, with various government regulations, including the Congressional Motor Boat Act of 1940. Your canoe falls into one of two categories: Class A—under 16 feet, or Class I—under 26 feet.

The U.S. Coast Guard is charged with administering maritime law and requires that each passenger, including yourself, be fitted with an approved life-preserving device. If your canoe exceeds 16 feet in length, the 1940 law requires that you have, and use when required, a whistle operated by mouth or other means that is audible for at least one-half mile. The 1940 law does not make this requirement of outboard-powered canoes under 16 feet, but the "Rules of the Road" require that you have the whistle. Whistles operated by a small aerosol can are obtainable at your nearest marine hardware dealer. Price, $3.50.

If you plan to operate your outboard-powered canoe on the inland waters of the United States between sunset and sunrise (not generally a good idea), then you are required to show two lights while under way: a white elevated light at the stern with a range of 2 miles and which is visible throughout all 32 points of the compass; and an elevated combination red (port) and green (starboard) light above the bow. The light must be visible for one mile and has to be seen through 20 points of the compass, 10 points (112°) on either side of the bow.

Your state requires that your motor-powered canoe be registered (there's a fee) and that the registration numbers be painted on the hull.

There are also the "Rules of the Road" which have to be obeyed.

We suggest that you secure two useful and inexpensive publications:

Recreational Boating Guide, U.S. Coast Guard Publication CG-340. Price, 40 cents from the Superintendent of Documents, Washington, D.C. 20402.

Basic Outboard Boating by Charles W. Rissell, American Red Cross. Price, 75 cents from your local Red Cross Chapter.

Muscle-powered canoes are exempt from the above regulations.

OUTBOARD MOTOR TROUBLE CHECKLIST

Hard to start
Out of gas
Clogged fuel line
Plugged vent in gas cap
Too much oil in gasoline (motor smokes)
Broken spark plug lead
Dirty plugs

    Dirty points
    Flooded (warm motor)
    Insufficiently choked (cold motor)
Motor knocks
    Carbonized cylinders
    Spark too far advanced
Motor overheated
    Blown exhaust gasket
    Defective water pump
Power loss
    Fuel line screens clogged
    Needs colder spark plug
    Adjust carburetor to obtain correct fuel mixture
    Improper fuel mixture (too much or too little oil)
Rough idle
    Adjust carburetor idle
    Needs hotter plug
    Blown intake valve gasket
Motor freezes
    No gear housing lubricant
    Rusted cylinder walls
    Propeller or prop shaft is bent
    Propeller fouled by weeds, debris, etc.
Excessive vibration
    Motor is not secure on transom
    Excessively rich carburetor mixture
    Damaged or fouled propeller
    Loose swivel brackets or loose steering gear tension
Propeller doesn't revolve
    Broken shear pin
    Damaged propeller
    Fouled propeller

     Most of the above problems are the result of in-attention to the motor. Always check the motor before leaving port. Institute regular motor check.

16
Portage and Posé

There are no easy portages.
—Pessimistic first-tripper

A man burdened beneath a heavy canoe—it gets heavier with every footstep—wearily drags himself along a bog pocked trail. . . . Other figures stagger under two packs. . . . The man with the canoe attempts to balance the craft on his head while one hand scratches bug bites and the other slaps at mosquitoes.

It isn't that bad, really, or at least not very often. It only seems that way now and then.

Throughout canoe country—except in the Northeast from Maine through the Adirondacks—"portage" has two meanings. "A portage" is a trail between two canoeable bodies of water. "To portage" is to carry canoe and gear over that trail. Voyageurs prefer the French-Canadian pronunciation of "por-TAZH" to the Anglicized "POR-tij." The word was derived from the French word, *porter*, to carry.

In the Northeast, "carry" is used instead of "portage." We prefer the latter in that "portage" means the two things noted above—and both are concerned with

One-man carry.

canoeing. "Carry," according to Webster, has more than twenty-five widely varied meanings. Some meanings have one or more subdivisions. Portagers use the word "carry" in a restricted sense: A "carry" means to literally "carry" the canoe by hand.

Why Portage?

To avoid shooting rapids (with the possibility of losing your outfit) which are, in your considered judgment, beyond your ability.

To avoid shooting rapids which are obviously impossible for even the most experienced whitewater men.

To avoid shooting over falls.

It is the only reasonable way to travel from one ca-

Two-man carry.

noeable body of water to another. Impassable rapids, swamps, ridges, and log-barricaded streams create a need for portages.

Some rivers or streams have alternate routes, at high-water level, or at normal, or low-water level.

We usually find portages a pleasant interlude. There seems to be a notion that all portages are several miles long. On a recent 220-mile voyage through northern Saskatchewan, there were nineteen portages. The shortest was less than 10 yards. There was one 1,400-yard portage, an unusually long one.

Portages—for us anyway—seem to average about a quarter of a mile. This is considered an easy portage in terms of distance. Portages between ¼ and ½ mile are moderate, and anything over a mile is considered hard.

Distance, however, is not the sole criterion. We've done some 200-odd yard portages that, because of the footing or steep grade, were more difficult and took longer than other portages twice or more as long.

The old voyageur's custom of taking a *pose'* (rest) every half mile was commendable. Even more commendable is our personal quarter-mile *posé*.

Many portages in canoe country are in good condition. Little-used portages on often-used voyaging routes may be an indication that a portage is not really necessary.

Location of Portages

In Canada's canoe country the beginning, or end, of a portage is often marked by a slashed tree. Frequently, portages are marked by poles used by Indians for drying fish or meat. Leave them alone. Campfire and tent sites may mark the beginning or end of a portage. The beginning of a portage trail is often marked by a break in the vegetation.

Remember that portages nearly always parallel the inlet or outlet that connect two canoeable bodies of water. River portages usually commence as near as possible to rapids or falls. It is sometimes necessary to pole or paddle through reeds or swamp grass to find the beginning of a portage.

If you are unable to locate the beginning of the portage (trail), your compass and map can be helpful. With these useful aids it is often possible to intersect the portage trail.

When it is impossible to locate the trail, even with your map and compass, walk to the body of water you wish to reach. Chart your course by map, compass, and pacing. If this method doesn't locate the trail, then take the last resort and axe a portage through the brush. When attempting to locate a portage, or to cut one, take along one of your packs. This will mean one less trek.

One-man portage: on the side.

Pick it up . . .

. . . throw it over . . .

. . . and position it on shoulder.

Portage Arrival

Unload the canoe. Move canoe, packs, and all gear away from the water's edge and to one side of the portage trail and landing. This keeps the landing clear for incoming or outgoing voyageurs.

Your packs (all Duluths look just about alike) should have something to identify them readily from those of another crew. Our packs are numbered from one upward. Boy Scout troop numeral patches are useful for this purpose.

A Duluth pack is always lifted by the ears. To lift it otherwise is the mark of a dude. The ears are the side flaps or side extensions. Lifting the pack by its ears prevents undue strain on the patch where the two shoulder straps are attached to the pack.

Portage Techniques

I prefer to portage the canoe by myself rather than to use a two-man carry. It seems easier. On most of my canoes I have substituted a commercial yoke for the center thwart. Two paddles lashed over the seats and thwarts and padded with sweaters or shirts make an acceptable yoke.

Scout the trail toting at least one pack. Take an axe to clear branches or underbrush from the portage. When you reach the far end, hang your pack in a tree. This will keep it safe from most small varmints.

In your scouting, note the location of low branches that you can rest your canoe against. Breathing spells are sometimes necessary.

Many portages are in mosquito and bug country. Apply an effective anti-bug repellent before commencing the portage. Use a spray repellent around your collar and cuffs.

There may come a time when you will have to haul your canoe up a steep mud or rocky slope to reach the portage. Scout the area so that you know exactly where the trail is before you haul up canoe and gear.

Paddles, fishing rods, gun cases, setting poles, etc., are carried in one hand. The other hand is always left free so you can grab a limb or other support should you slip on wet rock or a mud patch.

Voyageurs returning to their landing place for another portage should always yield the trail to burdened voyageurs. If the spirit moves you, and we hope it does, and the back is willing, you can lend a hand to burdened voyageurs heading toward your landing place.

17
Quick Water and Smooth

*Of course I've known fear but always fear
laced with exhilaration.*
—Dr. Charles Camsell, Canadian geologist,
explorer, and master canoeman

Canoe country, from Maine to Minnesota and
from Quebec to the Yukon, is a series of lakes laced together by rivers and streams. White water can be
avoided by a choice of route, portage, or tracking.
Rough-weather lake travel can be partially avoided by
staying ashore during high winds. But there will come a
time when, despite your precautions, you'll be caught
by wind and rain on some sizable lake.

Don't be alarmed. There are centuries-old techniques for coping with such conditions. Then, too, such
travel can be a source of exhilarating experiences.

When stowing gear for lake travel, trim your load
so that the bow is slightly higher than the stern. This
isn't a problem with us because I weigh twice as much
as Janet, so we shift the heaviest pack just aft of amidships. The slightly higher bow reduces the canoe's tendency to slice into the waves.

If the lake is large enough to require several hours (or days) of paddling, consider wrapping your packs except for flotation vests, sea anchor, bailing bucket, and foul weather gear inside your largest tarp. Lash the tarp to the thwarts.

Immediately when the wind rises, put on your vests and paddle from a kneeling position. This reduces wind resistance and you can put more power into each paddle stroke.

Riding a canoe in running seas requires the same delicate sense of balance of bike riders and bronco busters. There must be an instant response to the canoe's movement. This sense is usually acquired with experience. There is no practice here because each time it's the real thing.

It is not always necessary to run with or against the waves. It is possible, with a developed sense of balance,

White water ahead.

White water behind.

to ride parallel with high, running waves and not get swamped.

High waves frequently require that one man bail incoming water. When this is a constant chore, action must be taken to compensate for the loss of paddling power. You can't paddle and bail at the same time. This is where sea anchors come into play.

Tie about 15 feet of line to your largest kitchen pot. Throw the pot overside and behind the canoe. The slowing action stabilizes the canoe while you bail.

It is often necessary to cross a lake at right angles to running waves. Head the bow of your canoe into the wind then veer off 10 to 15 degrees from the direction you are heading. Maintain this position with a diagonal drawstroke. This reduces the possibility of swamping.

WHITE WATER

Whitewater canoeing and canoeing white water are not identical. "Whitewater canoeing," today, is the specialized sport of running rapids as dangerous as possible. This is usually done with specialized equipment like decked-over or spray-deck canoes which either have a shoe (shallow) keel or no keel at all. Much whitewater canoeing is done in the high, cold waters of spring. This necessitates wearing scuba divers' wet suits for warmth and protective crash helmets and flotation vests.

Much whitewater canoeing is competitive and is done near communities or along roads easily accessible to spectators. Little or no camping is associated with much competitive whitewater canoeing. A capsized canoe is an expected part of whitewater canoeing.

Canoeing white water is where voyageurs encounter rapids. They make a decision to run (or shoot), portage, or track (line). Sometimes the gear is portaged and the rapids run in an unloaded canoe.

Voyageurs in the backcountry have to be more cautious than whitewater canoeists in or near civilization.

Your canoe is your most important piece of voyaging equipment. In many instances, it is your only way in or out of an area. The terrain between you and the nearest help may be impassable swamp, high mountains, or miles of trackless forest.

WHAT IS A RIVER?

A river's speed is determined by its fall or downward slope. This fall or slope is determined by the general topography of the adjacent terrain.

Vermont's longest (New Hampshire owns all the Connecticut), the Big Otter, is a placid stream for most of its 90-odd meandering miles. It flows for nearly 60 miles (only four short portages around falls) through pastures and meadowland.

Suddenly, after the river narrows, it enters a gorge with steep rock walls. There are six portages within half as many miles. Then, once again, it enters the gentle, rolling meadowlands of the fertile Champlain Valley.

This river is typical in that throughout its rare, prolonged straight stretches, the main channel flows from the outside of one bend to the outside of the next bend.

In the few places where the bank of one side is lower than the other, the slowest current and shallowest water are close to the low bank. The converse is true of the high bank where the deepest water and fastest current are found.

International River Classification

The American White Water Affiliate, in conjunction with other organizations, has classified many rivers and sections of those rivers. One river, of course, may include several classifications. Guidebooks like the Appalachian Mountain Club's (AMC) *New England Canoeing Guide* have maps which give the category of all sections of more than 500 New England rivers. Some other state or regional guides classify rivers.

Grade I. Very easy. Waves small, regular; passages clear, sandbanks, artificial difficulties like bridge piers, riffles.

Grade II. Easy, rapids of medium difficulty, with passages clear and wide, low ledges; spray deck is useful.

Grade III. Medium. Waves numerous, high, irregular, rocks, eddies, rapids with passages that are clear though narrow, requiring expertise in maneuvering, inspection usually needed, spray deck needed.

Grade IV. Difficult. Long rapids, waves powerful, irregular, dangerous rocks, boiling eddies, passages difficult to reconnoiter, inspection mandatory first time, powerful and precise maneuvering required, spray deck essential.

Grade V. Very difficult. Long and very violent rapids following each other without interruption, riverbed extremely obstructed, big drops, violent current, very steep gradient, reconnoitering essential but very difficult. Spray deck essential.

Grade VI. Extraordinarily difficult. Difficulties of Grade V carried to the extreme of navigability. Nearly impossible and very dangerous. For teams of experts only during favorable water levels, and after close study with all precautions. Spray deck essential.

This classification would be most useful to voyageurs if it were applied to all, or most, rivers in canoe country. It is, however, mostly applied to New England rivers and those in other places where the emphasis is on competitive (whitewater) canoeing rather than canoeing white water as a matter of course in voyaging. The chart is included here as a matter of convenience for those who may voyage in that country where maps are marked with International River Categories.

We suggest that if you value your canoe and outfit, portage all rapids in Grades IV through VI. You might think twice about running rapids of Grade III. You can portage your outfit and run the rapids, but you can also lose or damage beyond immediate repair your only means of transportation out of the wilderness.

If you wish to practice whitewater canoeing—as opposed to canoeing white water—it is better if you don't undertake such rapids as those above Grade III on voyages. Do your sporty runs on those weekends in the spring when high water or frozen lakes make voyaging unfeasible. Should you wish to acquire whitewater skill, locate an experienced whitewaterman and induce him to take you along on an afternoon run.

READING THE WATER

Rapids trap the unwary. The roar of an outboard motor, wind from the wrong direction, or inattention may conceal the roar of the rapids. Always watch the current, which can quickly shift from slow to fast.

Many canoe maps have rapids marked on them. They are noted in most canoe-voyaging literature for a particular stream, but unless you make frequent refer-

We'd portage this one.

ence to map, compass, speed, and landmarks you may
be in difficult rapids before you know it.

Before approaching known rapids, land the canoe
and reconnoiter. Seemingly impassable rapids may
have a reasonably safe way through them. A study of
the waters may reveal such a passage. A V in the stream
heading downstream indicates a possibly passable
chute, while a V heading upstream indicates a rock or
other obstruction. Avoid upstream-pointing V's.

An upset canoe and the loss of food and equipment
is but an inconvenience in rural or semicivilized country. In the outback, such an upset can mean disaster, or
death. In 1955, one of six U.S. voyageurs following Ty-
rell's 1893 voyage of 800 miles to Baker Lake died of
exposure after his canoe upset in almost freezing water.

There are rapids which are impossible, or inadvis-
able, to run, and which cannot be portaged. Tracking or
lining may be the solution, or you might wade. When
wading rapids downstream always remain behind the
canoe. Your fragile craft is potentially a deadly missile.

You can ride through rapids at one of three speeds:
faster than the current, slower than the current, or at the
same speed as the current. You should go faster than
the current only in light or medium rapids. In swift water you should hold back (jam or backwater stroke) so
that you go slower than the current.

When close to a bank, keep the upstream end
closer to the bank than the downstream end. Otherwise,
the canoe may be pushed into the current broadside.
Never allow the canoe to get caught broadside. Always
keep it in line with the current. However, eddies can be
approached broadside or from the downstream side.

The outside of bends should be avoided. There
may be submerged logs or other obstructions.

If you hang up on a rock, jump onto it and, if possible, push the canoe clear and into main channel. Then get back into the canoe.

TRACKING OR LINING

When bank conditions allow it is possible to line or track a canoe up or down rapids. We carry four 50-foot lengths of ¼-inch braided nylon line for this purpose. A 50-foot length at the bow and stern usually suffices but there are times when we knot another 50-foot length onto both bow and stern lines. Sometimes one voyageur wades while the other handles both bow and stern lines.

There will come a time when you'll have to wade through rapids (up or downstream) while your partner lines the canoe, or you may both wade through shallow rapids. It's a wet and sweaty task but it may save portaging or no portage may exist. Wear your life jacket when wading in rapids.

While pushing a canoe through the shallow headwaters of Florida's Suwannee River it was necessary to wade frequently. This is water-moccasin (cottonmouth) country—and I don't like snakes. I wore my snakeproof leggings.

You may not be able to see where you are stepping, so tread cautiously when wading white water.

POLING DOWNSTREAM

The ancient and useful art of poling down shallow streams (6 to 18 inches deep) deserves wider popularity.

A pole can do something your paddle can't. It can bring the canoe to a complete halt. This is "snubbing."

I usually pole while Janet paddles. Before poling, we swap positions. She takes the stern position, while I move forward. Some polers prefer to have the bowman steer with a bow-steering stroke. They paddle from aft of amidships. Flotation vests may be worn while poling up or down stream.

In downstream work the pole is placed about 45 degrees forward of your upright body rather than about the same number of degrees aft as in poling upstream.

Brace your body. Set the pole's point on the bottom. When the canoe stops, it stops abruptly. The canoe tends to align itself with the current.

To move the craft sideways, move the pole's point away from the canoe and push. Repeat until the canoe is in the desired position. When the move is completed you'll be ready to move downstream on your pre-selected course.

To move slowly downstream, release the canoe. Let it move forward until the pole is abeam your body. Now lift the pole, move it 45 degrees forward. Snub. Repeat this operation until you've run out of the rapids.

POLING UPSTREAM

Poling upstream is infinitely easier than attempting to paddle upstream. Some rivers just cannot be "climbed" by paddling. Try paddling up Basswood River on the Quetico-Superior boundary—and then switch to poling up the remainder of the stream.

We use the climb-the-pole technique (explained in Chapter 14) for most upstream work.

To move canoe sideways, away from its present position, set the pole just abeam (opposite) your body's position and pull the canoe to it. Reverse this technique to move canoe in the opposite direction.

I usually work upstream with Janet in the stern-paddling position while I pole. When really rough upstream going is encountered we both pole, from the same side.

You don't have to rush while poling upstream. You'll have sufficient momentum from the preceding stroke to hold your position while making the next stroke.

Practice upstream and downstream poling. You'll be amazed at the efficiency, and you can well be proud of your accomplishment.

Part IV
Voyaging Techniques

18
Plans and Preparation

Fortunate is the expedition which has no adventures.

—Vilhjalmur Stefansson

"Roughly translated," Stef told us at his Vermont farm in 1951, "this means that inexperience combined with poor planning frequently means trouble."

Successful planning, barring unforeseen mishaps, is usually the key to successful voyaging, and that above all else means new experiences, new places, and happy memories. We may die in the poorhouse, but creditors can't auction off our memories.

Planning, selection, and purchasing new equipment is part of the pleasure of voyaging. This is a wonderful way to spend winter evenings.

Maps

Once you've decided where you are going, obtain the most detailed maps available of your route. (Sources of maps and other planning materials are noted in the appendices.)

These are usually the U.S. or Canadian government topographical maps with scales averaging about one inch to one-half inch per mile (see the next chapter).

Canoe maps show the location, name, and distance of portages. Portage distances may be marked in chains or rods. These are surveyor measures. One chain is 66 feet, one rod is 16½ feet. A few maps give the time (in minutes) the portage requires. These canoe maps usually have rapids and falls marked on them, also.

Always obtain official state or provincial highway maps for use in laying out your automobile route to and from the voyaging area.

Route Information

Obtain all possible data on your proposed voyage route. In New England, for instance, every canoeist should have the AMC guide. Secure all possible data from state or provincial governments. Other sources include local chambers of commerce, canoe clubs, federal, or crown agencies. These various sources may not be equal in reliability.

Hudson's Bay Co. will supply you with a map showing the location of their stores and trading posts.

Loop or One-Way Voyage?

Many canoe-country voyage routes are designed to bring you back to your starting point. This is convenient because you do not have to arrange for transportation for yourself and your canoe at the end of the voyage.

When a loop voyage is not possible or desired, we prefer to bring our car to the take-out point. First we leave canoe and supplies with a responsible party at our voyage departure point. We drive to the take-out point, and return to the put-out point, via jitney, hired car, or sometimes plane.

Sometimes two cars are required to simplify return transportation. On a recent three-day Big Otter voyage, Janet and I drove our car, carrying the canoe, and were followed by a friend in his car. Both cars rendezvoused at another friend's house situated about a mile from our take-out point. We parked the car without the canoe. The three of us drove to the put-in point. Janet and I shoved off in the canoe while our companion drove our rack-fitted car back to her own vehicle. She left our car and then drove her own car home. When we arrived at the take-out point, we beached the canoe and gear and walked to our car. I then drove it to the take-out point, loaded the canoe and gear, and headed homeward.

Check out canoe capacity before voyage.

Old Town

Checklist

Some days before departure, make a checklist of all required equipment and food supplies. A forgotten item may be a mere inconvenience on a voyage through relatively settled country, but the same missing item might have more serious consequences on an outback voyage.

Sometimes it is the less obvious items, like fresh flashlight batteries, that are left behind. But a friend once painstakingly checked all equipment and food items and then forgot to load his canoe. He didn't discover its absence until he was 500 miles away in Maine. Fortunately, he was able to rent a craft.

When you have all the gear and food together and it's the night before departure, check off each item as it goes into the proper pack or tote box.

FOOD STOWAGE

One standard 28x30-inch Duluth pack holds one week's food supply. Each meal of a day's three meals or two meals and lunch is loaded into its own separate plastic bag. The three one-meal bags are fitted into a larger one-day bag—on the bottom goes the lunch and snack bag, next the breakfast bag, and on top is the dinner bag. Seven of these bags fit into the Duluth pack along with a general food bag.

Before preparing dinner, a full day bag is removed from the top of the pack along with the general food bag. The night's dinner is removed from the day bag. After dinner, the day bag and general bag are put back in the Duluth.

Before breakfast, the current day bag and general food bag are removed from the Duluth. After breakfast the lunch and snack bag is placed atop the packbasket where, along with the stove and a cook pot, it will be handy for lunch.

After each meal, the empty meal bag is folded and placed in the day bag. After lunch the empty day bag and three empty meal bags are placed inside another day bag. Ultimately, they will be reused.

The general food bag contains screw-top, plastic-lined aluminum butter tin, combination salt/pepper shaker, West Berlin pumpernickel wrapped in foil. Screw-top, unlined aluminum canisters contain one-portion packets of mustard, catsup, sugar, cornmeal for frying fish, coffee, teabags, and individual packets of Coffee-mate.

After several sad experiences with supermarket-type bags, like Glad Bags, we adopted sturdy polybags designed for food storage and considerable reuse. Our Gerry one-meal bags are 6x12 inches. A packet of 15 bags weighs 2 ounces and costs $1. The one-day bags are 9x18 inches. Ten bags weigh 2 ounces and cost $1.

Also carried in the Duluth along with the seven one-day foodbags and the general bag is a small bag containing one week's supply of toilet paper at the rate of 7 to 9 feet per person per day; one Flip pad for cleaning dishes, and a Paket Soap tube (¾ ounce). This bio-degradable soap is usable in cold water and will usually last for a week of dishwashing. Price, 39 cents.

When packing for a voyage confined to the Boundary Waters Canoe Area of the Superior National Forest, we are cognizant of the regulations which prohibit using disposable tins, bottles, or plastic containers. Our reusable aluminum screw-top canisters, polybags, and bottles are allowed.

When we're about halfway through the second week's food supply, we are usually able to fit the empty first week's Duluth pack with its empty Gerry polybags, polybottles, and canisters into the bottom of the second week's food pack.

PERSONAL PACK

Janet and I each have a personal pack. These are Paul Bunyan model Duluths. My pack contains: sleeping bag in stuffsack, full-length (rolled) foam pad, clothing stuffsack, and one or two dittybag-type personal sacks. The dittybag contains pipe, tobacco, lighter fluid, paperback books, flashlight, toilet gear, nylon line, etc. Tent, saw, and axe are toted in this pack. Janet's pack, less tent, is about the same as mine—except no pipe— and she generally has two clothing stuffsacks rather than one. All items in this pack are carried in waterproof stuffsacks. The pack is plastic-lined.

Our final pack, a packbasket, contains an Optimus 111B stove, fuel bottles, Smilie nested pots (condiments inside), kitchen roll, steel frypan, coffeepot, and lantern. These items are all in waterproof nylon bags. The packbasket is usually stripped of its straps and fitted into a Duluth pack. The latter has a much more comfortable carrying harness.

Other equipment to be checked off:
Paddles (3)
Setting pole (1)
Fishing rods
Life-preserver cushions
Flotation jackets
Map case
Camera gear

We have a typed checklist for the contents of each pack. Items are checked off one by one. The packs and other gear are counted off as they are stowed in the car or station wagon. They are counted as they are loaded into the canoe. Canoe contents are checked before leaving campsites in the morning and while reloading at the end of portages.

A basic tenet in using Duluth packs is to pad the portion that rests against your back with soft items. Light items go into the bottom of the pack while heavier gear (normally the tent) rides in the top of the pack.

Remember the spare paddle and life preservers or jackets.

HOW MANY PACKS?

We have two personal packs, the kitchen gear pack, plus one food pack for each week of the voyage. The one food pack per week is based upon being entirely self-contained. A two-week trip down a semi-civilized river may only require one week's food pack.

How many packs will a canoe hold? Our recent 15-foot Grumman held two personal packs, kitchen pack, and two one-week food packs. Our 16-foot Old Town Royalex holds an extra (one-week) food pack. A 17-footer will hold up to four weekly food packs. The latter is rarely necessary.

The above loading is based on dehydrated or freeze-dried foods. We allow two pounds per person, per day. A seven-day food pack weighs about 35 pounds. This includes the general food bag and pack weight.

It is not always possible to obtain lightweight foods in the outback. This means a seven-day pack will be heavier. Hudson's Bay Company stores and posts stock regular groceries used by the local population, which often includes many canoeists. They do not stock freeze-dried or dehydrated foods but if they have sufficient notice beforehand they may be able to order them for you.

Canadian customs allows voyageurs to bring in two days' food supplies. A duty averaging 40 cents per day is charged for additional supplies. If you have special preferences in dried foods, it is worthwhile to bring your own and pay the small duty. Canadian stores devoted to backpacking supplies stock excellent dried foods. However, you may not have time to conduct shopping expeditions within the limited time allotted to your canoeing holiday.

CARTOP CANOE RACKS

Canoe manufacturers like Old Town and Grumman offer cartop canoe racks. Some racks are designed to tote two canoes. We are presently using one by Mark Forge ($19.95) and it could be improved. It should be designed and constructed so the plastic strips across the top of each carrying bar would not peel off. The plastic caps on either end of both carrying bars pop out unless they are secured with Phillips screws.

We bought this rack after someone stole our previous rack from the cartop. None other was immediately available, so we purchased this one.

The canoe should be tightly secured so that it doesn't move sideways. This is effected, on most rigs, by buckle-and-tongue tiedowns. We buckle one tiedown strap on one side of the cartop and then tie the down buckle on the opposite side.

The canoe must also be secured from fore-and-aft movement. Fore-and-aft tiedowns do not usually come with regular cartop racks. We use Grumman tiedowns.

Our setting pole is lashed onto the cartop alongside the canoe. Cartop racks, when nothing is on them to deflect the wind, make the devil of a racket. It is not necessary to remove the rack when the canoe is not lashed to

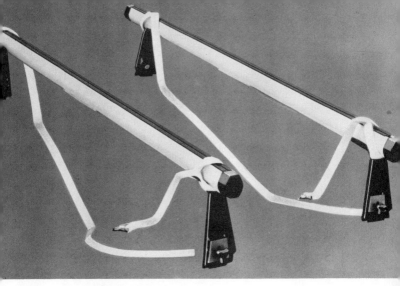

Cartop carrier (Mark Forge).

it. The setting pole is sufficient to prevent the ghastly whistling.

When you leave your car for several days at your destination, it is better to remove the rack and stow it in the car under a blanket. It's a problem to return with a canoe to a rackless car.

LOADING THE CANOE

The packs are normally loaded so that the canoe is on an even keel. I weigh 250 pounds and Janet about half that. This means that for level trim the heaviest packs must be loaded forward of amidships.

Packs are stowed and the spare paddle is lashed in position so that either of us can reach it readily. Map case and fishing-rod cases are also lashed to the thwarts. Seat-pack contents are checked.

Never load the canoe on land and then lift it into

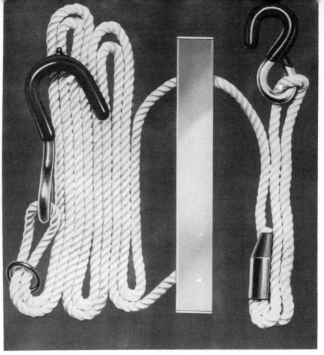

Grumman tie-downs.

the water. This can break its back. Sometimes the bow section is on land with the remainder of the canoe in the water. The best way is to have the canoe entirely afloat before loading. Try to have it parallel to the shore.

NOTIFICATION

Always let someone in authority know where you are going and when you expect to return. Allow time for being wind- or rainbound. In Canada it is required that the nearest officials be notified of your trip. This is usually the Royal Canadian Mounted Police.

In the Far North, the Mounties have the power to prevent a voyage if they are convinced you are inadequately outfitted and are inexperienced in bush travel. However, they can also be very helpful.

The regional office of the provincial Department of Natural Resources (DNR) will also accept your destination data. Their offices have regular forms to record this information.

Authorities suggest you leave the following information:

Number of canoes
Date of registration
Color of canoes (inside and outside)
Survival gear carried
Anticipated date of return or arrival at take-out
  point
Name and address of all members of party
Name and address of next of kin
Route to be followed

Ready to go.

19
Maps and Compass

Indian no lost. Wigwam lost.
                    —Alleged Indian adage

We voyageurs rarely "get lost," but sometimes we are not quite sure where we are in relation to a portage or lake exit. Many hours of searching can be avoided by using map and compass. Reading this chapter won't make you a successor to Prince Henry the Navigator, but you should be able to find your way confidently through the winding water trails of canoe country. Your possession of this knowledge should give you confidence and pride.

MAPS

It is surprising how many canoeists go voyaging without a map. Not only does such stupidity or sheer ignorance create problems, but there is a self-inflicted loss of a great deal of knowledge and pleasure.

The topographic map is the basic map—along with special canoe maps, available for only a few areas—used

1:24,000 scale (1 inch = 2,000 feet). Area shown is 1 square mile.

by voyageurs. Information contained on these maps can be readily discerned by looking at the map symbols shown in this chapter. Map sources for the U.S.A. and Canada are listed in Appendix VII (also Chapter 25 for the Quetico-Superior area).

The wide borders surrounding topographical maps contain information vital to reading the map. Once you have mastered map reading—and it's quite easy—you'll discover that topographical maps provide these data: dates, declination, descriptions, distances, directions, details, and designations.

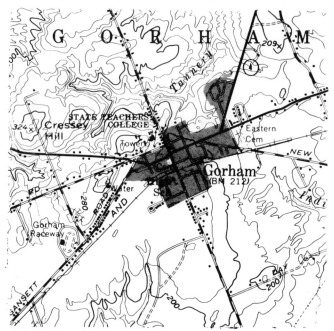

1:62,500 scale (1 inch = nearly 1 mile). Area shown is 6.75 square miles.

Scale

Topographic, hydrographic, and other maps used by voyageurs have a certain scale. The scale, which may be represented in several ways, indicates that a certain distance on a map represents so many feet, fractions of a mile, or miles on the ground. One inch on the map may represent 1,000 feet on the ground (large scale) while on other maps, one inch might represent one mile or 5000 miles (small scale).

The larger the number, the more distance is shown on the map. A map that has a 1:250,000 scale (4 miles

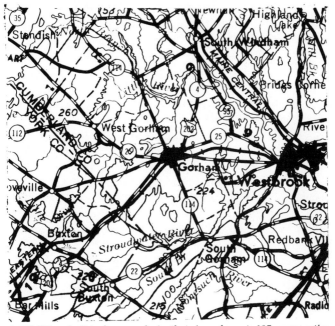

1:250,000 scale (1 inch = nearly 4 miles). Area shown is 107 square miles.

to the inch) has a smaller scale than one with a 1:62,500 scale (1 mile to the inch). The larger the scale the greater the detail that is shown. Thus, a map on which 1 inch represents ¼ mile reveals greater detail than one on which 1 inch represents 1 mile, or 4 miles.

Scale is relative, and can be a confusing concept. The simplest way to remember it is to realize that of two maps having the same dimensions, the large-scale map will show a smaller area but in a larger scale, with more detail. A smaller-scale map will show more area, but it will be physically smaller in relation to the actual territory it represents.

1:62,500 scale means that 1 inch on the map represents 62,500 inches (or approximately 1 mile). A mile has 63,360 inches, but 62,500 conveniently goes into 250,000, another widely used scale. The difference is so small as to be unimportant. Sometimes 1:62,500 is stated $\frac{1}{62,500}$. One inch equals one mile.

Much of the U.S. (some has never yet been topographically mapped) was originally mapped on the 1:62,500 scale. These were known as the 15-minute series because each map included 15 minutes of latitude vertically, and 15 minutes of longitude horizontally.

1:24,000 (sometimes expressed $\frac{1}{24,000}$) means that 1 inch on the map represents 24,000 inches or 2,000 feet. Much of the country is being remapped on this scale. It takes four of these 7.5-minute maps to cover the same overall area covered by one 15-minute (1:62,500) maps. Map features are, of course, shown in much greater detail in the new series.

1:250,000 (sometimes expressed $\frac{1}{250,000}$) means that 1 inch equals 4 miles. These maps, while on too small a scale for hiking or voyaging, are useful for providing an overall topographical view of a sizable area.

1:50,000 ($\frac{1}{50,000}$) scale is the basic scale for Canadian National Topographic maps. Unfortunately, in the North Country and Arctic where travelers badly need detailed maps, the scale often runs 4 miles to the inch (1:250,000). Quetico-Superior voyageurs are lucky; there are maps especially designed for them.

Map Symbols

Topographic maps, U.S. or Canadian, have conventions—symbols, colors, etc.—representing various features. (Variations are possible on older maps.)

> *1. Hydrographic features such as lakes and rivers are blue.*

Boundary: national .... ▬ ▬ ▬ ▬

    State .... ▬ ▬ ▬ ▬

    county, parish, municipio .... ▬ ▬ ▬ ▬

    civil township, precinct, town, barrio .... ▬ ▬ ▬ ▬

    incorporated city, village, town, hamlet .... ▬▬▬▬▬▬

    reservation, national or state .... ▬ · ▬ ·

    small park, cemetery, airport, etc. .... ▬▬▬▬▬

    land grant .... ▬ ·· ▬ ··

Wells other than water (labeled as to type) .... ○ Oil .... ○ Gas

U.S. mineral or location monument — Prospect .... ▲ .... ˣ

Quarry — Gravel pit .... ⊗ .... ✕

Mine shaft—Tunnel or cave entrance .... ▫ .... Y

Campsite — Picnic area .... 人 .... ⊼

Located or landmark object—Windmill .... ○ .... 🛆

Exposed wreck ....

Rock or coral reef ....

Foreshore flat ....

Rock: bare or awash .... * .... ⁕

Horizontal control station .... △

Vertical control station .... BM ×671 × ×672

Road fork — Section corner with elevation .... ⚊⚊429 +58

Checked spot elevation .... × 5970

Unchecked spot elevation .... × *5970*

Township or range line, U.S. land survey .... ▬▬▬▬

Section line, U.S. land survey .... ▬▬▬▬

Township line, not U.S. land survey .... ·················

Section line, not U.S. land survey ....

Fence line or field line .... ▬ ▬ ▬ ▬

Section corner: found—indicated .... + ... +

Boundary monument: land grant—other .... ▪ .... ▫

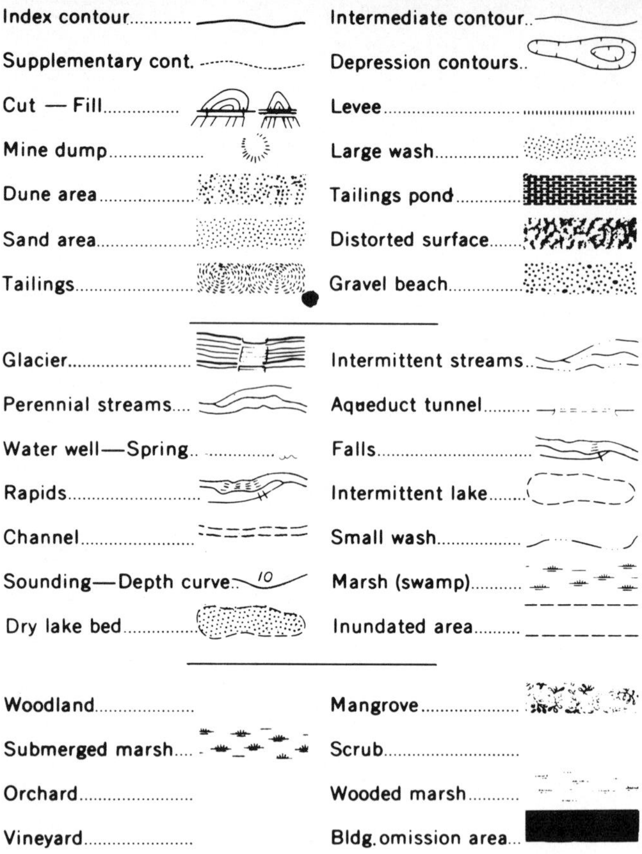
Index contour
Intermediate contour
Supplementary cont.
Depression contours
Cut — Fill
Levee
Mine dump
Large wash
Dune area
Tailings pond
Sand area
Distorted surface
Tailings
Gravel beach
Glacier
Intermittent streams
Perennial streams
Aqueduct tunnel
Water well—Spring
Falls
Rapids
Intermittent lake
Channel
Small wash
Sounding—Depth curve
10
Marsh (swamp)
Dry lake bed
Inundated area
Woodland
Mangrove
Submerged marsh
Scrub
Orchard
Wooded marsh
Vineyard
Bldg. omission area

2. *Vegetation features like forests are green.*
3. *Man-made features like houses are black or crosshatched.*
4. *Elevation features like contour lines are brown.*
5. *Special water features in blue are found on some topographic and canoe maps.*
6. *Some highways and political boundaries, in recent maps, are red.*

Hard surface, heavy-duty road	▬▬▬▬
Hard surface, medium-duty road	▬ ▬ ▬
Improved light-duty road	═══════
Unimproved dirt road	═ ═ ═ ═ ═ ═ ═
Trail	─ ─ ─ ─ ─ ─
Railroad: single track	┼──┼──┼──┼
Railroad: multiple track	▬┼▬▬┼▬▬
Bridge	──┤ ├──
Drawbridge	──┤○├──
Tunnel	──╗═══╔──
Footbridge	─ ─ ┤ ├──
Overpass—Underpass	┼ ‖ ‖═
Power transmission line with located tower	•─ ─ ─ ─ ─•
Landmark line (labeled as to type)	*TELEPHONE*
	──────────
Dam with lock	─┤ ▷├─
Canal with lock	═══◁──◁══
Large dam	▨▨▨▨▨▨
Small dam: masonry — earth	◁◁◁
Buildings (dwelling, place of employment, etc.)	▪■▦▦
School—Church—Cemeteries	▪ ꞏ ⊡ Cem
Buildings (barn, warehouse, etc.)	▫▢▨▨
Tanks; oil, water, etc. (labeled only if water)	• ● ● ⊘Water Tank

U.S. Army Corps of Engineers maps are primarily concerned with hydrographic features not always found on topographic maps, such as small streams. Some basic symbols are found on the back of some Corps maps.

Topographic maps formerly had an explanation of map symbols on the back. This material is now a separate free publication (map information source, U.S. Geological Survey, Reston, Va. 22092).

Canoe maps, like those published by the W. A. Fisher Company, Virginia, Minnesota, show rapids and portages. They usually have the length of the portage shown in rods.

Some maps show portage lengths in rods while others use yards. One rod equals 16½ feet. Some Canadian maps use the "chain" (66 feet) for portage length. When switching from one map type to another, always check the measurement used on portages; 10 chains are considerably different from 10 yards. Some portages are expressed in feet and occasionally in minutes (average time).

Contour Lines

Topographic maps indicate below the map scale the "contour interval." This may be 40 feet or 20 feet. Brown contour lines on the map show the elevation above sea level. Every fifth contour line is a darker brown. If the contour interval is 40 feet, the next darker line is a higher (or lower) elevation by 200 feet. The actual elevation, when indicated, is on the darker lines. Thus, the elevation on any given contour line may be readily determined.

When lines are so close together that they are almost indistinguishable, the terrain is very steep. When they are widely separated, the terrain is almost flat or rolling.

Dates

Each U.S. Geological Survey National Topographic Series map contains one or more dates. These dates indicate the year the original survey was made and the dates when the map has been updated. There is also the date that the declination degree was made.

Writer's map measurer, Silva Explorer III TD compass, and case.

COMPASS

You can navigate through much of canoe country with only a map, but once you get into the outback, the use of a compass becomes imperative to keep your voyage on course.

The compass of yesteryear—marked North, East, South, and West and sometimes with the intercardinal points of Northeast, Southeast, Southwest, and Northwest—has been replaced (except on some cheaper or special-purpose models) with the 360 degrees of the circle. The 360 (or 0) degrees is North, and reading clockwise, 90 degrees is East, 180 degrees is South, and 270 degrees is West.

For many years, the average outdoorsman who bothered to take along a compass—he usually doesn't know how to use it—purchased a pocket-watch-type compass. This compass type is still useful, if you know how to use it, but it is being largely replaced by the orienteering compass.

Orienteering Compasses

Nearly thirty years ago in a little sports shop off Stockholm's Sturaplan (Big Square), I bought a Swedish-made Silva orienteering compass. I have been using them ever since. I still have my original one but have since graduated to a more advanced model. This orienteering compass is the most efficient and easy to use handheld compass I have ever owned.

This compass is mounted on a durable 2¼x5-inch transparent base. There is an inch scale along the 2-inch end and a millimeter scale along the 5-inch side. Some models, like the 4-inch-long Voyageur model, have map scales. A magnifying lens is built into the baseplate. This is useful for discerning fine map details and for separating closely spaced contour lines. The side of the baseplate is useful for measuring and for drawing resection lines. The north end of the needle is luminous. The compass housing bottom is transparent and has meridian lines useful for plotting a course. The baseplate can be used as a protractor. The aluminum band of the compass housing is graduated from 360 to 0 degrees in 2-degree increments. Just forward of the compass housing is a place to read your sight or bearing. The rotating compass band is useful in determining bearings and for declination adjustments.

This particular Silva model has a liquid-damped needle which reduces needle fluctuation time to a minimum. This is particularly useful for canoe travel when the compass rests on a map on an unsteady deck at your feet.

This orienteering compass was devised in 1930 in

Sweden by Bjorn Kjellstrom, now a U.S. resident. Orienteering, a rapidly growing sport in America and Canada, has long been popular in Europe. It is competition in route finding, under sometimes difficult conditions, with map and compass.

Components of Silva compasses sold in the U.S. are made in Sweden but are assembled in LaPorte, Ind. Boy Scouts and groups interested in survival training are leading Silva compass users. The orienteering compass has become the standard for many backpackers and other outdoorsmen, including voyageurs.

One factor to consider in selecting a compass is its "damping" action. "Damping" as applied to compasses is the method used to stop the oscillation or swinging of the needle.

In the standard non-damped compass, the needle swings from side to side around until it comes to rest. This is the slowest to use and the least expensive.

In the induction-damped compass, the needle swings within a copper or aluminum bowl which generates electricity. As the needle swings, the electrical energy flow ceases. The needle action halts. Average stopping time, 18 seconds.

The liquid-damped compass has the fastest needle-halting technique. Average stopping time, 5 seconds.

The Silva Explorer, Type I now sells for $13.40. However, mine has an adjustment for magnetic declination. This is the Explorer, Type I-TD with an automatic declination adjustment feature. Price, $17.30. The leather case is $4.50 additional.

Two excellent but less expensive models are the Voyageur, Type 2 (4x2 inches), price $11.15, and the Explorer III, Type 3 (2x4 inches), $7.25. Both are liquid-filled, have inch and millimeter scales, magnifying lens, and luminous needle points.

A fine compass is worth its cost. We know sportsmen who record their incomes in six figures. They spend thousands of dollars on fine shotguns, flyrods, and other outdoor equipment. Paradoxically, they use cheap compasses, some costing less than a dollar.

Beware of compasses located in the handles of hunting knives and other odd places.

American-made Leopold and Taylor compasses are well made but the ones I've seen do not have all the features of the Silva and consequently they are not as versatile or efficient.

Using the Compass

Many outdoorsmen own compasses but very few know how to use them. Most only know that the compass needle points north. Actually it doesn't. The needle points to a slowly shifting point on the earth's surface—the north magnetic pole (or the south magnetic pole, when you're below the equator).

Instructions that come with Silva compasses are remarkably clear. Fifteen minutes of fascinating reading and study and you can (aided by a topographic map) determine your location and determine the identity of a distant object like a mountain peak, a bay, or river delta. This knowledge, so easily acquired, makes for great confidence when wilderness voyaging. It can open a whole new world for your exploration.

Declination: Your compass needle, with one exception, does not point to true north.

The magnetized needle points toward the north magnetic pole, which is located 1,400 miles south of the true north pole. The position of the magnetic north pole was first visited nearly 150 years ago by Sir James Ross and is constantly shifting.

Only along the agonic line, the line running directly north from the equator through the magnetic north pole to the true north pole, does your compass needle indicate true north.

At all points east—for about 180 degrees—of the agonic line the compass needle points northwesterly toward the north magnetic pole. This is west magnetic declination.

The reverse is true of all points west of the agonic line, where the needle points northeasterly. This is east declination.

The U.S. Coast and Geodetic Survey regularly publishes a map showing the current position of the agonic line. Lines running roughly parallel to the agonic line are called isogonic lines. The map usually shows the isogonic lines at 10-degree intervals.

At the bottom of a Geological Survey topographic map is the declination that was valid for the year the map was last corrected. The change from the last map date until the time you are using the map is slight; two or three degrees of difference will not affect your fundamental reckoning.

Bearing and azimuth. A bearing is the way to go. "Azimuth," another word for bearing, comes from the Arabic word *as-samt,* "the way." Your compass, indicates 360 degrees (or ways) to go. Your bearing, or azimuth, is one of these 360 directions you can go.

Orienting your compass. Turn the compass until the magnetic north-south needle is superimposed on the arrow engraved into the compass baseplate.

How to take a bearing. I live in an area where the current annual declination is about 15 degrees west. I point the compass plate in the general direction of north. I swing the needle until it is exactly over the arrow stamped into the baseplate of the compass housing.

The compass band now reads 0 or 360 degrees. The declination is 15 degrees west. I adjust the compass band until it reads 15 degrees. This gives a reading of true north. In plotting a course of 90 degrees (due east) I add 15 degrees to 90 degrees to give a magnetic bearing of 105 degrees.

When declination is west you add your declination, but when your declination is east, you subtract. This holds true only when you work from land to map.

When working from map to compass, your field bearing (magnetic) must have west declination subtracted and east declination added. This gives you a true map bearing or azimuth.

MISCELLANEOUS EQUIPMENT

A map case is essential for canoe travel through country where maps are required. It keeps charts dry and from blowing away or to pieces. There are several such cases on the market. Mine (3 ounces) came from Thomas Black and Sons. Its folded size is 9¼x6½ inches. Routes can be traced with a chinograph pencil on the face of the transparent plastic case. Price, $1.39. Spare maps that can't fit into the case are usually carried in a short aluminum watertight fishing rod case.

A map measurer is a useful gadget, providing about the only handy, accurate method for reading winding, wiggling, river mileage from a map. Set the scale adjustment and roll the wheel along your course. Your mileage or kilometer reading is recorded on the dial. Price, $2.35.

20
Bugs, Bears, Band-Aids, and Bad Weather

Anyone can camp when the weather is going just right. The camper who can travel in the rain, keep himself and his equipment dry and cook a warm meal when he wants one is in another class. . . . There are few more buoyant moments on any canoe trip than the one when the sun finally breaks through and canoeists start to dry out.

—Mark Fisher, *The Quetico-Superior Canoeist's Handbook*

The British admiral Sir Francis Beaufort (1774-1857) was a sailor, not a voyageur, but he performed a signal service to voyageurs everywhere. Sir Francis gave us the Beaufort Scale, which enables meteorologists with instrumentation as well as folk with no more equipment than basic powers of observation to determine how fast the wind is blowing. No small craft warning lights or flags are flown in the outback, but anyone can estimate the approximate wind speed to determine if the waters are safe to go voyaging.

BEAUFORT SCALE

Beaufort number	Velocity (mph)	Description	Indications
0	0–1	Calm	Smoke rises vertically
1	1–3	Light air	Wind direction shown by smoke drift but not by waves
2	4–7	Slight breeze	Wind direction shown by smoke but not by waves
3	8–12	Gentle breeze	Wind felt on face, leaves rustle, ordinary wave moved by wind
4	13–18	Moderate breeze	Dust and loose paper, also small branches, are moved
5	19–24	Fresh breeze	Small trees in leaf begin to sway
6	25–31	Strong breeze	Large branches in motion; whistling in telegraph wires
7	32–38	Moderate gale	Whole trees in motion

8	39–46	Fresh gale	Twigs break off trees; progress generally impeded
9	47–54	Strong gale	Slight structural damage occurs, chimney pots removed
10	55–63	Whole gale	Trees uprooted; considerable structural damage
11	64–72	Storm	Very rarely experienced; widespread damage
12	73–up	Hurricane	

Only experienced voyageurs should venture forth, and in a following wind only, when the Beaufort Scale number is above 6. All hands should stay ashore or head for the nearest shore or lee side of an island when the Beaufort Scale hits 8.

Forecasting

You cannot predict day-to-day weather patterns, but before voyaging into unknown country, secure climatic data. Knowledge of the area's climate, the weather patterns over the years, will guide you in choosing appropriate clothing. Temperatures in the North may reach into the 80's during the day but take a sharp dip at night. Fort Yukon has registered 100 degrees F. Some areas have a rainy season, so check the weather records for average monthly rainfall.

City folk are apt to discount weather sayings. However, those of us brought up in rural America where weather can spell crop success or failure, or who have spent time at sea or in the outback, place considerable reliance on basic weather lore.

We have found the following to be usually reliable:

> Red sky at night,
> Sailor's delight.
> Red sky at morning,
> Sailors take warning.
>
> Evening red,
> Morning gray,
> Sends the traveler
> On his way.
> Evening gray
> And morning red,
> Stays the traveler
> Home in bed.

While a recent guest on an educational TV program as a weather folklorist, I discussed the above weather lore with U.S. Weather Bureau meteorologist, Jack Hummel. He said that it has a scientific basis. A red evening sky means that a high-pressure area has arrived or is approaching. This means good weather.

The following weather lore also has validity:

> When the dew is on the grass
> Rain will rarely come to pass.

A ring (or circle) around the moon means rain (or snow). The number of stars within the circle does not, however, correctly forecast the number of days before it storms.

Check local weather patterns. A southwest wind may bring rain or fair weather.

Learn to recognize cloud formations that herald

Don't do this. Pull canoe farther onto shore.

approaching storms. This includes thunderheads (get off the lake!) and a mackerel sky.

Your canoe, be the weather foul or fair, should always be hauled onto the beach and secured so that it will not blow into the lake or river. A safe procedure is to move it behind some trees or bushes. In heavy winds, secure the canoe with lines.

Secure the tent—all lines taut but not too taut. Dry firewood should be placed under the canoe or brought into the tent. Be careful not to puncture the tent floor.

Paddling during a rainstorm often calls for frequent bailing.

Wet canvas packs should always be thoroughly dried at the first opportunity. The same is true for canvas tents, to prevent mildew and rot.

Saplings (1- to 2-inch diameter) can be cut and laid inside the door. This elevates packs.

We try to wrap all packs inside a nylon tarpaulin before we set out to paddle in the rain.

THE BUG PARADE

The three prime canoeing months—June, July, and August—are also bug months. June is usually the worst, while August sees the fewest bugs and the most people. July is in between.

Deerflies (*brulot*) don't just bite. They like to gouge out pieces of your flesh.

Blackflies are bothersome, but unlike the mosquito, they have the decency to retire at nightfall.

Sand flies, tiny but torturous—the little critters' bites burn.

Allow at least one pocket-sized container of bug dope per person per week. Two is a better allowance in June.

Bugs are bad news, but a tightly zippered tent with mosquito netting is a major defense against the critters. Spray the inside of your tent with a non-DDT bug killer about half an hour before retiring. Spray the atmosphere inside the tent, but don't spray bug killer directly on the inner tent fabric. This is especially true of nylon tents. The bug killer can adversely affect the fabric. Now crawl outside and zipper the door shut but leave the flaps open.

Do not bring an insecticide containing DDT into

canoe country. DDT is harmful to animals, notably insects which provide food for birds and fish.

Bugs are rarely bothersome on lakes and rivers, but can be hell on portages. Wear long-sleeved shirts and apply bug dope generously around your collar and cuffs. Some bugs, such as blackflies, may crawl under your clothing, so anoint your ankles.

If possible select a bug-free campsite.

BEAR FACTS

Black bears may be pleasant to watch in a zoo, but they are a confounded nuisance in camp. Bears know that voyageurs tote food, so avoid heavily traveled canoe trails whenever possible. It's so much easier to break into a tent and rip open food packs than to search for victuals in the wilderness. Whether or not you are in the tent seems to make little difference to the bear. He even seems to be interested in your reactions.

If it can be avoided, do not take food or food packs into your tent. Hang up your food packs.

Whenever possible during rainy weather, do your cooking on a stove under the kitchen tarp and not in the tent. Rain does, however, kill scent so it is to be hoped that the rain will last through supper and almost to breakfast time. You might, under these conditions, eat inside your tent.

Bears can sometimes be frightened off by a campfire, by shining flashlight beams in their eyes, by banging pans, or by yelling. On the other hand, they might take umbrage and charge you.

If you're skittish about bears (we've never had much trouble with them), camp on a nearby island, if there is one. Bears can swim, but they probably won't make the effort.

Some voyageurs put gear and food packs under the canoe and line up their pots and pans along the bottom of the upended craft. A bear will be frightened by the rattling pots and pans and this usually scares it away. At least you'll know that it has arrived. Your visitors, however, may not always be bears. The first and only time we attempted this technique we were aroused by our kitchenware bounding down the rocky slope into the lake. The flashlight revealed an old acquaintance (not friend), a porcupine with all his 30,000 quills.

A final admonition about bears. Don't worry too much about them. They can run and climb faster than you can, and remember, discretion is always the better part of valor.

OTHER VARMINTS

Porcupines, in my experience, have never become the problem on voyages that they are on backpacking treks in the Appalachian, Green, and White mountains. We take proper precautions. Porcupines love salt and will chew anything that carries its smell or taste. This includes paddles, axe handles, and sweat-stained leather packstraps. We suspend paddles from the lower branches of a nearby tree with a piece of nylon parachute cord.

Another reason for not bringing food packs into the tent are chipmunks, squirrels, and mice. They have small appetites, but it's a nuisance to have them gnaw holes in food packets and then sharpen their teeth on your moccasins.

CANOE-COUNTRY MEDICINE

First aid is usually the only form of medicine in

wilderness voyaging where the nearest doctor may be three days away by canoe. He might be able to reach you by air in an hour if he knew of your predicament, but he won't know. You need a basic medical kit to handle the situation, and the contents are considerably different from bathroom-shelf medications.

It is beyond the scope and space of this book to prescribe treatments and remedies for voyageurs. Secure a copy of the American Red Cross First Aid Manual ($1. at your local ARC chapter) and concentrate on ills that voyageurs may be heir to:

Exposure
Heat exhaustion
Heat stroke
Burns
Axe wounds
Poison ivy

Medical Kit

A first-aid kit is what the name implies. It is designed to give basic treatment until the doctor arrives. In the wilderness, the contents of the medicine chest must be more extensive. Here are suggested items to be included in a wilderness voyaging medical kit:

Eight 3x3-inch gauze pads
One roll 1-inch gauze bandage
One roll 2-inch gauze bandage
One Ace elastic bandage
One triangular bandage
One eyecup
Four ounces boric acid (plastic bottle)
Bandage scissors
Tweezers
Needle for puncturing blisters

Some of the items below require prescriptions from your family physician:

> *24 penicillin or Acromycin tablets (for infection)*
> *24 Lomotil tablets (for diarrhea)*
> *1 small tube pontocaine-neohydeltrasol with applicator (for eye infection)*
> *12 morphine tablets, or codeine.*
> *Sterile suture packet with nylon suture and 3–0 and 5–0 needles*
> *Scalpel blade*
> *Mosquito clamp (hemostat)*

All the above items are usful, but when you need it, nothing will ever seem as welcome as morphine.

Discuss the proper administration and dosages with your doctor. We use Camphophenique, transferred to a plastic bottle, for bug bites.

Bring along a laxative, in case it is needed.

Snakebite Kit

Maine is reportedly the only one of the 48 contiguous states not inhabited by venomous snakes. Rattlers of the cane brake, pygmy, and giant Florida diamondback varieties are confined to the South. Timber rattlers spread throughout the country. I've never seen a rattlesnake in Vermont, though the state pays an annual bounty to several residents of one town, West Haven, where the snakes are all collected in an abandoned slate quarry.

The Cutter Compact Snake Bite kit is standard. It is light (1½ ounces), about the size of a 16-gauge shot shell, and inexpensive. Price, $3.

This kit contains three suction cups, knife blade for making the two traditional X-shaped slashes (one centered over each of the two fang punctures), lymph constrictor, and antiseptic. Memorize the instructions before your departure. We heard of a solitary hunter who was so scared following a snakebite and his shakes were so severe that he couldn't hold steady enough to read the fine print of the instructions. It turned out that the snake was not poisonous. The hunter didn't know the difference between the twin-fang punctures of a venomous snake and the horseshoe (U-shaped) bite of a nonvenomous reptile.

Each voyageur should tote his personal snakebite kit. Before heading into new country, determine what venomous snakes inhabit the area. Learn to identify them. The coral snake (its bite is almost invariably deadly) requires a different antivenin than do rattlers, or the water moccasin. The latter snake is often called "cottonmouth" because his open mouth is white inside. The cottonmouth's bite is rarely fatal, but produces several weeks of unpleasant illness. Regardless of the type of snake, the following precautions are recommended:

When in snake country, consider wearing antisnake leggings. These are easy to put on but hot to wear and usually extend above the kneecap. Some are made of lightweight aluminum. Mine are stainless-steel mesh sandwiched between two layers of canvas.

Before stepping ashore, examine the immediate area carefully.

Look on the other side of a log before stepping over it.

When gathering squaw-wood (dead sticks) examine the ground carefully. The cottonmouth with its black body can be mistaken for a stick.

Keep the mosquito netting door of your tent zipped at all times.

Don't visit the latrine at night without examining the ground with your flashlight.

If you are bitten, don't panic. Florida is a snake-infested state but only three people die in an average year from snakebites.

Do not under any circumstances drink liquor once you have been bitten. Alcohol hastens the flow of venom through the body.

Use your snakebite kit immediately.

Move as little as possible. A snake bitten backpacker usually has to hike out. You can get to the nearest civilization resting on the deck of your canoe.

It is important to identify the type of snake that bit you. The doctor will want to know. Hospitals in snake-infested country usually carry basic antivenins.

21
The Voyageur in Action

It is late afternoon and you are unloading the canoe. This is a stirring moment. This is your first camp.

Now comes the work of setting up camp. Everyone does it somewhat differently, but here are the ways, evolved over many years, that work well for us.

Janet hands the packs out of the canoe to me. They are then laid on the beach. The canoe is carried, not dragged, to a place where it will be safe from the wind.

On exposed sites like a low peninsula, we anchor it with line and rocks.

Some yards back from the shore, we locate a fairly flat tent site. The cookfire, if we are to have one, is best located near the water. It's safer and there is less distance to tote water.

The two personal packs which include tent and sleeping gear are brought to the tent site. The current week's food pack and kitchen packbasket are laid out on a tarp near the fireplace site.

The stove comes out of the kitchen pack. Slightly less than 1 quart of water is placed in the smallest (1½-quart) pot. The stove is lighted, and the pot is placed on it. The water boils in about five minutes. This gives us

Lash pack straps around thwart(s).

time to unpack the tent, spread it out, and place the poles and pegs in their respective positions. When the water is boiling, instant soup is dumped into the pot.

By the time the tent is up (no more than seven to ten minutes, unless there is a high wind), the soup is sufficiently cool to drink. Pipe and cigarettes are lighted.

Janet unpacks the personal bags, takes the sleeping bags out of the stuffsacks, fluffs them up, and hangs them up to air. She unrolls the full-length foam sleeping pads. They may go into the tent or be left out for us to stretch on after dinner around the campfire.

She commences building the fireplace while I saw, chop, or collect firewood. Tinder and kindling are collected first. After the fireplace is ready, Janet starts the fire while I continue gathering wood. Once the fire is underway, the 4½-quart utility pot, about three-quarters full of water, is placed on the grate.

I put the kitchen gear near the fireplace along with the current food and kitchen packs. The remaining food packs are usually suspended from a line between two trees as protection from bears or other critters.

It's now time for the traditional drink of 151-proof Hudson's Bay Company rum, cut with water.

We may now swim or fish. Once the water boils, it is placed on the back of the grate to keep warm. If there's fresh fish for supper, it's cleaned and the entrails left for the gulls.

After dinner, Janet does the dishes while I check the canoe, hang up the current food bag, and put the sleeping bags into the tent. Sleeping comes early in canoe country.

After a predawn coffee in the sleeping bag, I build a fire or light the stove.

While I make breakfast (no longer than 10 minutes), Janet stows all the personal gear. Sleeping bags are aired. They are the last items to be packed. This airing takes out some of the body moisture that didn't evaporate during the night.

Loading the packs.

After breakfast, the tent is struck, dew is wiped off the outside of the fly, and the tent and fly are stowed. Food packs are taken down. The line from which they were suspended is coiled and placed in a personal pack.

The packs are placed aboard the canoe. Several buckets of water thoroughly drench the fire. The fire-place is left for the convenience of future voyageurs. This is common canoe-country courtesy.

Rainy weather calls for different techniques. We rig a tarp for cooking and dining, unless we're fairly sure this is not bear country or if the rain drives beneath the tarp. In such cases we cook inside the tent.

FIREWOOD

Camping writers from Kephart to anybody's brother-in-law usually include long lists of trees that make desirable firewood. They are generally listed in order of desirability. This is fine and dandy but for two major factors.

Many of these texts were written (Kephart hasn't been revised for nearly sixty years) when Americans were predominantly rural residents. Today, only 5 percent of us make our living from farm and forest. Many city dwellers don't know a palm from a pine tree.

It is of little help to the canoeist, or to any other camper, to say that live oak is a fine, long-burning cook-fire wood when the nearest live oak may be 1,500 miles away. We have to use, for better or worse, whatever is in the immediate vicinity of our campsite.

Fortunately, however, most of the best canoe country lies within that vast belt predominated by coniferous (evergreen) trees like pine (red, white, and jack), cedar, and spruce. Two hardwoods, both readily identifiable, that are strewn through much of canoe country are poplar (aspen) and white birch.

Lightly lash spare paddle to thwarts and carrying yoke.

Hardwoods take longer to ignite but they burn longer. Evergreens are easier to ignite but burn rapidly. They also throw off more sparks that have to be watched. A rule of thumb: hardwoods have leaves, and evergreens, excepting cedar, have various types of needles.

Cutting Firewood

Look for upright dead trees. This wood will be drier and sounder than fallen deadwood. Make sure a dead tree is solid enough so that part of it won't break off and fall on you during the chopping or sawing process.

Small branches on fallen trees are often clear of the ground and, hence, dry. They are good for kindling.

We rarely bother with dead trees that are more than 6 inches in diameter. It is usually easier to saw dead wood and then use the axe for splitting into readily burnable pieces.

FIREPLACES

Many campers build circular fireplaces. Don't follow their example. Rectangular grates require, for maximum efficiency, a rectangular fireplace.

Your fireplace should be about the same size as your grate. Use rocks whenever possible, or green logs when they are not. In our case, this is 15x24 inches. This holds simultaneously our 7½-inch-diameter 4½-quart utility pot, 10-inch-diameter frypan, and 6-inch-diameter 2½-quart pot or coffee pot.

The stone walls supporting the fireplace should be as level as possible. A tilted grate fouls up frying operations. One end of the fireplace should be a sizable stone which is easy to remove for inserting your firewood. With the stone removed, you can bake bannock in an upright frypan. A solid wall shields the flame from the wind.

If all of your cooking, or most of it, will be done over a fire, then lay in a goodly supply of dry wood. Place your next morning's supply under the upturned canoe or under a tarp. We usually fix breakfast over the gas stove because it saves time, but if it rains during the night or in the morning, a bright fire dries things out and is cheery after dismal weather.

Use dry pine needles and twigs for tinder. Once it is blazing, add some thumb-sized pieces of softwood. This is followed by split pieces of softwood like pine or spruce. If hardwood like birch is available this can be added once the fire is well under way.

KITCHEN TECHNIQUES

Once the cook fire is blazing brightly, we fill the 4½-quart pot, our largest, with water. When the water

The fireplace in action.

boils, the pot is shoved to a far corner of the grate to keep it moderately hot. This is our tea kettle-utility pot. From it we draw water for cooking, coffee, and dish-washing. When water is dipped or poured out it is replaced with cold water. On those occasions when we have something other than a one-dish dinner, we don't always succeed in having the main dish, say fried fish, finish at the same time the potatoes or vegetable is done. We take the vegetable in its pot, usually the 1½-quart one, and float it in the utility pot. This keeps the second dish hot until ready to serve with the fish or other course.

Frying

Heat frypan. Dump shortening (butter, bacon grease, vegetable oil, olive oil, or oleomargarine) into the skillet. After frying is finished, pour remaining grease into the screw-top aluminum canister that serves

as grease container. After doing this, fill frypan with hot
water. It will be easier to clean.

Never cool frypan or pots by dunking in lake or
stream. This will warp them.

Reflector Oven Baking

These are used by tyro' campers who have had an
oven supplied by the outfitter or by those who enjoy
fancy cooking in camp. We enjoy gourmet cooking, but
on the trail we prefer to keep our culinary tasks as
simple and easy as possible. Nowadays we rarely, if
ever, tote a reflector oven. If desired, one can readily be
improvised by using aluminum foil. Our baking is usually confined to baking bannock in the frypan.

Baking with a reflector oven requires a different
kind of fire than is used for cooking. It means waiting,
or the work of setting up a special fire. However, we
deny no man his right to starve to death while waiting
for fancy foods to finish baking.

It is possible to remove one long side of your fireplace to provide heat for the oven. Don't try this if it
will make your grate unsteady.

Here are the requirements for successful baking:
1. A hot fire and little smoke.
2. The center of the oven shelf should be no more than
   8 to 12 inches from the fire. Exact distance depends
   on size of oven.
3. The bottom edge of the oven, not the edge of the
   oven shelf, should be level with, or slightly below, the
   base of your fire or fireplace.
4. Funnel heat to the oven by placing several stones on
   either side of the oven.
5. The inside top and bottom of the oven's insides
   should be shiny bright to ensure maximum reflection

of heat. It is better if the under surface of the shelf is blackened so that it absorbs heat.

Once the coffee is ready we pour it into another pot, usually the 1½-quart one, dump the grounds from the coffee pot, rinse it out, and then pour the coffee back into it. Set the coffee pot on a warm corner of the grate. This keeps the coffee warm, but prevents it from becoming bitter.

Kitchen Chores

There are two basic schools of camp-pot cleaning. Some don't clean off the soot because the blackened pot heats up more rapidly than a shiny one. Housewifely tyros scour the pots until they are almost like new ones.

We steer a middle course. Loose soot is wiped off, but the pot is not scrubbed. Pots, frypan, coffee pot, and grate are toted in their own nylon sacks.

Pots are scoured inside with Chore Girl or Flip. Sand and gravel will also do a good job. Use non-detergent soaps. It is not necessary to foul up the water by washing pots and pans in the river or lake. It can be done on the shore.

FIRE PREVENTION

Fires from natural causes like lightning cause enough damage, so let's not add to the millions of acres destroyed annually through man's carelessness.

In some Canadian provinces, it is illegal to smoke while walking through the woods. One can, however, sit down to rest and smoke.

Poorly arranged or neglected cook fires account for many forest fires, as well as those not put out before leaving the campsite.

Canadian law requires that all campfires be built on mineral soil (dirt) or rocks.

There should be a cleared space at least 3 feet in radius all around the cook-fire site.

The fire should be enclosed by stones or green logs.

Cook fires should be small, and campfires should not be much larger.

Voyageurs, unlike some backpackers, rarely suffer from a water shortage, so there is absolutely no excuse for not thoroughly dousing and then drowning all cook fires or campfires before leaving camp.

Never leave a cook fire unattended.

Exercise caution when using gasoline stoves and lanterns.

Cigarettes should be broken up and the tobacco scattered or thumbed into the dirt.

Pipe dottle should be thoroughly extinguished.

"Dead" matches should be broken in two and the ends put into the fireplace or shoved into the ground. (A cigarette lighter reduces fire hazards.)

GARBAGE DISPOSAL

Most state, provincial, and national forests, parks, and wilderness areas have specific regulations about garbage and trash disposal.

Some areas require that all unburnable garbage, and trash like foil, cans, and bottles, be brought back to civilization. Some areas provide plastic garbage bags to take along with you. They may provide containers for disposing of your garbage and trash at the end of the voyage. Areas like Superior National Forest-Boundary Waters Canoe Area have regulations that prohibit unburnable packages, tins, and bottles.

In the more remote areas of the North Country, garbage may be legally disposed of by burying to a minimum depth of 18 inches.

The best solution to the undisposable bottle, foil-packet, and tin-can problem is to plan your food supply so that none of these items is included in your outfit.

Many outfitters, notably those in the Quetico-Superior area, only provide food items in disposable packets.

The only liquids we normally tote—wine, rum, olive oil, and maple syrup (stove fuel is carried in aluminum bottles)—are carried in reusable poly bottles. They are unbreakable and much lighter than glass containers.

Soups like Swiss-Knorr or Maggi are transferred from foil packets to polybags.

Well-planned menus leave little or no garbage. Gulls clean up fish scraps.

Where the law allows you to bury trash and garbage, first flatten out tins and then eliminate traces of food smell by burning the tins in the fireplace. Bury tins and garbage to a depth of at least 18 inches. Cover burial site with rocks if any are available. All this is to discourage animals from digging up the trash.

Sanitation

The folding GI shovel, obtainable in most war-surplus stores, is a standard item among voyageurs. Its primary function is to dig a latrine some distance from your tent and at least 100 feet from the nearest water. For an overnight stop, dig a hole about 18 inches deep. Each time it is used, shovel a layer of dirt into the hole.

Always prepare a proper latrine. Any other behavior is not sanitary, safe, or courteous, as others may soon use your campsite.

22
A Voyageur's Notebook

If a man can pack a heavy load across a por-
tage, if he can do whatever he has to do with-
out complaint and with good humor, it makes
little difference what his background has been.
And if he can somehow keep alive a spark of
adventure and romance as the old time voy-
ageurs seem to have done, then any expedition
becomes more than a journey through wild
country. It becomes a shining challenge and
adventure of the spirit.
      —Sigurd F. Olson, *The Lonely Land*

Here are some miscellaneous thoughts, and practical hints, on various aspects of voyaging.

FISHING

Much of North America's canoe country is fish
country. Northern lakes and streams provide some of
this continent's best smallmouth, walleye, lake trout,
and landlocked salmon fishing. Some streams offer rain-
bow, brook, or brown trout fishing.

Pike and bass are prime country fare.

Fishing tackle should be kept light and minimal. This is difficult for confirmed anglers, but you'll be surprised how little tackle you can get along with.

My basic spinning rod, good for 90 percent of North American freshwater fishing, is a two-piece Orvis bamboo 3⅝-ounce 7-foot rod. Rod and spare tip are carried in an aluminum rod case. I use 6-pound-test nylon line.

The following lures have taken smallmouth and bigmouth bass, various trout, and walleyes: white and red Dardevle, Mepps Agilla, Rapala, and Orvis Fearsome Foursome. These are broad spoon, regular spoon, narrow spoon, and fish spinner. Sometimes, in bass country, we take along Uncle Josh's porkrind bait. Hula poppers and Hula dancers (¼ ounce) are bass plugs of proven effectiveness.

My fishing tackle, rod excepted, fits into my Tackle-Pak jacket, and tackle includes a lightweight collapsible net.

Sometimes I take a second rod. This may be my 5-foot, 1½-ounce bamboo spinning rod for $\frac{1}{16}$-ounce lures with 2-pound-test line, or my 2-ounce, 5-foot-9-inch bamboo rod for ⅛-ounce lures and 4-pound-test line.

Our lures have single hooks. Favorite lures which have not been fitted with single hooks have the trebles removed and replaced with singles. It may be my imagination but I seem to get more bites with single-hook lures than with the same lures fitted with trebles.

A canoe trip involving portages is no place for a heavy, oversize tackle box. I use a small Orvis box (10x5x2 inches) that holds about two dozen spoons, spinners, plugs, hooks, and swivels.

Use care when fishing from your canoe. Usually one voyageur casts or trolls at a time. The bowman should make sure his rod or line doesn't hit his partner. Fore and aft anchors, if you need them, can be jury-rigged rocks and your nylon parachute cord.

Don't make sudden or jerky movements. Fishing is more fun than trying to get back into your canoe, wet clothes and all.

HUNTING

The moose, an ugly but majestic critter with semi-aquatic habits, is probably the foremost game animal for North American canoe hunters. Ontario is both prime moose and canoe country. Bring your own canoe and outfit, or rent a rig from an outfitter who usually supplies a guide.

There are few more thrilling experiences than to

hear, and then see, an experienced moose caller bring a mighty bull moose into rifle range.

Moose hunting in the Ontario moose season sometimes sees snowfall and fairly coolish weather, so take along some warm clothing like lightweight down parkas, Maine hunting boots (rubber bottoms, leather tops in the lightweight version), warm trousers, and wool stockings. Your sleeping bag should be rated to at least 0°.

Many of our duck-shooting acquaintances use canoes for their wildfowling, but very few go canoe camping during the all-too-brief season. This is partly because they think it is too cold to camp out.

Only one man should shoot at a time. Take turns. Shoot mallards, not men. There are no excusable hunting accidents. Wounds and fatalities are caused by stupidity and carelessness.

Some of our most memorable days and nights afield have been on late-fall canoe hunts for moose, duck, and even deer. A big tarp is rigged as a lean-to, or an open Baker or Adirondack tent is pitched with pots simmering on the gasoline stove, while the campfire in front of a rock or a stack of green logs throws light and warmth into the tent.

CAMERA TIPS

Voyageurs' cameras, spare lenses, accessories, and film must be protected against breakage, dust, damp, water, and excessive heat.

The simplest and least expensive but least convenient method is to stow them in waterproof plastic bags and stow the bags in the middle of your pack. However, if you want to make shots en route, then some other method has to be found.

Regular metal waterproof camera boxes by Halliburton cost $75 and up. They are lined with a foam plastic which can be cut to accommodate your lenses, cameras, film tins, and accessories. They are insulated.

Small plastic waterproof fishing-tackle boxes make excellent camera cases, especially if lined with polyfoam. Price, $3.50 to $5.

Orvis offers a protective camera bag in two sizes. The plastic bag (Velcro-sealed) protects the camera from breakage by the air pocket formed when bag is sealed. The 11x15-inch bag costs $9.50. The 13¾x24-inch bag is $12.95.

Insulated refrigerated bags designed to keep beer and food cold for several hours without ice are waterproof in some versions. We've used a 16x10x6-inch bag with good results. Price, $6.50. A large version by an-

Kids like canoe camping, too.

other maker measures 10x18x12 inches and costs $14.50.

Your camera container should be secured to your seat or thwart so that in the event of capsizing, the outfit won't float away.

FAMILY VOYAGING

Children can enjoy canoeing—ten years seems to be about the minimum age—but they should not be taken along unless they know how to swim. They should wear life jackets at all times.

Family camping with two kids requires two canoes. One adult and one child per canoe.

Outfit each kid with his or her own Dacron sleeping bag (Gerry's Quetico is first rate), pack, sleeping pad (shorty size will do), canteen, plate, fork, spoon and jackknife. A small tent with flaps and screening provides their shelter. Meals and community living is done in the Mom-Dad tent.

Today's kids are finicky about food. They'll have to learn to like, or at least eat, freeze-dried foods. For the first few days, you might take along some hamburger, hotdogs, and marshmallows.

Many kids enjoy fishing. Take along their spinning tackle, or if they don't have any, then get them a spinning or a spin-casting outfit.

Kids should have their own specific chores in camp: gathering squaw wood, helping build the fireplace, fetching water, and helping with the dishes.

Take along a game or two for those rainy days, which can be hell on tempers unless there is something to occupy everybody.

Show the kids how to use an axe, build a fire, and tie a few basic knots. Explain axe and knife safety.

Before shoving off on your voyage make sure the kids know how to swim and how to help upright a capsized canoe.

Permissiveness as practiced by too many of today's parents has no place on a canoe trip. The Old Man's word is law. When you say "Jump," they have to learn to jump immediately and ask why later.

SURVIVAL GEAR

Janet and I both carry beneath our seats or lashed to the thwarts a fanny pack containing survival items. Both of us always carry on our persons a sheath knife and waterproof match safe along with our Zippo cigarette lighters.

Most survival items were discussed in Chapter 9. They include (between both packs):

Basic first-aid kit
Fire ribbon
Nylon line

Ontario Indian guide calling up moose.

Silva orienteering compass
Topographical maps (if available)
Shooting/sun glasses
Rain/wind parka
2-inch roll of adhesive tape
Swiss Army knife
Flashlights (2)
Anti-bug dope
Anti-surnburn cream
Snakebite kit (in poisonous-snake country)
Emergency fishing tackle (including nylon line, hooks, sinkers)
Repair kit (insulated handled, needlenose, wire-cutting pliers; screwdrivers (2), small file, copper wire

A distress-signal kit ($6.95) contains three 1-ounce red flares. Each flare (visible in daylight) rises several hundred feet. The flare burns out before descending. This eliminates fire hazard. Flares are rustproof and will float. You'll probably never need one, but if you ever do you'll be glad you took them.

Radios and tape decks have no legitimate place in the wilderness. Exception: In the Far North, a radio could be useful for receiving time signals. These are useful only when you are navigating with a sextant.

Part V
Where to Go Voyaging

23
Canada: A Voyageur's Paradise

Here then is an immense tract of country,
which the Supreme Being, the Lord of the
whole earth has given to the Deer, and other
wild animals; and to the Red Man forever.
— David Thompson, explorer,
writing in 1796

Canada, the world's second-largest country, has more freshwater rivers and lakes than any other nation. Its 291,571 square miles of fresh water could provide several lifetimes of voyaging.

Canadian voyaging ranges from cruises through pleasant countryside, to much-used canoe trails in some of the more readily accessible parks, to the lonesome lakes and rivers of the Arctic and sub-Arctic regions.

It is possible to canoe Canada from the Atlantic to the Arctic Ocean with no more than 150 miles of portages.

Canoeists contemplating voyages throughout northern Canada should be expert paddlers, have a knowledge of winds, lake and river travel, be able to read map and compass, and have a working knowledge of camping and woodcraft. Maps and compasses are a necessity. Rations must be carefully planned and definite arrangements made for resupply.

Voyageurs into the Canadian wilderness must notify the Royal Canadian Mounted Police of their route, destination, and estimated time of arrival. Friendly, helpful Mounties can deny you permission to enter a wilderness area if they believe the trip to be beyond your skill and know-how or if your equipment and rations are improper or inadequate.

ALBERTA

To the voyageur, past and present, Alberta is the crossroads of the continent. Here the Mackenzie, the Mighty Mac, with its major rivers, the Peace, Hay, Athabasca, and Slave, begins the long journey to the Arctic Ocean. Most of the rivers are canoeable.

The Mighty Mac is 5 miles wide through its lower reaches. Occasional trading posts and settlements are dotted along its bank. It is the waterway along which nearly 300,000 tons of freight are carried annually into the Northwest Territories.

In Central Alberta, the North and South Saskatchewan Rivers flow east into Hudson Bay via Lake Winnipeg and the Nelson River.

At the extreme southern edge of the province, the Milk River dips below the U.S.-Canadian frontier to commence its long southward flow to the Gulf of Mexico as a tributary to the Missouri and Mississippi.

BRITISH COLUMBIA

This province has, in the Rockies, the genesis of the

Fraser, named after the Vermont-born Tory and explorer Simon Fraser, and the Finlay, a tributary of the Mackenzie.

Lake Bowron Provincial Park is a major voyaging area. Seven-to-twelve-day voyages can be taken through primitive country.

MANITOBA

This is another great voyageur's province. Here, Hudson Bay is the ultimate destination of the great rivers like the Burnwood, Nelson, and Red River of the North, and exciting lesser streams like God's River (and Lake) and the Seal.

British Columbia: Bowron Lake Provincial Park.

Manitoba: Lake Country.

Here, too, are some of North America's largest lakes: Winnipeg (9,465 square miles), Winnipegosis (2,100 square miles), Manitoba (1,825 square miles), and Cedar (538 square miles).

The Assiniboine is a major stream near the U.S.-Canadian frontier.

Most lakes and streams are navigable for canoes.

There are, of course, numerous portages.

The northern half of the province is sub-Arctic tundra. This is where the North begins.

NEW BRUNSWICK

New Brunswick, the smallest mainland Canadian province, has only 519 square miles of water. Until recently, guides were required for trips in this first-rate Atlantic salmon country.

The Parks Branch, Department of Natural Resources (Canada), now lists 26 approved canoe trails, ranging from 12 to 100 miles.

Courtesy to the salmon fisherman is requested by the Parks Branch. "Pass to the side of the pool the fisherman is casting over."

Fire-building permits are not issued during dry spells. Campers must tote a gasoline or gas stove or eat cold rations.

Some noted New Brunswick canoe trails:

Restigouche River: 93 miles, Cedar Brook to Christopher Brook, Campbellton. Intermediate canoeing skills required.

St. John River (middle): 74 miles, Beechwood to Mactaquac Provincial Park. Intermediate canoeing skills required.

LABRADOR

"The Land That God Gave Cain" is now part of Newfoundland. Voyages require a high degree of canoemanship and a considerable knowledge of wood- and campcraft. Guides, and rightly so, are required for some interior voyages. Too many voyageurs, not all of them foolhardy, have perished in the past. Food, equipment, and planning are of an expeditionary nature. This challenging country separates men from boys.

NEWFOUNDLAND

This province has not yet developed many canoe trails. Most canoeing revolves around camps or guides catering to Atlantic salmon fishermen.

NORTHWEST TERRITORIES

This is probably the world's greatest canoe country. One rarely has to camp among other voyageurs. The Mackenzie is the major stream here. One can sell his canoe in Aklavik or Tututoyaktuk, the end of the voyage, and fly back to Edmonton. The territories have 51,465 square miles of fresh water.

The Mackenzie Basin has a much milder climate than the rest of the Northwest Territories, which includes North America's northernmost mainland and the offshoot islands like Baffin Island, Ellesmere Island, Victoria Island, Stefansson Island, Banks Island, and all others claimed by Canada.

Major mainland streams include Coppermine and Hanbury's River. Here are the mighty lakes, Great Slave, Lesser Slave, and Great Bear.

Summer is about two months long here and the water temperature rarely rises above 50 degrees F.

ONTARIO

Ontario, Canada's second-largest province, is dotted with thousands of lakes and slashed with myriad streams.

Ontario's waters include the Canadian portion of Lakes Superior, Huron, Erie, and Ontario, and Niagara Falls, along with the frontier-divided lakes of Lake of the Woods and Steep Rock Lake.

Northern provincial streams flow northwestward into Hudson Bay, Albany, Attawapiskat, Moose, Severn, and Winisk. Southern streams drain into the St. Lawrence system. Major interior lakes include Nipissing and Nipigon.

It is on the northern shores of Lake Superior that Grand Portage lies, a 9-mile portage, over the Height of Land. It was here that the great Montreal canoes came from that city with supplies for the men of the north, who exchanged their furs for powder, ball, and other necessities.

PRINCE EDWARD ISLAND

Canada's smallest and only offshore province has almost no freshwater canoeing areas. One could, of course, circumnavigate the island. Saltwater voyaging off the lovely beaches would be a pleasure.

QUEBEC

One of every 6 Canadian square miles lies within La Belle Province, and one of every 8 of its square miles is water.

Quebec's southern border stretches from New England and upper New York State northward to near the Arctic Circle. Its northern tips lie farther north than Cape Farewell, the southern tip of Greenland.

Here we have the mighty St. Lawrence, one of the continent's great river systems. The French and Indian origin of more than 80 percent of the habitants is revealed in the river names: Saguenay, St. Maurice, Ottawa, Richelieu. English settlers are remembered by rivers like Fort George and Rupert. Both flow into James Bay.

Quebec: Parc de La Verendrye.

Voyages through northern Quebec of necessity take on the aspects of expeditions.

The province's park system has both semi-wilderness and wilderness canoeing. Major parks with hundreds of miles of marked canoe trails, and many more miles of wilderness, include: Parc de La Verendrye (5,257 square miles), Parc des Laurentides (4,060 square miles), Parc de Port-Cartier (3,250 square miles).

These parks are all within a day's drive from Montreal. They include both stream and lake voyaging. Portages are usually short and well marked.

SASKATCHEWAN

The name of this province comes from Sis-Sis-Katchewan-Sepie, or "Big Angry Water," and has 31,520 square miles of water. Muskeg (bog) covers much of the northern half of the province. This is superb voyaging country.

The Saskatchewan Government Tourist Bureau publishes 27 free and comprehensive booklets on canoe voyages (see Appendix V).

Many provincial rivers run eastward through Manitoba into Hudson Bay. The famed Churchill River is a notable example.

The confluence of the South and North Saskatchewan Rivers lies near Prince Albert. The Saskatchewan then flows east through Manitoba's Lake Winnipeg and Nelson River into Hudson Bay.

Notable lakes include Athabasca, La Ronge, Reindeer, and Wollaston.

Prince Albert Park (1,500 square miles) has the justly famed and pleasant Waskeisu loop voyage. Route: Waskeisu Lake, Wakeslu Narrows (portage via miniature railway), Kingsmere Lake, Ajawaan, Sanctuary, Lavallee, Wabeno, Wassegam, Tibiska, Crean, Herat, and Wakeslu Lake.

YUKON TERRITORY

Here lies the genesis of the mighty Yukon River system. Voyageurs, tired of portaging, can canoe 450 miles along the Yukon from White Horse to Dawson. The Yukon runs 2,000 miles from its source to the Bering Sea.

Various runs include: Quiet Lake (Canol Road) to Carmack on the Yukon: 200 miles down through Big Salmon Lake, down Big Salmon River to Carmack.

Carmack to Dawson City: 250 miles downstream.

Watson Lake to Dawson: 1,000 miles via Frances River, Frances Lake, Finlayson River, Finlayson Lake

(5-mile portage to Campbell Creek), Campbell Creek, Campbell River, Pelly River (Hoole Canyon portage), Yukon, Dawson.

Voyaging through this country requires expert paddle know-how and a good knowledge of river lore and woodcraft.

Voyaging time is limited between ice break-up in mid-June to freeze-up in late August or early September.

Water temperature rarely exceeds 50°F.

24
U.S.A.: The Far Corners

The Northeastern U.S. from Maine through Michigan to Minnesota is the traditional U.S. canoe country. Another state, in our opinion, should be added to this distinguished roster: Florida.

Every state, even New Mexico, has some canoeable water. Many states have only flat water. This rarely appeals to experienced voyageurs. Sometimes, a flat-water cruise is taken along a river because of its historic, social, or dramatic significance. Details of possible voyages will be found in those publications listed in the several appendices and through the several sources also listed therein.

ALASKA

The Yukon courses for nearly 1,000 miles from the Yukon frontier to the sea. Its major tributary is the Tanana.

Many Alaskan rivers are quite inaccessible except by air. You need a big bankroll in this bog state.

The Kenai Peninsula has the 120-mile-long Swan Lake cruise.

Canoe country: an after-supper paddle.

The Gulkana River trip is 25 miles from put-in at Paxton Lake to take-out at Sourdough. This route parallels a caribou migration trail. There are few, if any, more magnificent sights in all North America than to see thousands of caribou thundering across the tundra.

ARKANSAS

The Ozarks offer many two- and three-day canoe-camping cruises. Some streams are too low after mid-July for pleasant or exciting cruises.

Some notable streams: Buffalo, Eleven Point, Quachita (many dams), Little Missouri, and Big Piney Creek. Mulberry River in the Boston Mountains has fairly decent white water in the spring.

CONNECTICUT

The Connecticut and Housatonic Rivers are major canoeable streams.

FLORIDA

Florida, the nation's least developed canoe state, has the nation's greatest flat-water voyaging routes.

Some rivers: Appalachicola (it is the Chattahoochee in Georgia) Caloosahatchee, Kissimmee, Myyakka, Ockwahlaha, Peace, Perdido, St. Johns, St. Mary's, Steinhatchee, and Withlacoochee.

The Suwannee rises in southeastern Georgia's Okefenokee Swamp and flows 250 miles to the Gulf of Mexico, where its waters mingle with those from far-away Saskatchewan. In this century only a few white men (this writer among them) have ventured from Okefenokee to the Gulf.

The voyage need not end where the Suwannee flows into the Gulf. Continue a few miles south along the Gulf Coast, past Cedar Key to the Withlacoochee and then upstream (it's easy flat-water paddling) through a series of lakes to the lovely Ockwahlaha, thence into the St. Johns, and down to Jacksonville. This voyage, which takes one almost twice across Florida, is about 750 miles long.

The Everglades, that mysterious region of water and sawgrass up to 8 feet tall, has no counterpart in the world. The River Everglades flows southeast from Lake Okeechobee. Everglades National Park, the country's second largest, has hundreds of miles of canoe routes, and here in the subtropics one can see bird, animal, and reptile species found nowhere else in North America.

Florida publishes maps of some rivers but no canoeing information. Data on specific rivers can some-times be obtained by writing Jim Floyd, Chief, Infor-mation and Education Division, Florida Freshwater Fish and Game Commission, Tallahassee, Florida. The Forest Supervisor, Ocala National Forest, Ocala, Flor-ida, has details and maps of the Ockwahlaha.

ILLINOIS

The Illinois River is the longest, 275 miles, but not the most attractive river within the state.

The Mackinaw is probably the pleasantest run: 60 miles from put-in at Mackinaw to the Illinois River.

As a high school student, Ernest Hemingway ca-noed the now heavily polluted Des Plaines.

Spoon River, made famous by poet Edgar Lee Masters in his *Spoon River Anthology*, offers 125 miles of attractive country from Elmore to Havana.

MAINE

This foremost canoe state with more than 5,000 riv-ers and over 2,200 lakes provides flat and white water. There is the Allagash Wilderness Waterway, probably this country's most famed canoe route. There are lakes like Sebago, Moosehead, Allagash, Belgrade, Moose-lookmeguntic, and the Rangeley chain. Here are the Androscoggin, Kennebec, St. Croix, St. John, and Saco.

The Damariscotta loop offers saltwater canoeing in lovely coves and along the rocky, rugged coast.

Guides are not required but are useful in some areas. Here are the itineraries of some outstandingly re-warding voyages:

Allagash Wilderness Waterway: East Seeboomook to Fort Kent, 156 miles, 10-28 days. Via Allagash and

St. Francis, over the West Branch of the Penobscot River, several lakes, the Allagash and St. John rivers. Six portages (or carries, as they are called in Maine).

East Branch: Greenville to Grindstone, 140 miles, 14-21 days. Via Kokadjo, Ripogenue Dam, Chesuncook Dam, Whetstone, Burntland and Grindstone Falls, over several lakes, Umbazookus Stream and the East Branch of the Penobscot River. Twelve carries.

Dead River and Moosehead Waters: Stratton to Rockwood, 87 miles, 8-14 days. Via Flagstaff, Dead River, and Jackman. Over Dead River, Spencer Lake, Fish Pond, Attean Lake, Wood Pond, Moose River, Brassua and Moosehead Lakes. Eight carries.

Rangeley Lakes: Rangeley Village to Upton, 50 miles, 7 days. Via Oquossoc and Haines Landing over Rangeley, Mooselookmeguntic, Upper Richardson, and Umbabog Lakes.

Maine: packbasket country.

St. Croix River: Danforth to Calais, 108 miles, 10-21 days. Across Spednic Lake and St. Croix River (guides useful here).

Fish River chain of lakes: St. Agatha to Fort Kent, 65 miles, 7-21 days. Over Cross, Square, and Eagle Lakes and Fish River. Guides useful.

Upper Kennebec: Forths to Bath, 7-14 days. Cross Dead River, Wyman Lake, and Kennebec River; dangerous whirlpools in lower river. Guides useful.

Lower Kennebec: Loop trip, Gardiner to Gardiner, 100 miles, 8-21 days. Via Cobbossee Stream, Pleasant and Horseshoe Streams, Cobbosseecontee, Annaessacook, Maranacook and Messalonskee Lakes, and Kennebec River.

Belgrade Lakes: Waterville to Oakland, 40-100 miles, 7-14 days. Via East, North, Great, Ellis, McGrath and Long Ponds, Belgrade Lakes, Belgrade Stream, and Snow Pond.

MASSACHUSETTS

The Connecticut River flows through rural and urban areas. Millers' River offers some rural campsites. The Housatonic River flows through pleasant countryside.

Massachusetts and neighboring Connecticut are probably not states that an outsider would visit solely for canoe voyaging. Exceptions are Connecticut River voyageurs passing through on their way to Long Island Sound from points in Vermont and New Hampshire.

MICHIGAN

Here, Ernest Hemingway learned to hunt, fish, and canoe. There are canoeable streams throughout the state, but the real outback lies along the Upper Peninsula and the upper portion of the "Hand."

Many Michigan waterways, as many as Maine or Minnesota, are described in a booklet published by the state (see Appendix V).

MINNESOTA

Once known as Minnay Sotor, this mis-called "state of 10,000 lakes" (it has almost 15,000) is canoe country par excellence. There are also 15,000 miles of river canoe trails.

Here, too, is the 2,000,000-acre Superior National Forest, and 1,036,000 acres are reserved for canoes alone. No airplanes, no stink of trail bikes, outboard motors, and best of all, no water skiers.

A major voyage through this country is the 235-mile International Boundary route with 9 miles of portages. This route, which starts at Grand Portage, requires a minimum of three weeks. Better allow four weeks.

This superb canoeing wilderness is abutted by Ontario's Quetico Provincial Park.

Minnesota rivers are too numerous to mention within our allotted space, but two particularly fine ones are the Vermilion and the Kawishi. A special booklet is available on the famed Crow Wing Canoe Trail.

NEW HAMPSHIRE

This is mostly short, sporty, springtime white water country. There is a section of the Androscoggin below Berlin suitable for voyaging. The Connecticut River rises in northern New Hampshire and forms the Vermont-New Hampshire border for about 230 miles.

NEW JERSEY

This is not a state one would travel a few hundred miles to solely for voyaging, but New York City area residents can practice paddle dipping in Garden State streams.

The Delaware River, jointly owned by New Jersey and Pennsylvania, provides a 180-mile voyage from Hancock, N.Y., to Camden, N.J.

Overnight cruises might include:

Toms River: 20 miles from Holmeson to Toms River (town).

Wading River: 25 miles from Chatsworth to tidewater (Great Bay).

Great Egg River: 35 miles from Braddock to tidewater (Great Bay).

Ramapo River: 20 miles from Suffern, N.Y. to Two Bridges on the Passaic River.

Hackensack River: 20 miles from New Bridge to Newark Bay.

Raritan River, south branch: 16 miles from Flemington Jct. to Somerville: usually too low after mid-July.

Ranacos River: 25 miles from Brown's Mills to Delaware River (near Riverside).

The pleasantest short New Jersey cruise is Millstone River: 32 miles from Princeton to Bound Brook on the Raritan River. Continue on Raritan to New Brunswick. Portage to Delaware-Raritan Canal. Return to Princeton.

NEW YORK STATE

Except for the prime canoe country of Maine, Minnesota, and Florida, New York State, notably in the Adirondack Forest Preserve, offers some of this nation's finest canoe routes. These are but a few hours' drive from any point within the Boston-Washington complex. Take I-87, the Northway, north from Albany.

The New York State Department of Environmental Conservation has established a series of Adirondack Forest Preserve Canoe Routes, complete with campsites including lean-tos and tent sites.

Recommended canoe routes have some alternate sections.

Detailed description of these routes is included in *Adirondack Canoe Routes* (see Appendix VI).

Major routes include: Fulton Chain, Raquette (Snowshoe Lake), Long Lake, Tupper Lake, and Saranac Lake.

The Department of Environmental Conservation publishes a list of boat liveries where canoes can be rented. Arrangements can also be made for returning canoes to the liveries.

The Upper Hudson River provides good camping areas and whitewater running.

In the fall of 1972 the Old Town Canoe Company, Old Town, Maine, published an interesting booklet detailing a 100-odd-mile, five-day journey made around the waters of New York City by six men in three canoes.

History-minded voyageurs might try the Mohawk River, which courses the entire state in the north-south regions.

TENNESSEE

This is the best canoeing state in the south. The 117-mile-long voyage along the Buffalo River is probably the state's most scenic canoe voyage or float trip. Superb smallmouth bass, bream, and channel cat fishing is to be found early in the morning and in the evening.

Put in at Henryville Bridge (1 mile east of Henryville on County Rd. #6230). The voyage ends at Link Bridge or Buzzard Cave on Duck River 3 miles from the mouth of the Buffalo River.

The Tennessee is a major American river, but there are too many motorboats.

VERMONT

Vermont streams east of the Green Mountains are largely whitewater streams with short runs during spring high water. Two streams cut through the mountains, the Lamoille and the Winooski. West of the mountains is the Big Otter (sometimes called Otter Creek) that provides nearly 100 miles of mostly flatwater voyaging. It is the state's longest river. Canoe voyages of several days' duration can be made on the Lamoille and Winooski.

Physically, Vermont and New Hampshire share about 230 miles of the 400-mile-long Connecticut River, but legally the river belongs to New Hampshire. The upper sections of the river have excellent rips and some

Wisconsin waterways.

good runs. Downstream there are several short portages. This is a fine canoeing stream.

WISCONSIN

A voyageur could spend a lifetime of canoeing vacations in this state and never retrace his route.

The state has at least 48 major canoe routes all of which are described in *Wisconsin Water Trails* (see Appendix VI). Notable routes include:

> *Manitowish River Trail:* High Lake to Rest Lake via more than a half-dozen lakes.
>
> *Rock River Trail:* Highway 49 to Illinois state line.
>
> *Yahara River Trail:* Through Madison's famed four lakes.
>
> *Peshtigo River Trail:* Highway C to Green Bay provides wilderness and white water along with leisurely paddling.

Fox River Trail: From Portage to Wolf River covers routes of the old fur traders and voyageurs.

Wolf River Trail: Post Lake to Shawano is considered the state's best whitewater voyage.

25
Quetico-Superior Country

But I don't want to leave. I'll always remember this place and long for it a little. Islands of gold and green. the wind in great branches, an owl's call in the rainy dusk, the scent of our wood smoke drifting across the moonlight. It will be like a lost kingdom. . . . I should very much like to live here forever. It's sorcery. It's not our world at all: it's like another star.

 —Florence Page Jacques, *Canoe Country*

Northwest of Lake Superior and southwest of Lake of the Woods lies one of the world's great canoe regions. It is a wilderness upon which no houses or roads can be built, and throughout its southern portion, motorboats are not allowed. This is a wilderness, but we consider it semiwilderness, at least through the summer months, as up to 100,000 canoeists take to its water trails. Fortunately for those of us who enjoy solitude, there are lakes and rivers which the great lovers of togetherness avoid.

Quetico lies within Ontario's Quetico Provincial Park. The southern section, the northern part of Superior National Forest, is the Boundary Waters Canoe

Area (B.W.C.A.). The combined area of more than 2,000,000 acres contains thousands of lakes tied together by streams and rivers—enough canoe routes to last more than one man's lifetime. There is no air pollution. You can drink from the rivers and lakes. Rigid regulations prevent the region from becoming a garbage dump.

First trippers have no cause to worry. The portages are well marked. Special area maps note the locations of rapids. You don't even have to portage, though you'll be missing a unique experience, but can spend your holiday exploring a lake. Lac La Croix has more than 250 islands, and there are others with similar numbers. Many of these islands provide camping sites. You can stay on the beaten trails or you can fare forth into more remote areas where you are unlikely to meet your fellow man.

You can come to the Quetico-Superior with nothing but your credit cards or cash. Local outfitters and shops will supply clothes, footgear, canoe, and all canoe gear. If you don't know how to canoe, the outfitters will provide an afternoon's instruction. That will be adequate for a fortnight's voyage. You'll be an advanced canoeist, though not necessarily expert, when you return from the wilderness.

Some voyageurs confine their canoeing to either Quetico or Superior, but most cover at least some of both areas during their voyage. Our last voyage through Quetico—we left from Ely—covered about 135 miles in Canada and about 10 miles in the United States.

The two areas, though in different countries, have similar regulations. A major difference is that outboard motors are allowed in Quetico but not in the B.W.C.A. The Border Lakes, on both sides, allow power boats. The use of outboards in Quetico is not as prevalent as might be expected. Many voyageurs are unwilling or have no desire to portage, with a motor, into the remote lakes.

U.S. citizens must check with both Canadian Customs and Immigration when entering Canada. You do not have to check through Canadian Customs or Immigration upon your return to Minnesota, but do have to clear U.S. Customs and Immigration in Ely upon your return to the States. Have identification with you.

Dogs and cats can be taken into Canada or back into the U.S. provided that you have a veterinarian's certificate showing that the pet has been vaccinated against rabies within the past twelve months.

August has the best weather and the fewest bugs of the three main canoeing months. June is usually too buggy while July has fewer bugs and not as many voyageurs as August. May, September, and October have no bugs but some bad weather can be expected. These months do have one outstanding virtue: you meet fewer people.

Throughout the summer months, the days are warm and nights are comfortably cooler.

No firearms can be taken into Quetico. The state of Minnesota has jurisdiction over fish and game within B.W.C.A.

License Fees: Minnesota Nonresident Fishing: Individual (all season), $6.50. Husband and wife (all season), $10. Individual (3-day), $3. Ontario Nonresident Fishing: Individual (all season), $8.50; Individual (3-day), $4.

Strict rules govern the use of aircraft in the area. Landing places, save for emergencies, are limited to specified areas. Write the regulatory agencies (addresses below) for current aircraft and motorboat regulations.

Writer's Quetico camp.

QUETICO

U.S. residents enter Quetico from the B.W.C.A. or from the north. The park's main entrance (you can reach it by car) is Dawson Trail (off Highway 11). There is road access to the park (headquarters are here) at Nym Lake. One lake (Batchewaung) must be crossed and two portages made before the park itself is reached.

Beaverhouse Lake and La Croix Cabin are two major entry points by water from the Canadian side.

Voyageurs arriving by water from the U.S. must check into the country and the park at: Cache Bay, Saganaga Lake; Ottawa Island, western Basswood Lake; Prairie Portage, eastern Basswood Lake; or Sandpoint Lake. These four stations issue park travel permits. Also located at these sites are Canadian Customs and Immigration Stations (see below).

Canadian Customs

Whether you enter Canada from B.W.C.A. or through any regular port of entry you are subject to the following duties:

Food: First two days free and 20 percent duty thereafter. This averages about 40 cents per person per day.

There is no duty on your camping or sporting equipment. It is assumed that you will return with it.

Park Fees: Canoeists enter Quetico at entry points listed above. There is a daily fee of $2 per day per canoe. For periods of ten days or more the flat rate is $20 per canoe.

Information

Voyageurs entering Quetico from Canada can secure additional information about the park and its routes and regulations by writing:

The Park Supt.
Quetico Provincial Park,
Dept. of Lands and Forests
Atikokan, Ontario

Ask for the following free publications: "Quetico Provincial Park," "Canoe Routes through Quetico," and Quetico map.

Information on Canadian-side outfitters can be secured from:

Atikokan Chamber of Commerce
Atikokan, Ontario

Fort Frances Chamber of Commerce
Fort Frances, Ontario

Thunder Bay Chamber of Commerce
Thunder Bay, Ontario

The Quetico Foundation, a nonprofit organization devoted to preserving Quetico's wilderness, also has information. Write:

Quetico Foundation
Suite 305
200 Bay Street
Toronto, Ontario

BOUNDARY WATERS CANOE AREA

This northern section of Superior National Forest is administered by the U.S. Forest Service, which issues free permits to voyageurs. Roving rangers check campers to see if they are violating regulations such as illegal campsites, litter, or illegal containers (see below).

Current (April, 1973) regulations:

Obey all state laws and regulations (notably concerning hunting and fishing).

Leave a clean campsite.

Do not pollute lakes and streams.

Burn all combustible garbage. Pack out unburnable items.

Use cord instead of nails and wire (saves trees).

Obtain firewood away from campsite and back from the lake (or stream) shore.

The use of firearms is discouraged. Use your camera. Firearms are not illegal, but there is no legal hunting during the usual canoeing months of June, July, and August.

No disposable containers, including bottles and tins, can be brought into the Boundary Waters Canoe Area.

One party per campsite; no more than 15 campers per site. (That's too many, in our opinion.)

Whenever possible, select an existing campsite where it is not necessary to clear additional brush or trees. It is illegal to cut live trees or brush (including boughs for the obsolete bough bed).

Build fires only at fireproofed sites. (The Forest Service provides fireplaces at many campsites). When leaving or breaking camp make sure fire is *out*. Drown it.

Some U.S. Forest Service campsites are outfitted with tables, fireplaces, and latrines. This is to reduce the cutting of live trees and to ensure that human waste doesn't seep into the lake or river.

The basic source of Boundary Waters Canoe Area information can be obtained from:

Supervisor, Superior National Forest,

Box 338

Duluth, Minn. 55801

Free camping permits can usually be secured through your outfitter from the Voyageur Visitor, Ely, Minn., or from one of the following district ranger offices (all addresses are in Minn.): Aurora, Cook, Ely, Tofte, Grand Marais, Two Harbors, Isabella, and Virginia.

Write Forest Supervisor, Duluth, Minn. for following (free) material: "Boundary Waters Canoe Area," "Canoeing-Camping in the Boundary Waters Canoe Area," and large multicolored map.

OUTFITTERS

Centrally located Ely, Minn., is the prime outfitting place and most popular point of departure for the Quetico-Superior canoe country. Toward the western end of the region lies Crane Lake and at the eastern end is Grand Marais. For information, write:

Ely Chamber of Commerce
Ely, Minn.

Crane Lake Chamber of Commerce
Crane Lake, Minn.

Grand Marais Chamber of Commerce
Grand Marais, Minn.

The chamber of commerce will supply you with a list of local outfitters and accommodations that you'll need for the eve of your departure.

Superior National Forest and Quetico Provincial Park have automobile campsites.

Voyageurs who have outfitted in the Quetico-Superior country are spoiled when it comes to outfitters in other areas. Our personal experience has been confined to Canadian Waters. We were very satisfied.

It is not necessary to bring your canoe, camping outfit, or food. These outfitters for a daily per-person fee ($10–14) supply canoe, paddles, life preservers, packs, sleeping bags, tent, cooking and basic camp gear plus lightweight foods. Lower rates are available for groups.

If your time is very limited, they will fly you to a remote area and you can return via canoe to the home base.

Outfitters like Waters feed you and put you up overnight at the beginning and end of your voyage. They have facilities to stow your valuables and will issue for a few cents per day a policy covering the canoe and camp gear.

About 100,000 voyageurs utilize the Quetico-Superior area every summer. It is surprising how many folk show up for a wilderness voyage without ever having been canoeing or camping. Instructors can provide the basic canoeing techniques in one afternoon.

You can bring your own canoe and camp gear and pick up your food from the outfitter or bring your own gear and food and rent a canoe. Many people just fly in with a few basic items of clothing and rent the entire outfit including canoe, food, and camp gear.

Ely outfitters suggest you bring the following items, or buy them in Ely:

> Hiking boots
> Wool socks
> Tennis shoes or moccasins
> Chino trousers
> Wool shirt
> Swimming trunks
> Light rain shirt
> Brimmed hat
> Sun glasses
> Sunburn lotion
> Toilet kit
> Flashlight
> Basic first-aid kit
> Camera and film
> Fishing tackle
> Compass
> Towel and washcloth

Some Notes on Outfitters

Lightweight freeze-dried foods are packed in Duluth packs. One week's food supply to a pack. Outfitters, unless requested, do not include breakfast for the first day or dinner for the seventh day. These meals are usually eaten the morning of your departure and the evening of your return at your outfitting point. We usually bring our own grub but on those occasions when we use an outfitter's prepacked food bags, we ask them to include the two extra meals. They may come in handy if you get windbound.

Paddling and portaging make for heavy appetites. Outfitters want repeat business, so they pack an abundance of food. Left-over food belongs to you.

Outfitters like Canadian Waters send you a week's menu. You have certain options like tea, coffee, cocoa, etc.

Outfitters are much happier if you return your cooking pots free of soot. Be careful of the tent. Don't punch holes in it.

Your outfitter will help you plot a canoe route which they think is within your capacity. Many first-trippers are over-optimistic when it comes to estimating their daily mileage.

Canoe-country camping.

PARTIAL OUTFITTING

Voyageurs who do not wish to be completely outfitted can rent on a daily basis any item including a canoe. These are the 1973 daily rental fees of one outfitter. It is quite possible that subsequent rates will be
slightly higher.

Item		*Daily rate*
Grumman aluminum canoe— standard weight		$6.00
Grumman aluminum canoe— light weight		7.00
Alumacraft Quetico canoe		6.00
Johnson Sea Horse motors 2 HP		3.50
Johnson Sea Horse motors 4 HP		5.00
Canoe carrying yoke	furnished	.50
Paddle	free with	.20
Car top canoe carrier	canoe	.50
Platform portage wheel		2.00
Packsack		.60
Gas pack (5 gal. capacity)	furnished	.60
Gasoline can (2½ gal.)	free with	.20
Gasoline can (5 gal. fits gas pack)	motor	.35
Tarp—10′ x 10′		.85
Tents:		
6 x 7 (2 people)		2.50
7½ x 9 (3 people)		3.50
8 x 10½ (4 people)		4.50
9 x 12 (5–6 people)		5.50
Sleeping bag with liner—single		1.00
Sleeping bag with liner—double (for two people)		2.00
Foam sleeping bag		.50

Poncho	.35
Camp saw	.35
Camp shovel	.35
Gas lantern—with carrying case	1.00
Gas stove—	
1-burner	.50
2-burner	1.00
Reflector oven with baking pan	.75
Aluminum griddle	.35
Fireplace grate:	
small	.35
medium	.45
large	.60
Life jacket or cushion	.50

Rates for the following are based upon a per-person-per-day charge:

Cooking kit–complete with pots, pans, cups, plates, silverware, can opener, and other utensils	.75
Ultra-light food supplies	5.00

Rates subject to Minnesota sales tax.

A deposit of $10 per canoe is required for reservation of equipment on a partial outfitting basis. All rental charges computed on calendar-day basis.

MAPS

No other canoe country with which we are familiar has such an abundance of maps as the Quetico-Superior country.

Before going into detailed section maps, we suggest you purchase two overall maps:

Quetico-Superior map (sometimes called the Minnesota-Canadian Wilderness Map). Size: 21x34 inches. Scale: 1 inch = 3 miles. Price: $1. Printed on water-resistant paper. W. A. Fisher Co., publisher. This map gives an overall view of the Quetico-Superior region. Use this map for planning your overall route.

Quetico Provincial Park map. Size: 30x40 inches. Scale: Portage lengths in yards. Price: $1. This map, printed on non-water-resistant paper, is an excellent choice for planning a route that includes only Quetico Provincial Park.

Once you have decided on your overall route (your outfitter may suggest reasonable changes) the next step is to procure detailed sectional maps of your proposed route. A set of 15 maps covers the region. You probably won't need more than three or four. Size: 17x22 inches. Scale: ⅝th inch = 1 mile. Price: 35 cents per sheet. Maps are printed on water-resistant paper. Portages show on roads. W. A. Fisher Co., publisher.

Map Designations

The above maps include:
101 West Rainy Lake
102 East Rainy-Kabetogma Lakes
103 Beaverhouse-Quetico Lakes
104 Jean-Pickerel Lakes
105 MacKenzie-Upper Shebandowan Lakes
106 Lower Shebandowan Lake
107 Crane-Sand Point-La Croix Lakes
108 Crooked-Agnes Lakes
109 Seagull-Saganaga-Northern Lights Lakes
110 Arrow-Rose-Mountain Lakes
111 Vermilion-Trout Lakes
112 Burntside-Basswood Lakes
113 Moose-Knife-Insula Lakes
114 Lakes adjacent to the Gunflint Trail
115 North-South Fowl Lakes-Pigeon River

Border Lakes Maps

The chain of border lakes—the Grand Portage route of the voyageurs—has been surveyed by the U.S. Corps of Engineers. Size: 17x22 inches. Scale: 1 inch = ¾ mile. Anyone contemplating a voyage which includes any of the border lakes should obtain these maps. Price: $1. Portages are given in yards. Rapids are shown in considerable detail. Contour lines are given for areas along lake and river banks.

Any voyageur going up or down the Basswood River should purchase a special map for this river. The Corps of Engineers map measures 17x22 inches. It is very detailed. 1 inch = ⅙ mile (6 inches = 1 mile).

The most commonly used Corps of Engineers maps (plus Basswood River) are:

> Eastern Basswood Lake
> Western Basswood Lake
> Crooked Lake
> La Croix
> Knife Lake
> Saganaga Lake

U.S. Geological Survey topographical maps show the usual topographic features plus most portages and some campsites. Most maps are 1:24,000 scale (3 inches = 1 mile). Size: 22x27 inches. Price, 75 cents. The following sheets are available:

> Alice Lake
> Angleworm Lake
> Astrid Lake
> Coleman Island
> Crab Lake
> Dutton Lake
> Ely
> Ester Lake

Fourtown Lake
Friday Bay
Iron Lake
Kawishiwi Lake
Kebekabic Lake
Lake Agnes
Lake Jeanette
Lapond Lake
Ogishkemmuncie Lake
Perent Lake
Shagawa Lake
Shell Lake
Snow Lake
Takucmich Lake

Four topographical maps have a smaller scale—1:62,500, or about 1 inch = 1 mile. Size: 17x21 inches. Price: 75 cents.

Basswood Lake
Ensign Lake
Forest Center
Gabbro Lake

Map Notes

Canadian and American maps showing Quetico do not show Quetico campsites. Fisher, U.S. Geological Survey, and some Corps of Engineers maps show campsites on the American side.

We use U.S. Geological Survey maps as our base maps and add details from other maps. If we ever had to walk out we would know what the terrain was between ourselves and civilization. Fisher maps do not show terrain details (other than lakes and rivers). We also take along Corps of Engineers maps when traveling through the Border Lakes.

The above maps can be obtained from the Pack-sack Press, Box 177, Winton, Minn. 55796, or from Canadian Waters, Inc., Sheridan St., Ely, Minn. Fisher maps can also be obtained from the W. A. Fisher Co., Virginia, Minn.

If you plan to use U.S. Geological Survey topographical maps, it would be wise to secure Fisher's sectional maps. These are updated annually.

Canadian Topographical Maps

Maps with the scale of 2 inches = 1 mile or 4 inches = 1 mile can be obtained from the Map Distribution Center, Department of Mines and Technical Surveys, Ottawa, Ontario. Write for descriptive list and current prices.

BOOKS ABOUT QUETICO-SUPERIOR COUNTRY

Anonymous: "Canoeing from Ely," Packsack Press, Winton, Minn. (current). This eight-page mimeographed sheet is useful to anyone canoeing or planning to canoe from Ely. 50 cents.

Anonymous: *Auto Campgrounds of the Superior National Forest,* Packsack Press, Winton, Minn. (current). Includes U.S. Forest Service map of the area. $2.25.

Bolz, Dr. Arnold: *Portage into the Past,* University of Minnesota Press, St. Paul, Minn., 1959. Interesting quotations and background of the voyageurs and explorers. Details from author's 1957 voyage along the Grand Portage-Rainy Lake Route. $5.00.

Coatsworth, Emerson S.: *The Indians of Quetico*, A Quetico Foundation Publication. Distributed by the University of Toronto Press, 1957. $2.50. Interesting reading for Quetico voyageurs.

Denis, Keith: *Canoe Trails Through Quetico*. A Quetico Foundation publication. Distributed by the University of Toronto Press, Toronto, Ont., 1959. A must book for all voyageurs. Paperback, $3.50.

Dewdney, Selwyn, and Kidd, K. E.: *Indian Rock Paintings, Great Lakes.* A Quetico Foundation publication. Distributed by the University of Toronto Press, Toronto, Ont., 1957. This is the authoritative book on the paintings found throughout the Quetico-Superior area. $6.75.

Fisher, Mark: *Quetico-Superior Canoeist's Handbook,* Packsack Press, Winton, Minn., (current). Useful for first trippers $1.95.

Jacques, Florence Page: *Canoe Country*, University of Minnesota Press, Minneapolis, 1938. (7th printing, 1967.) This delightful book evokes many images of the Quetico of some thirty-five years ago. Illustrated by writer's husband, Francis Lee Jacques. $4.50.

———— *Snowshoe Country,* University of Minnesota Press, Minneapolis, Minn., 1944. Quetico-Superior country by snowshoe and dog sled. $5.00.

Litteljohn, Bruce M.: *Quetico-Superior Country.* Paperback. This is a reprint of two Canadian Geographical Journal articles. Ontario Foundation Suite 305, 200 Bay St., Toronto, Ont. $1.50.

Meen, V. B.: *Quetico Geology,* A Quetico Foundation publication. Distributed by the University of Toronto Press, Toronto, Ont., 1959, $2.50.

Morse, Eric V.: *Canoe Routes of the Voyageurs*, Minnesota Historical Society, St. Paul, Minn., 1962. One of Canada's most experienced and knowledgeable modern voyageurs provides data on the ancient routes of today's canoe country. $1.75.

Nute, Dr. Grace Lee: *The Voyageur*, Appleton Century, N.Y., 1931. (Now reprinted by the Minnesota Historical Society, St. Paul, Minn.) This is the fascinating story of the great voyageurs and explorers through the Quetico-Superior country. A must for the romantic and history-minded voyageur. $5.00.

_____ *Rainy Lake Country*, Minnesota Historical Society, St. Paul, Minn., 1950. $3.50.

_____ *The Voyageurs' Highway*, Minnesota Historical Society, St. Paul, Minn., 1941. $3.50.

Appendices
Appendix I:
Canoe Manufacturers

There are at least 75 canoe manufacturers in the U.S. and Canada. To list all of these makers would only confuse prospective purchasers. There were only a few manufacturers in the days when wood-and-canvas, or Peterborough types were just about all that was available. The manufacture of such craft required skill and craftsmanship. The advent of aluminum and plastics brought many new firms into the field. Many were drafting board nightmares and some are even dangerous in their design. Their advertising was and still is dangerously misleading.

We have deliberately excluded those makers.

We have also deliberately excluded some others because they specialize in whitewater canoes. Many of these highly specialized canoes are not suitable for canoe camping and voyaging. This doesn't mean that many fine cruising canoes like those by Old Town, Chestnut, Grumman, and Alumacraft's Quetico model are not adequate for canoeing white water, as opposed to whitewater canoeing, the highly competitive sport.

The writer has used and found satisfactory those products marked with an asterisk (*). This does not imply that products by other manufacturers may not be adequate.

Aluminum Canoes

Aluma Craft Boat Co.* (Quetico canoe)
Div. of Alpex Corp.
1551 Central Ave., N.E.
Minneapolis, Minn. 55413

Chestnut Canoe Co.,
Fredericton, New Brunswick

Grumman Boats,*
Grumman Allied Industries,
Marathon, N.Y. 13803

Lund Boat Co.,
P.O. Box 10,
New York Mills,
Minn. 56567

Mirror Aluminum Co.,
1516 Washington St.,
Manitowoc, Wis. 54220

Fiberglass Canoes

Chestnut Canoe Co.,
Fredericton, New Brunswick

Chicagoland Canoe Base,
4019 North Narragansett Ave.,
Chicago, Ill. 60634

Industrial Fibreglass Products,
Ludington, Mich. 49431

Mountain Ash Fibreglass Co.,
Hudson N.Y. 12534

Old Town Canoe Co.,*
Old Town, Maine 04468

Riverside Fibreglass Canoe Co.,
Box 5595
Riverside, Calif. 92502

Royalex Canoes

Old Town Canoe Co.,*
Old Town, Maine 04468

Wood-and-Canvas Canoes

Chestnut Canoe Co.,*
Fredericton, New Brunswick

Old Town Canoe Co.,*
Old Town, Maine 04468

Appendix II:
Camp Equipment Sources

Key

A—Manufacturers of quality sleeping bags, packs, tents, clothing, etc.
B—General outfitters supplying their own products or products by other manufacturers like stoves, cook kits, food containers, etc.

Some manufacturers like Gerry offer catalogs but do not sell by mail. Their catalogs, however, usually list retailers by state. Voyageurs not handily located can order by mail from outfitters like Eastern Mountain Sports who stock a wide variety of sleeping bags, packs and about everything you might need.

Alpine Designs—A
    (formerly Alp Sport)
3245 Prairie Ave.,
P.O. Box 1081,
Boulder, Colo. 80302

Eddie Bauer—B
417 East Pine St.,
Seattle, Wash. 98122

L. L. Bean—B
Freeport, Maine 04032
(packbaskets)

Thomas Black & Sons—A,B
930 Ford St.,
Odensburg, N.Y. 13669

Thomas Black & Sons—A,B
225 Strathcona Ave.,
Ottawa, Ontario
(high-quality British products)

Camp Trails—A
3920 West Clarendon Ave.,
Phoenix, Ariz. 85109
(no sleeping bags)

Charles Orvis—B
Manchester, Vt.,
(waterproof camera bags & mfrs. of fine fish-
    ing tackle)

Coleman Products—A,B
Wichita, Kansas
(retail outlets only—widely available—noted
    for stoves & lanterns—most tents and
    sleeping bags designed for car campers)

Colorado Outdoor Sports Corp.—A,B
P.O. Box 5544,
Denver, Colorado 80217
(Gerry products)

Eastern Mountain Sports—B
1041 Commonwealth Ave.,
Boston, Mass. 02215

Gokey Company—B
21 West 5th,
St. Paul, Minn. 55102
(snake-proof boots)

Herter's, Inc.—A,B
Rural Route 1,
Waseca, Minn. 56093
(just about everything)

Hudson's Bay Co.,—B
Hudson's Bay House,
Winnipeg, Manitoba
(You can buy supplies and reoutfit at most

any HBCo. post. They also make the famed post blankets and distribute spirits in the States including a fine 151 proof rum.)

Pacific Tent—A
P.O. Box 2028
Fresno, Calif. 93721

P. & S. Sales,—B
P.O. Box 155
Tulsa, Okla. 74101
(war surplus)

Recreational Equipment, Inc.,—B
1525 11th Ave.,
Seattle, Wash. 98122
(a cooperative)

Seattle Tent and Fabric Products Co.—B
900 North 137th St.,
Seattle, Wash. 98133

Sierra Designs—A
4th and Addison Sts.,
Berkeley, Calif. 94710

Skihaus of Vermont—B
Middlebury, Vt., 05753

Ski Hut—A,B
1615 University Ave.,
Berkeley, Calif. 94703
(Trailwise products)

Smilie Company—B
575 Howard St.,
San Francisco, Calif. 94105
(classic canoe country cook pots)

Waters, Inc.—B
Sheridan St.,
Ely, Minn. 55731
(a major source for canoe and camp gear)

Kitchen roll	1
Fire Ribbon	5
Kitchen two-tined fork	4
Reflector, oven (rarely used)	16
Aluminum plate	5
Coleman lantern	62
Lantern case	48
Insulated cup, 12-ounce	2
Fork and spoon set	2½
Flip pot cleaners	5

Personal Gear

Item	Ounces
Mallory flashlight (AA) with batteries	3½
Batteries (AA), 2 spare	1½
Mallory flashlight (C) with batteries	6 or 7½
Batteries (C), 2 spare	4½
Nylon parachute cord, 550-pound test, 50 feet	3
Plastic jug, 2½-gallon	5
Anti-bug dope	2
Lip salve	1
Anti-sunburn lotion	1
Snakebite kit	3
Sheath knife	7
Sheath	3
Stone	1
Complete	11
Binoculars (7x50)	23
Case	12
Monoculars (8x30)	8
Case	3
Sven saw	16
Axe	74
Sheath	3
Adhesive tape, 2-inch, without cover	4
Toilet kit	8
Toilet tissue	6
Bandannas (2)	1
Band-Aids (6)	1
Aspirin	1

Candle lantern, round	5
Candle lantern, flat	7
Candles	1 (each)

Bedroll

Item	*Ounces*
Sleeping bag	50
Shorty foam pad	18
Long foam pad	50
Single shell	11
Double shell	23
Sleeping bag stuffsack	5½

Appendix V:
Information Sources for
U.S.A. and Canada

This section includes some local and national information sources. Agencies known to have specific canoe-trip publications are marked with an asterisk. States listed but with no asterisk either have no specific canoe trip information or material may be in preparation.

Alaska: Dept. of Economic Development, Alaska Travel Div., Pouch E, Juneau 99801

Alberta: Government Travel Bureau, 1629 Centennial Bldg., Edmonton*

Arkansas: Publicity & Parks Commission, 412 State Capitol Bldg., Little Rock 72001*

British Columbia: Dept. of Travel Industry, Parliament Bldg., Victoria*; Canadian Government Travel Bureau, 150 Kent St., Ottawa, Ontario*

Connecticut: State Park & Forest Commission, Hartford 06115

District of Columbia: National Capitol Region, National Park Serv., 1100 Ohio Dr., S.W. Washington, D.C. 20242

Florida: Development Commission, 107 West Gaines St., Tallahassee 32304

Georgia: Dept. of State Parks,
7 Hunter St., S.W., Atlanta 30334

Illinois: Dept. of Conservation, Boating Section
State Office Bldg., Springfield 62706*

Indiana: Dept. of Natural Resources, Division of Water,
609 State Office Bldg., Indianapolis 46204

Iowa: Conservation Commission,
East 7th & Court Ave., Des Moines 50309*

Kentucky: Dept. of Public Information,
Division of Tourist & Travel, Capitol Annex Bldg.,
Frankfort 40601*

Maine: Forestry Dept., Augusta 04330;
Dept. of Economic Development,

State House, Augusta 04330*;
Park & Recreational Commission,
State House, Augusta 04330*
(Allagash Wilderness Waterway & Baxter State Park)

Manitoba: Dept. of Tourism & Recreation,
Tourist Bureau, Norway Bldg., Winnipeg*

Maryland: Dept. of Forests & Parks,
State Office Bldg., Annapolis 21404

Massachusetts: Dept. of Natural Resources,
Div. of Parks & Forests,
100 Cambridge St., Boston 02202

Michigan: Dept. of Conservation,
Stevens T. Mason Bldg., Lansing 48926*

Minnesota: Dept. of Business Development,
State Capitol, St. Paul 55101*

Missouri: Commerce & Industrial Development,
803 Jefferson Bldg., Jefferson City 65101

Montana: Advertising Dept.,
State Highway Commission, Helena 59601

New Brunswick: Travel Bureau,
Box 1030, Fredericton*

Newfoundland & Labrador: Tourist Development Office,
Confederation Bldg., St. John's*

New Hampshire: Dept. of Economic Development,
Concord 03301*

New Jersey: Dept. of Conservation & Economic Development,
520 East St., Trenton 08609*

New York: State Conservation Dept.,
State Campus, Albany 12226*

Northwest Territories: Tourist Office,
400 Laurier Ave. West, Ottawa, Ontario*

Ohio: Dept. of Natural Resources,
1500 Dublin Road, Columbus 43212*

Ontario: Dept. of Tourism & Information,
185 Bloor St., East, Toronto*

Oregon: State Highway Dept.,
Travel Information Division, Salem 97310

Pennsylvania: Dept. of Forests & Waters,
State Capitol Bldg., Harrisburg 17101

Quebec: Dept. of Tourism, Fish & Game,
12 Ste Anne St., Quebec City*

Quetico Provincial Park: Attn. The Superintendent,
Dept. of Natural Resources, Atikokan, Ontario*

Saskatchewan: Tourist Development Bureau,
Power Bldg., Regina*

Tennessee: Dept. of Conservation,
Division of State Parks, 2611 West End Ave.,
Nashville 37203*

Texas: Parks & Wildlife Dept.,
John H. Reagan Bldg., Austin 78701

Vermont: State Board of Recreation,
Montpelier 05601;
Dept. of Forests & Parks,
Montpelier 05602

Virginia: Dept. of Conservation & Economic
Development,
911 East Broad St., Richmond 23219*;
Commission of Game & Inland Fisheries,
P.O. Box 1642, Richmond 23213*

Washington: State Parks & Recreation
Commission,
522 South Franklin,
Olympia 98501

Wisconsin: Conservation Dept.,
Box 450, Madison 53701

Wyoming: Travel Commission,
2320 Capitol Ave., Cheyenne 82001;
Bureau of Land Management, Dept. of
Interior,
318 P.O. Bldg., Lander 82520

Yukon Territory: Dept. of Travel &
Publicity,
Box 2703, Whitehorse*

Appendix VI:
Guidebooks for U.S.A. and Canada

This list contains state, provincial, and regional publications, and some privately published ones, currently available about our canoeing rivers. F = Free.

ALASKA

Anonymous: *Alaska's Gulkana Basin* (F); *Alaska's Gulkana Float Trips* (F); Bureau of Land Management, P.O. Box 2511, Juneau, Alaska. 99801.

Anonymous: *Swan Lake Canoe Route Map,* Bureau of Sport Fisheries, U.S. Fish and Wildlife Service, P.O. Box 500, Kenai, Alaska. 99611 (F)

BRITISH COLUMBIA

Anonymous: *Lake Bowron Provincial Park,* Parks Branch, Dept. of Recreation and Conservation, Parliament Bldg., Victoria, B.C. (F)

CONNECTICUT

Canoe Guidebook Committee: *A.M.C. New England Canoeing Guide,* Appalachian

Mountain Club, Boston, Mass. 1971, $6.00. Best detailed coverage of Conn. rivers.

CONNECTICUT RIVER

Anonymous: *Canoeing on the Connecticut River,* Vermont State Board of Recreation and Water Resources Dept., Montpelier, Vt. 1964. (F). Covers in detail the Connecticut River from the Vt.–P.Q. frontier to the Vt.–Mass. border. Divided into nine sections, each with its own map. This should be used in conjunction with the *A.M.C. New England Canoeing Guide.*

Anonymous: *Down River,* New England Electric System, 20 Turnpike Rd., Westborough, Mass. 01581. (F). A pleasant canoe voyage down the Connecticut from Pittsburgh Landing, N.H., to French King Bridge, Mass.

Anonymous: *Welcome to the Happy Valley,* New England Electric System, 20 Turnpike Rd., Westborough, Mass. 01581. (F) Useful data on Connecticut River recreation.

Canoe Guidebook Committee: *A.M.C. New England Canoeing Guide,* Appalachian Mountain Club, Boston, Mass. 1971, $6.00. Most detailed account of Connecticut from source to its mouth. Should be supplemented by *Canoeing on the Connecticut River.*

Foster, Elmer R.: *Connecticut River Guide,* Connecticut River Watershed Council, 497 Main St., Greenfield, Mass. 01301. $2.00. Another must for Connecticut River voyageurs.

ILLINOIS

Anonymous: *Illinois Canoeing Guide,* Boat Section, Illinois Dept. of Conservation, Springfield, Ill. (F)

INDIANA

Anonymous: *Canoe Trails in Indiana.* Dept. of Conservation, 612 State Office Bldg., Indianapolis, Ind. 46209 (F)

IOWA

Anonymous: *Iowa Canoe Trips,* Iowa Conservation Dept., East 7th and Courts Sta., Des Moines, Iowa. (F)

MAINE

Anonymous: *Allagash Wilderness Waterway*, Maine State Park and Recreation Commission, State House, Augusta, Maine 04330 (F)

Bearse, Ray: *Maine: A Guide to the Vacation State*, Houghton Mifflin Co., Boston, 1969. $7.95. A chapter devoted to Maine canoe trails. Book contains historical matter and legends of the cities and villages along Maine waterways.

Canoe Guidebook Committee: *A.M.C. New England Canoeing Guide,* Appalachian Mountain Club, Boston, Mass. 1971, $6.00. Best detailed coverage of Maine's lakes and rivers.

MASSACHUSETTS

Bearse, Ray: *Massachusetts: A Guide to the Pilgrim State*, Houghton Mifflin, Boston, Mass. 1971. $10.00. Contains history and legends of every Bay State town and city along its waterways.

Canoe Guidebook Committee: *A.M.C. New England Canoeing Guide*, Appalachian Mountain Club, Boston, Mass. 1971, $6.00. Best detailed coverage of Bay State's rivers.

MICHIGAN

Anonymous: *Michigan Canoe Trails*, Michigan Tourist Council, Steven D. Mason Bldg., Lansing, Mich. 48926 (F)

MINNESOTA

Anonymous: *Wilderness Crow Wing Canoe Trail.* Vacation Information Center, Dept. of Business Development, State Capitol, St. Paul., Minn. 55101. (F)

MISSOURI

Hawksley, Oz: *Missouri Ozark Waterways*, Div. of Commerce and Industry, Jefferson Bldg., Jefferson City, Mo. 65102. $1.00.

NEW BRUNSWICK

Anonymous: *Guide to Canoe Tripping in New Brunswick*, Parks Branch, Dept. of Natural Resources, Fredericton, N.B. (F) Describes highlights of 125 canoe routes.

NEW ENGLAND

Canoe Guidebook Committee, *A.M.C. New England Canoeing Guide*, Appalachian Mountain Club. (Three folding maps in end pockets.) Boston, Mass., 1971. $6.00. This is the third revised, much-enlarged edition of *Quick-Water and Smooth: A Canoeist's Guide to New England Rivers*, by John C. Phillips and Thomas D. Cabot (Stephen Daye Press, Brattleboro, Vt., 1935). This handy 600 pp. pocket-sized guide covers in detail more than 500 New England rivers. It is a must for any New England canoeist, voyageur or white water buff.

NEW HAMPSHIRE

Canoe Guidebook Committee: *A.M.C. New England Canoeing Guide*, Appalachian Mountain Club, Boston, Mass., 1971, $6.00. Best detailed coverage of New Hampshire rivers, including the Connecticut.

NEW JERSEY

Anonymous: *Canoe Runs in New Jersey*, N.J. Dept. of Conservation and Economic Development, Trenton, N.J. (F)

Cawley, James and Margaret: *Exploring the Little Rivers of New Jersey*. Rutgers University Press, New Brunswick, N.J. 1965. $4.50 (cloth) $1.95 (paper).

NEW YORK

Anonymous: *Adirondack Canoe Routes*, State of N.Y. Conservation Dept., Div. of Conservation Education, Albany, N.Y. 12226 (F).

Anonymous: *Lake George*, N.Y. State Dept. of Environmental Conservation, Albany, (F). Campsites, public-owned lands, etc.

Anonymous: *Public Campsites in the Forest Preserve Park Region*, State of N.Y. Dept. of Environmental Conservation, Albany, (F). The Adirondack Region.

Anonymous: *Public Use of the Forest Preserve*, N.Y. State Dept. of Environmental Conservation, Albany, (F). The Adirondack Region.

Anonymous: *Register of Guides,* State of N.Y. Dept. of Environmental Conservation, Albany, (F)

Grinell, Lawrence I.: *Canoeable Waters of New York State*, Pageant Press, N.Y. $5.00. Basic for New York State voyageurs.

OHIO

Anonymous: *Ohio Canoe Adventures*, Ohio Dept. of Natural Resources, Div. of Watercraft, Ohio Depts. Bldg., Columbus, Ohio. (F)

ONTARIO (Quetico Routes, see Chapter 25)

Anonymous: *Northern Ontario Canoe Routes*, Ontario Dept. of Lands & Forests, Queen's Park, Toronto, Ont. 50 cents. This 84-page book highlights 125 canoe routes.

Anonymous: *Southern Ontario/Quebec Canoe Routes*, Trent Publishing Co., Box 479, Lakefield, Ont. $5.50.

QUEBEC

Anonymous: *Les Parcs Du Quebec (Quebec Parks),* Tourist Branch, Parliament Bldgs., Quebec City, P.Q. (F). Secure this book and then write for maps and details of the parks you are interested in.

RHODE ISLAND

Canoe Guidebook Committee: *A.M.C. New England Canoeing Guide,* Appalachian Mountain Club, Boston, 1971. $6.00.

SASKATCHEWAN

This province publishes many comprehensive canoe guide books, all free. Write Saskatchewan Tourist Development Bureau, Power Bldg., Regina, Sas.

VERMONT

Bearse, Ray: *Vermont: A Guide to the Green Mountain State.* Houghton Mifflin, Boston, 1968. History and legends of the state's waterways.

Canoe Guidebook Committee: *A.M.C. New England Canoeing Guide.* Appalachian Mountain Club, Boston, Mass., 1971. $6.00. Detailed coverage of Vermont rivers.

WISCONSIN

Anonymous: *Wisconsin Waterways.* Wisconsin Tourist Office, Madison, Wis. n.d.

Appendix VII:
Map Sources for U.S.A. and Canada

U.S. topographical maps—"topos"—are available by mail from three basic sources:

Mississippi River (East)
Distribution Section
U.S. Geological Survey,
Washington, D.C. 20242

Mississippi River (West)
Distribution Section
U.S. Geological Survey,
Federal Center,
Denver, Colo. 80225

Alaska
U.S. Geological Survey,
520 Illinois St.,
Fairbanks, Alaska

Distribution sections supply free an index map of the state or states for which you wish topos.

Many local stores, usually stationers, carry topos for their particular state but when traveling from New York City to Minnesota or Maine your quickest source is the nearest USGS distribution center. Remember that government agencies, even good ones like USGS, are slow to respond, so don't wait two weeks before your holiday to order a state index.

The U.S. Corps of Engineers has maps of lakes and rivers with which Corps projects are related. The Corps has many regional offices. For the address covering the region you want to visit write:

Map Information Office,
U.S. Army Corps of Engineers,
Fort Belvoir, Va. 22060

For Great Lakes Area, including Boundary Waters Canoe Area, Superior National Forest, write:

U.S. Corps of Engineers
Box 1027,
Detroit, Mich. 48231

* Quetico-Superior map sources are listed in Chapter 25.

CANADIAN SOURCES

Map Distribution Center,
Dept. of Mines and Technical Surveys,
Ottawa, Ontario.
Free indexes showing available topographical maps. Yukon and Northwest Territorial maps can be obtained here.

PROVINCIAL MAPS

Director, Technical Division,
Dept. of Lands & Forests,
Edmonton, Alberta

Director, Surveys and Mapping,
Dept. of Lands and Forests,
Victoria, British Columbia

Director of Surveys,
Dept. of Mines and Natural Resources,
Winnipeg, Manitoba

Dept. of Lands and Mines,
Fredericton, New Brunswick

Dept. of Mines and Resources,
St. Johns, Newfoundland

Dept. of Mines,
Halifax, Nova Scotia

Surveys Branch, Dept. of Lands & Forests,
Quebec City, Province of Quebec.

Surveys and Engineering Division, Dept. of
    Natural Resources,
Toronto, Ontario

Controller of Surveys, Dept. of Natural
    Resources,
Regina, Saskatchewan

Appendix VIII:
Some Books for Voyageurs

Many excellent books on canoeing and related subjects are published by the authors themselves or by small publishers and are not usually available through most bookstores.

Adney, Edwin Tappan, and Chapelle, Howard T.: *Bark Canoes and Skin Boats of North America*. Smithsonian Institution, Washington, D.C., $3.75. Order from Government Printing Office, Washington, D.C. 20402. Make check payable to the Superintendent of Documents. The ultimate source book. Fascinating and informative.

American Red Cross Staff: *First Aid Textbook*, American Red Cross, Washington, D.C. 1957, 4th ed. (39th printing), $1. This book, while it deals more with first aid than with back-country medicine where help may be days away, is still a must for every canoeist.

Anderson, Luther: *A Guide to Canoe Camping*, Reilly, Chicago, 1971, $4.95. Useful, but Riviere and Rutstrom are better.

BSA: *Canoeing Merit Badge Book*. (paper), Boy Scouts of America, New Brunswick, New Jersey. 45 cents. The economy guide to canoeing. The basics are here.

Handel, Carl W.: *Canoe Camping*, Ronald Press, N.Y., 1965. $4.00. Comprehensive but somewhat outdated.

Hassenfuss, Joseph: *American Red Cross Canoeing Manual,* Doubleday, N.Y., 1959 (paper), $1.75. This book, despite its overly cautious approach, is the best single book on basic canoe techniques. Every canoeist should read it. The brief chapter on canoe camping is somewhat outdated. The book has one ecologically unsound chapter on "How To Build a Birch Bark Canoe." Today, one doesn't strip bark from a tree to make a canoe. Such a suggestion could start a run by Boy Scouts on our remaining birch trees. The chapter on canoe repair, mostly wood-and-canvas, is excellent.

Malo, John: *Wilderness Canoeing,* Collier Books, N.Y., 1971 (paper), $3.95. Save your money and buy Bill Riviere and/or Cal Rutstrom.

——— *Malo's Complete Guide to Canoeing and Canoe Camping,* Quadrangle Books, Chicago, 1969, $6.95. Save your money and buy Riviere or Rutstrom.

McNair, Robert: *Basic River Canoeing* (paper), Buck Ridge Ski Club, Swarthmore, Penn., undated, $1.25. A basic whitewater and canoeing book.

Merrill, Bill: *The Survival Handbook,* Winchester Press, N.Y., 1972. $5.95. This is a must book for all back-country travelers.

Mountaineers, The: *Mountaineering First Aid* (reprinted from *Mountaineering: The Freedom of the Hills*), The Mountaineers, Seattle, 1967. 50 cents. This small 24-page paperback, though designed for mountaineers, is one of the best basic back-country medicine books I know. It is far superior to any first-aid kit booklet and in some respects is much more useful than the far heavier and bulkier American Red Cross *First Aid Textbook*.

Olson, Sigurd F.: *The Lonely Land*, Knopf, N.Y., 1961, $5.95. This description of a 500-mile, three-week voyage along the Churchill River conveys the true essence of the wilderness and canoeing more than any other book I know. A must book for all voyageurs.

Riviere, Bill: *Paddle Pole and Portage*, Van Nostrand, Reinhold Co., N.Y. 1969. $6.95. Only 20 pages (pp. 148–68) are devoted to canoe camping gear but there is a wealth of basic canoe technique data. Both beginner and expert can profit from this book. Bill uses the "practical" rather than the "pussy-footing" American Red Cross approach.

——— *Family Campers Cook Book*, Holt, Rinehart & Winston, N.Y. 1965. $4.95 One of the best general outdoor cookbooks.

Russell, Charles W.: *Basic Outboard Boating*, The American Red Cross, Washington, D.C., 1964 (paper), 75 cents. A must for every canoeist who considers using an outboard.

Rutstrom, Calvin: *North American Canoe Country*, Macmillan, N.Y. 1964. $6.95. This excellent book contains only 28 pages (pp. 171–99) on canoe camping but there is a wealth of fascinating anecdotes and canoe know-how.

Sevareid, A. Eric: *Canoeing with the Cree*, Minnesota Historical Society, St. Paul, 1967, $4.25. Noted newsman and commentator's 1930 voyage from Minnesota to Hudson Bay.

Thoreau, Henry: *The Maine Woods,* Houghton Mifflin Co., Boston (paper, Sentry edition), $2.25. His 1846 voyage through Maine in a birchbark canoe.

——— *A Week on the Concord and Merrimac Rivers,* Houghton Mifflin Co., Boston (paper) $2.25. A classic.

Urban, John T.: *White Water Handbook for Canoe and Kayak,* Appalachian Mountain Club, Boston, Mass., 1965. $1.50. Concise but comprehensive.

Whitney, Peter Dwight: *White Water Sports,* Ronald Press, N.Y., 1960, $4.00. A basic work.

Epilogue

THE FINAL HAZARD

Your canoe is sliding through a chute. Suddenly, it capsizes. The ground where you pegged out your tent was destitute of lumps but suddenly one appears. A frying pan or axe disappears. A portage marked twenty yards turns out to be 200 yards. You awaken to a quiet, breezeless day and that is wonderful because this is your last day out and there is a plane to catch in the evening. You finish stowing gear in the canoe, when a stiff breeze springs up. Its intensity increases. You are windbound for three days—the last two without food.

The explanation for these hazards is simple. They are created by the Mamaygwessey, the little men with round noseless heads, long, dangling arms and six fingers and six toes. The existence of the little men—the Leprechauns of the North—is confirmed by their portraits on hundreds of pictographs through much of canoe country.

I can't help you cope with the Mamaygwessey. But I wish you the best of luck.

Index

Photograph Credits

Many of the photographs reproduced in this book came from the author's own collection—those on pp. 53, 66, 70, 71, 73, 74, 82, 84, 117, 138, 142, 144, 148, 153, 156, 160, 184, 190, 202, 214, 233, 241, 243, 251, 261, 270, 271, 273, 275, 313, 319. The others came from various sources, as follows: Betty Bradish, 76, 207, 240; Col. John A. Bradish, 9; British Columbia Dept. of Tourism, 290; Chestnut Canoe Co., 46, 209, 221; Dikmar Studios, 77, 81, 89,· 146, 163, 165, 178; Florida Development Commission, 15; Gerry, 79; Grumman Boats, 64, 67, 192, 205, 208; Hudson's Bay Co., 12; Janet, 214, 216, 217; Manitoba Tourist Office, 291; Minnesota Tourist Bureau, 107, 109; Old Town Canoe Co., 47, 68, 299, 302; Ontario Natural Resources Dept., 6, 222, 226; Province of Quebec Dept. of Parks, 295; Saskatchewan Tourist Office, 2; Trailblazer by Winchester, 101; Wisconsin Development Agency, 51; Mark Forge Products, 239.